Sport and Communities

Over the past three decades there has been widespread commitment to an under-standing that sport can play a key role in community development. The role of sport within communities has been promoted with a wide range of goals in mind. These include environmental outcomes, encouragement of civic pride, enhancement of perso-nal confidence and self-esteem, and the promotion of social cohesion, as well as the fostering of a fit and healthy workforce.

To address these issues, a number of programmes have been funded and supported to develop the role of sport in communities worldwide and to increase participation and access to sport and physical activities in disadvantaged areas. In addition we are wit-nessing the development of new sports communities through social media including Twitter and Facebook.

The belief is that we need to revisit the concept of 'community and sport' and investigate our current understanding of these terms in view of the evolving role of sport in a range of national settings. This book will present a platform upon which this process can begin and offer a fundamental re-evaluation of the relationship that cur-rently exists between sport and communities throughout selected parts of the world.

This book was previously published as a special issue of *Sport in Society*.

David Hassan is Professor of Sport Policy and Management at the University of Ulster. He is the current Deputy Executive Academic Editor of *Sport in Society*, an interna-tional, peer-reviewed journal published by Taylor & Francis Ltd. (an imprint of Rou-tledge). In December 2006 he was presented with the Award of Distinguished Research Fellowship by the University of Ulster in recognition of his outstanding contribution to research. Dr Hassan's research expertise concerns the relationship between sport and national identity, the politics of sport and sport governance.

Sean F. Brown received his PhD in 2013 from Northeastern University, Boston, USA. His primary research interests include sport and community, social capital and urban sociology. He currently works as a Postdoctoral Fellow at the University of Chicago, where he is exploring links between social capital and low-income families.

Sport and Communities

Edited by
David Hassan and Sean F. Brown

Routledge
Taylor & Francis Group
LONDON AND NEW YORK

First published 2014
by Routledge
2 Park Square, Milton Park, Abingdon, Oxon, OX14 4RN, UK

and by Routledge
711 Third Avenue, New York, NY 10017, USA

Routledge is an imprint of the Taylor & Francis Group, an informa business

British Library Cataloguing in Publication Data
A catalogue record for this book is available from the British Library

ISBN 13: 978-0-415-57165-4

Typeset in Times New Roman
by Taylor & Francis Books

Publisher's Note
The publisher accepts responsibility for any inconsistencies that may have arisen during the conversion of this book from journal articles to book chapters, namely the possible inclusion of journal terminology.

Disclaimer
Every effort has been made to contact copyright holders for their permission to reprint material in this book. The publishers would be grateful to hear from any copyright holder who is not here acknowledged and will undertake to rectify any errors or omissions in future editions of this book.

Contents

SPORT IN THE GLOBAL SOCIETY – CONTEMPORARY PERSPECTIVES

Series Editor: Boria Majumdar

SPORT AND COMMUNITIES

Sport in the Global Society – Contemporary Perspectives
Series Editor: Boria Majumdar

The social, cultural (including media) and political study of sport is an expanding area of scholarship and related research. While this area has been well served by the *Sport in the Global Society* series, the surge in quality scholarship over the last few years has necessitated the creation of *Sport in the Global Society: Contemporary Perspectives*. The series will publish the work of leading scholars in fields as diverse as sociology, cultural studies, media studies, gender studies, cultural geography and history, political science and political economy. If the social and cultural study of sport is to receive the scholarly attention and readership it warrants, a cross-disciplinary series dedicated to taking sport beyond the narrow confines of physical education and sport science academic domains is necessary. *Sport in the Global Society: Contemporary Perspectives* will answer this need.

Titles in the Series

Citation Information

The chapters in this book were originally published in *Sport in Society*, volume 17, issue 4 (January 2014). When citing this material, please use the original page numbering for each article, as follows:

Chapter 7
Sport and community integration in Northern Ireland
David Hassan and Rachael Telford
Sport in Society, volume 17, issue 4 (January 2014) pp. 89–101

Chapter 8
Women's toplessness on the Red Mile, Calgary, May–June 2004
Mary Valentich
Sport in Society, volume 17, issue 4 (January 2014) pp. 102–115

Chapter 9
Volunteer roles, involvement and commitment in voluntary sport organizations: evidence of core and peripheral volunteers
Caroline Ringuet-Riot, Graham Cuskelly, Chris Auld and Dwight H. Zakus
Sport in Society, volume 17, issue 4 (January 2014) pp. 116–133

Chapter 10
Epilogue: the not-so-hidden complexity of the sport-community connection
Sean F. Brown
Sport in Society, volume 17, issue 4 (January 2014) pp. 134–138

Please direct any queries you may have about the citations to
clsuk.permissions@cengage.com

Sport and communities: an introduction

David Hassan

Ulster Sports Academy, University of Ulster Jordanstown, Shore Road, Newtownabbey, County Antrim BT37 0QN, UK

While there has been considerable academic and popular coverage of the perceived importance of community identity in the lives of ordinary citizens, such analysis is problematical due to a conceptual and theoretical deficiency around the very use and understanding of the term. There has been a failure to fully operationalize and thus objectify (for measurement) some of the contributing elements of this term, which is of concern to sports scholars as it is often sport that is used as a proxy measurement of the precise strength of a community's vibrancy and connectedness. The latter part of this introductory piece details common themes and issues of note that emerge throughout the course of the ensuing compendium of published works, which essentially cohere around issues of sport in society, volunteerism and identity.

Introduction

It seems that there is near-universal agreement regarding the importance of community identity in the lives of everyday citizens. This appears even more pronounced when, amid a growing sense of dislocation on the part of some, traditional forms of connecting individuals with established and real communities – in the geo-political sense – are themselves becoming more difficult to define. Of course, there are many and varied forms of communities and these are established along a diverse set of identity markers, often cohering around common interests or causes, and they can exist in a physical or virtual space. One of the most readily available means of demonstrating a sense of community identity is through involvement in sport. Support for a local sports club, representing it in regional or national competitions, volunteering to ensure its survival or simply recognizing its importance in the lives of others are all examples of how sport can serve to offer a focal point for an otherwise increasingly fragmented society (Collins 2003, Collins 2004). What is remarkable therefore, amid this broad agreement concerning the centrality of community identity, is the failure of most to properly define and capture what they mean through the use of the term. An inability to agree a logical basis for future research in this field does little to assist the arguments of those who suggest that an erosion of community identity is taking place, and while some can perhaps offer anecdotal evidence to support their assertions, they are otherwise unable to present any empirical evidence to substantiate their beliefs.

It should be said that this entire premise – the assumption that any threat to one's participation and engagement in community life is best resisted – is based on the received wisdom that remaining part of a community, either physically or virtually constituted, is inherently desirable. This represents something of a value judgement but equally is a commonly held view often informed by an at-times irrational assumption that the unrelenting advance of modernization automatically equates to the 'loss' of something valuable or constitutes a societal advance 'away from' that which is considered worth holding dear. There is also a misplaced belief that a concomitant sense of anxiety, again concerning the erosion of community-based identities, somehow represents a recent phenomenon. In fact, this is far from the case. Questions of identity have always been appropriated broadly into two fields – those who argue 'community' can only be understood with reference to a territorially based interrogation of the term and, in contrast, advocates of a broader definition of the concept, which includes members of established, evolving or emerging social networks constituted by like-minded personnel who take little account of national or regional boundaries.

Irrespective of how the term is understood, there nevertheless remains a considerable debate concerning the perceived importance of community identity and, it seems, an equally worthwhile examination of whether the term is best understood as an empirical concept, i.e. one that can be measured and thus tracked, or an analytical concept, regarding the importance of what might otherwise be understood as an 'imagined' sense of identity. Simply put, in the absence of an objective set of measures against which individuals may wish to gauge their sense of identity, it is difficult to establish the rise, fall or even presence of a sense of community identity. Moreover, if we accept the seemingly pre-eminent claims in support of a preservation of community-based identities, where precisely this leaves other forms of identity construction, among them social, gender or national forms, and all of which invoke a strong sense attachment, inclusion and comparative homogeneity, is another issue.

Sport and community identity

Building on this theme, it is too often claimed, in the absence of any serious supporting evidence, that sport exercises a role in maintaining a sense of community identity. Moreover, in the opinions of some, sport may even promote and enhance this imagined sense of identity (Commission on the European Communities 2007). This is an often universally held view, again in spite of the lack of an agreed conceptual or theoretical understanding of what is meant by community identity. In a similar vein, there exists a variously and largely untested thesis suggesting that involvement in sports or the mere presence of sporting opportunities that accentuate the presence of a community is again inherently desirable. On this basis, large amounts of financial support from sovereign governments have been deployed to underwrite policy decisions of an occasionally questionable form, often aimed at using sport to address isolation, division or marginalization 'away from' such imagined communities. In fact, it is only comparatively recently that a more critical body of academic literature has emerged and persuaded those engaged in this practice to pause, reflect and seek a more empirically considered way forward (Coalter 2007a, 2007b). This is important not only for sport's role in society but also for the substance of society itself as the ready conflation of desirable outcomes thought to emerge from involvement in sport are readily overwritten onto society as a whole. It is as if the mere provision of sport creates, through a process of extension, a 'better' society, defined by a more socially responsible population, a reduction in anti-social behaviour and a more enlightened approach, for example to the plight of ethnic minorities.

As a result, it could be argued that sport's role in the production and reproduction of community identities has in fact been somewhat overstated. There are a range of other similarly sized bodies existing in most communities that present opportunities for groups to cohere around, which do not retain some of the exclusionary practices often witnessed around sport. Then again, few elicit the emotion of sporting attachment, especially those designed to promote partisanship. Much of this may prove to be ephemeral, jingoistic or even exclusionary but, in fairness, there is perhaps something surrounding this process that merits the recognition of sport's capacity to encourage a common cause, to reflect on one's attachment to a broader aspiration or simply to experience a sense of meaningful association in their lives. This in turn gives rise to a range of other desirable outcomes, including volunteerism, the production of social capital (both bonding and bridging) and enhanced levels of integration more generally (Nicholson and Hoye 2008). Indeed, volunteers are widely regarded as being a core component of locally based, national and international sporting delivery. A widely held view, evidenced within some current literature, suggests that the majority of sporting organizations worldwide would simply fail to operate in an efficient and effective manner were it not for the work of volunteers. Thus, it could be argued, the focus should be less on the elusive attachment to community identity per se and more on the maintenance or creation of a better society for all through the role sport plays in encouraging willing volunteerism (with all its commensurate benefits) within the population at large.

The collection

It is of little surprise therefore that a collection examining sport's contribution to society would contain a number of articles dealing specifically with the place of volunteers. It begins with the work of Matt Nicholson, who considers the relationship between sport and non-sporting community-based activities and their respective levels of perceived social support. In so doing, he draws upon a vast empirical data-set and thus confidently concludes that the role played by sport in the production of social capital, relative to other community-based activities, has perhaps been overstated. Using a multidimensional scale of perceived support as a means of measuring social capital, Nicholson argues that sport occupies something of the middle ground in relation to community-based social capital production and is certainly not the sole platform upon which this may emerge as a by-product of volunteer activity.

This issue of sport's role in the production of social capital is further unpacked by Brown who, through a discrete but no less insightful, examination of a Little League baseball club in New Mexico demonstrates the often overlooked capacity of young children to generate social capital for their parents. The former's participation in sport, in this case Little League baseball, creates a context in which parents, with broadly similar aspirations for their children, come together, socialize and establish bonds. While these bonds may be of varying strengths, Brown's work nonetheless makes an extremely valuable contribution because it highlights mechanisms and strategies employed by parents, vicariously deployed through their children's sporting lives, to expand their own social networks and generate enhanced levels of social capital.

The strong empirical nature to this collection continues through the work of Jamie Clelland and his critical analysis of the role played by local government authorities in the UK when advancing strategies designed to increase participation rates in sport among ethnic minority groupings. There has been a long-held view that local borough councils in Britain could do more to respond to the challenges of multiculturalism, which remains a common concern among advocacy groups operating across a range of European countries. Yet Cleland notes that despite their best efforts, barriers to participation still remain and leaders of organizations representing minority groups are becoming increasingly exasperated at the failure (or reluctance) to make proper sporting provision for members of societies as a whole.

Thereafter, the collection returns briefly to the motivations volunteers cite with regard to their involvement in youth sport activities. Volunteerism at this level rarely presents the opportunity for discernible levels of recognition and so, for many, their generosity of time, expertise and spirit is worthy of particular note. A qualitative enquiry undertaken by Engelberg, Skinner and Zakus, colleagues at Griffith Business School, Australia, revealed there to be four distinct types of volunteer-commitment profiles, each emphasizing aspects of their motivation for volunteerism in slightly different and discrete ways.

This focus on youth sport compliments the work of Roult whose examination of the impact on the physical health and well-being of a community that the location of an outdoor skating rink may exercise offers some remarkably insightful findings. It concludes that the construction of a community sports facility can indeed encourage citizens to become more physically active, including those who were previous non-participants; however, building such an outlet is not in itself sufficient to secure long-term goals in this regard. Rather, it must be complimented with other forms of advocacy and broad encouragement, which, when viewed in the round, lead to engagement in programmes designed to address worrying levels of inactivity, diabetes and broader population health concerns.

The long-standing work around sport's role in encouraging greater community integration and cultural understanding in Northern Ireland is reviewed in the contribution made by Hassan and Telford, based at the University of Ulster. In particular, their work examines developments, in what is now a mercifully post-conflict setting, around promoting enhanced relationships between the majority Protestant community and the minority Catholic community, using sport as a 'hook' to establish closer, more considered bonds. Of course, many of those involved, either directly or indirectly, in the inter-ethnic violence that defined life in Northern Ireland for much of the latter part of the twentieth century constitute subsections of the population typically referred to as being 'hard to reach'. Often this term defines adolescent members of working class, urban communities in Belfast (and elsewhere) who are not in full-time education, training or employment and, in the case of some, may be involved in low-level criminal activity within their immediate locales. The thesis advanced by Hassan and Telford is that often it is sport that infiltrates the cultural and social lives of these young people and, to confirm this view, they provide examples from Northern Ireland demonstrating how this is can be shown to be the case.

The penultimate article in the collection, written by Mary Valentich from the University of Calgary, examines some of the remarkable outworkings of the ice-hockey play off finals during 2004 in Calgary in which public attention was drawn to the propensity of women to remove their clothing during the celebrations surrounding the hockey series. Valentich interrogates attitudes towards this unprecedented reaction to sporting success and examines some of the reasons that may have led to their behaviour in the first place.

Finally, the collection draws to a close with a somewhat more sedate examination of volunteerism, which remains a consistent theme of this compendium, in the non-profit sports sector. This research work, undertaken by Caroline Ringuet, Graham Cuskelly, Chris Auld and Dwight H. Zakus, builds on the published work to date by successfully categorizing volunteers as being either 'core' or 'peripheral', suggestive of the potential to draw a meaningful distinction between such individuals in the context of future volunteer recruitment, retention and assignments.

References

Coalter, F. 2007a. *A Wider Social Role For Sport: Who's Keeping Score?* London: Routledge.

Coalter, F. 2007b. "Sports Clubs, Social Capital and Social Regeneration: Ill-Defined Interventions with Hard to Follow Outcomes'?'." *Sport in Society* 10: 537–559.

Collins, M. 2003. *Sport and Social Exclusion*. London: Routledge.

Collins, M. 2004. "Voluntary Sports Clubs and Social Capital." In *Volunteers in Sports Clubs*, edited by G. Nichols and M. Collins, 105–118. Eastbourne: LSA.

Commission on the European Communities. 2007. *White Paper on Sport*. Brussels: Commission on the European Communities.

Nicholson, M., and R. Hoye, eds. 2008. *Sport and Social Capital*. Oxford: Butterworth-Heinemann.

Sport, community involvement and social support

Matthew Nicholson, Kevin Brown and Russell Hoye

Centre for Sport and Social Impact, La Trobe University, Melbourne, Australia

This paper examines the relationship between involvement in sport and non-sport community activities and perceived social support. This paper reports on a large cross-sectional survey administered in the state of Victoria, Australia ($N = 1833$), which collected data on involvement, selected demographic variables and the multidimensional scale of perceived social support (MSPSS). The findings reveal that sport and non-sport community activities have a small but significant predictive effect on the overall MSPSS, as well as on the 'friends' and 'significant other' subscales: less than having a partner, being female or being born in Australia, but more than being employed full time, being highly educated or attending religious services. The findings do not appear to support the proposition that involvement in sport organizations is associated with or produces higher levels of social capital (measured via perceived social support) relative to involvement in other types of voluntary associations.

Introduction

It is often claimed that sport is social glue, which serves to cohere, build and strengthen communities,[1] but this proposition, which underpins broader arguments about sport's impact, is largely untested. Skille made similar observations, noting that there is a general belief in sport's potential for good, but that a range of sport scholars have been sceptical of the blind faith of policy-makers, referring to 'the lack of evidence for the causal link between sport participation and the societal benefits of it'.[2] Sport organizations are often identified as important community nodes in the creation and maintenance of social benefits and outcomes by politicians, policy-makers and advocates of sport. These benefits, which theoretically originate in community sport organizations, are often aggregated across entire communities: capacity building, the reduction of crime and youth delinquency, empowerment of disadvantaged groups, improvements in confidence and self-esteem, and an increase in social integration and co-operation.[3] As Coalter has argued, however, evidence for sport's role in facilitating social outcomes is undermined by both conceptual and methodological weaknesses and little or no consideration of sufficient conditions.[4]

In *Bowling Alone*, Putnam used the distinction between bowling in teams and bowling alone as both a concrete example of a decline in social capital and a metaphor for a broader decline in social capital within American society.[5] The somewhat forlorn figure of the solo bowler on the cover of the book succinctly juxtaposed sport and the absence of social networks and their concomitant benefits. However, the prominent place of sport in Putnam's work on social capital has also served to popularize the notion that sport, in its ideal form, played fairly between groups of well-connected happy people, is an ideal vehicle for the creation of social capital. Indeed, as part of a discussion of bridging social capital, Putnam declared that 'team sports provide good avenues for social capital creation'.[6] Community sport organizations are only one type of voluntary organization, yet their potential to deliver social benefits has been emphasized over other organizations of comparable size and capacity, particularly by policy-makers, in large part because sport is a highly visible and popular activity among both children and adults, and has a significant network of human and physical resources. The adherence to sport's special potential for good is also perhaps the result of an enduring belief that there is a socializing process unique to sport.

Despite the prominence of sport organizations in broader discussions about the development and maintenance of social capital, there is a lack of clarity about whether sport is more or less able to contribute to these benefits and outcomes than other types of community organizations, and a lack of knowledge about the ways in which different types of voluntary associations contribute to making their members more (or less) trusting, more (or less) prepared to engage in civic participation or more (or less) socially connected.[7] The lack of clarity about whether community sport organizations are more or less effective at facilitating social capital benefits and outcomes was the starting point for a broader research project, of which this paper forms one part. As such, in this paper, we are concerned with exploring whether involvement in sport and non-sport community organizations leads to greater levels of perceived social support, which can be considered one benefit or aspect of an individual's social networks.

Social support, social capital and sport

Described variously as the most frequently studied psychosocial resource[8] and one of the three most important constructs in mental health research,[9] social support has become a popular academic construct, particularly in health and psychology research. Despite the acknowledgement that social support is multidimensional and therefore difficult to measure,[10] research has demonstrated that social support is positively correlated with physical health,[11] as well as with mental health and general well-being.[12] Social support has been interpreted as functions performed by significant people within a social network,[13] a coping resource and a social fund upon which people might draw,[14] communication between recipients and providers,[15] an exchange of resources intended to enhance the well-being of the recipient[16] and knowing that one is loved and that others will do all they can when a problem arises.[17] What is common to all of these understandings of social support is the existence of a social relationship, a network of social relations or an exchange, which takes place within a network. Similarly, there is an increasing agreement that social capital is created by, manifest within and used by and through social networks. A common ground for social capital theorists is the concept of social networks. As Putnam noted, 'the core idea of social capital is that social networks have value'.[18]

In order to examine the relationship between social support and social capital more closely, it is important to explore definitional aspects of both concepts. In particular, we are interested in the proposition by Bourdieu that social capital is 'the aggregate of the actual or potential resources which are linked to possession of a durable network of more or less institutionalised relationships of mutual acquaintance and recognition'.[19] This definition emphasizes social relationships (or networks) and the resources that are made available through them. This basic premise of social capital has been extensively debated since Bourdieu's intervention. Coleman identified that social capital constituted 'a particular kind of resource' and 'inheres in the structure of relations',[20] while later Portes noted a growing consensus in the definition of social capital – 'the ability of actors to secure benefits by virtue of membership in social networks or other social structures'.[21] Bourdieu argued that the volume of social capital available within a social network

7

depends on the size of the network of connections that an individual can mobilize and the volume of capital possessed by the membership of the network.[22] Importantly, those within the network have access to the resources made available through the network, while those who are not members of the social network have no access and are therefore disadvantaged, particularly if there are finite resources within a community that are only accessible through the network. Portes and Landolt argued that it is important to distinguish between the sources and benefits of social capital; to confuse or conflate them might lead only to the conclusion that the successful succeed.[23] In other words, Portes and Landolt's position, based on Bourdieu's notion of capital, power and the inequitable distribution of resources, is that strong social networks, the source of social capital, do not necessarily or in any automatic way lead to a greater access to resources or benefits, particularly when a community is economically disadvantaged. In this respect, social capital might simply optimize the potentiality of access to limited resources.[24]

This notion of the available resources within a social network holds if economic or financial resources are considered exclusively. The proposition alters, however, if the definition of resources is broadened to include non-economic aspects of a person's quality of life. Putnam defined social capital as 'social networks and the norms of reciprocity and trustworthiness that arise from them'.[25] He did not refer directly to resources, but rather noted that 'life is easier in a community blessed with a substantial stock of social capital',[26] because social networks foster reciprocity and trust and facilitate communication. In this respect, the social network is a conduit for a range of outcomes (such as increased trust), which might in turn result in further outcomes (such as emotional support in a time of need), which in turn might result in further outcomes (such as improved mental health). This line of reasoning could be extended further, but even these three tiers of social capital benefits are sufficient to illustrate that a social network can make available non-economic, yet useful, resources.

Thoits' definition of social support as a coping resource and a social fund upon which people might draw,[27] Shumaker and Brownell's definition of social support as an exchange of resources intended to enhance the well-being of the recipient[28] and interest in the role of social support as a coping resource[29] are all pertinent in the context of an understanding of social capital as access to a broadly defined set of resources available within a social network. The social network that delivers social support usually consists of significant others, such as a partner, family, friends and co-workers.[30] Thus, an individual's social network, which might be drawn from a range of associations, could provide a non-economic resource, which might in turn provide other benefits, such as improved health and well-being. It is unlikely that social support would exist or be available outside a social network, given it requires a relationship in order to exist, and while it is also likely to be finite, given the personal and time constraints of the membership of the network, it is not likely to be as scarce as the financial resources referred to by Bourdieu[31] or by Portes and Landolt.[32] Focussing on social support enables an examination of a particular benefit or outcome made possible by the existence and operation of a social network. In this respect, we consider social support to be an aspect of social capital, as well as a resource made possible by the existence of social capital.

The relationship between social capital and sport has only recently attracted academic interest.[33] Although some of this research is empirical,[34] much has focused on conceptualizing the potential linkages between social capital and sport, a reasonable approach given that Putnam implicitly tied the two together through his analysis of the decline in bowling leagues.[35] Many studies of the relationship between sport and social capital have used generic social survey and participation data to draw correlations between the two, and although participation in sport is attractive as a proxy for social capital, as Nicholson and Hoye's discussion of this issue illustrated, sport participation trends are only useful as one of a series of social indicators.[36] Importantly, 'the notion that participation is a valid proxy for social capital does not account for the way in which the social capital produced through these interactions is used'.[37]

Very little of the literature that has examined the relationship or connections between sport and social capital has resulted from purposely designed large-scale cross-sectional surveys. Rather, as noted previously, generic social survey data have been interrogated, or small qualitative studies within specific population cohorts have been conducted. These studies have yet to build a body of evidence from which valid or reliable generalizations are able to be made about engagement in sport and its social benefits.

Research into social support within sport has largely focussed on the benefits to athletes and elite athletes in particular: its relationship to assisting with injury recovery,[38] reducing anxiety and stress[39] or enhancing performance.[40] By contrast, this paper is not concerned with the benefits of specific social support provided by coaches and parents to athletes or players. Rather, it is concerned with examining the concept of social support more broadly, and exploring whether involvement in community sport and non-sport organizations, as participants, administrators, coaches, officials or general volunteers, leads to higher levels of perceived social support.

Method

Sample

A sample of $N = 5655$ residents in the State of Victoria, Australia, was randomly selected using the Victorian *White Pages* (2009) telephone directories as the sampling frame.

Measures

Data were collected on levels of involvement in community sport and other third sector organizations, selected demographic variables and the multidimensional scale of perceived social support (MSPSS).[41] The MSPSS consists of 12 items, which measure perceived social support from family, friends and a significant other, using a seven-point Likert scale (very strongly agree to very strongly disagree):

(1) There is a special person who is around when I am in need.
(2) There is a special person with whom I can share my joys and sorrows.
(3) My family really tries to help me.
(4) I get the emotional help and support I need from my family.
(5) I have a special person who is a real source of comfort to me.
(6) My friends really try to help me.
(7) I can count on my friends when things go wrong.
(8) I can talk about my problems with my family.
(9) I have friends with whom I can share my joys and sorrows.
(10) There is a special person in my life who cares about my feelings.
(11) My family is willing to help me make decisions.
(12) I can talk about my problems with my friends.

Items 1, 2, 5 and 10 comprise the significant other subscale; Items 3, 4, 8 and 11 comprise the family subscale and Items 6, 7, 9 and 12 comprise the friends subscale.

Measures of involvement within the study included the number of organizations, length of time involved with an organization, number of hours per week spent engaged with an organization and organizational role (player, coach, administrator or other volunteer). We also collected data on the type of organization (traditional club, fitness-oriented business or recreational club) and whether the sport was team-based or individual. Demographic variables included age, gender, employment status, education level, marital status, gross annual income, housing arrangements and frequency of attendance at religious services.

Data collection and analysis

The sample was surveyed by means of self-administration questionnaires via direct mail with two reminders following the standard 'tailored design method' for mail surveys recommended by Dillman.[42] The survey was administered between February and March 2009. A total of 1833 responses were received giving a response rate of 32.4%, which is at the high end of the response range for similar surveys.[43] The data were analysed in SPSS (PASW Statistics 17) using both univariate and multivariate procedures.

Results

Univariate

The sample consisted of $N = 1833$ respondents. Table 1 illustrates the demographic profile of the respondents. Compared to the general population, the sample was similar in several respects, including the proportion of men and women, the proportion of Australian and non-Australian born and the proportion that was married. The sample differed relative to the general population in terms of the median age, the proportion working full time and the proportion living outside Melbourne. The proportion of sample that was female was 48% compared to the population statistic of 50.9%;[44] 73.4 % of the sample was born in Australia compared to 71.1% for Victoria[45] and the sample proportion that was married was 50.9% compared to the population statistic (Victoria) of 50.1%.[46] The sample (median age = 55.0 years) was older than the population (Victoria, median age = 37.0 years at June 2009).[47] A total of 31% of the sample was aged 65 years or above compared to 13.7% for Victoria in 2006.[48] Half (49.6%) the sample was aged over 55 years compared to 24.5% for Victoria in 2006.[49] While patterned unit non-response by younger age groups is a well-known effect in survey research,[50] which can be exacerbated in the context of a mail-based survey using a sampling frame taken from telephone directories,[51] it nevertheless needs to be taken into account in assessing the results reported here. The sample also contained proportionately fewer people working full time (38.4%) to the population (Victoria = 60.1%)[52] though the median individual annual income was higher (sample median = \$30–60K compared to Victoria, median = \$23,712).[53] The sample had proportionately more Victorians who lived outside Melbourne (51.6%) than the population of Victoria in 2004 (27.6%).[54]

Respondents were grouped into four types according to their organizational involvement. 'No involvement' was the modal category (50%) followed by 'sport involvement only' (20%), 'other organisation involvement only' (18%) and 'both sport and other organisation involvement' (12%). Table 2 shows the participation rates of the sample in sport and community organizations.

The results for this study are comparable to previous studies that have used the MSPSS scale. The results within this study were as follows: overall scale ($M = 5.61$, SD $= 1.21$,

Table 1. Demographic details of sample.

	Sample $N = 1833$
Age	Mean = 56 (SD = 16)
Gender	
Male	52%
Female	48%
Country of birth	
Australian	73%
Non-Australian	27%
Marital status	
Married/*de facto*	68%
Other	32%
Residence	
Melbourne	48%
Rural	52%
Housing arrangements	
Living with partner	68%
Other	32%
House ownership	
Own outright	51%
Paying off mortgage	33%
Private rental	12%
Boarding or similar	3%
Public rental	2%
Education level	
Postgraduate degree	10%
Bachelor degree	16%
Diploma	18%
Secondary education	45%
Other	11%
Employment status	
Full time	38%
Part time	20%
Unemployed	3%
Not in labour force	38%
Annual income	
Nil	6%
Up to $10,000	8%
$10,000–$30,000	32%
$30,000–$60,000	28%
$60,000–$100,000	18%
Over $100,000	8%
Religious attendance	
Several times a week	3%
Once a week	13%
Two or three times a month	4%
Once a month	5%
Less than once a month	17%
Never	58%

$N = 1700$), family subscale ($M = 5.55$, SD $= 1.44$, $N = 1751$), friends subscale ($M = 5.41$, SD $= 1.31$, $N = 1771$) and significant other subscale ($M = 5.83$, SD $= 1.40$, $N = 1764$). Dahlem, Zimet, and Walker reported similar results in their study of 154 American college students: overall scale ($M = 5.58$, SD $= 1.07$), family

Table 2.   Participation rates of the sample in sport and community organizations.

Sport participation (32% of sample)		Community participation (31% of sample)	
Number of organizations		Number of organizations	
One	67%	One	56%
Two	23%	Two	25%
Three	6%	Three	12%
Four or more	4%	Four or more	7%
Primary organization type		Primary organization type	
Traditional club	73%	Social services	22%
Fitness business	16%	Religion	21%
Recreational	11%	Education	12%
		Culture/arts	12%
		Philanthropy	12%
		Environment	10%
		Health	7%
		Housing	1%
		Law	1%
		International	1%
Involvement type		Involvement type	
Player/participant	64%	Participant	55%
Volunteer	20%	Volunteer	19%
Administrator	9%	Facilitator/leader	18%
Coach	7%	Administrator	8%
Involvement tenure in primary organization	Median = 8 years	Involvement tenure in primary organization	Median = 8 years
Involvement hours per week in primary organization	Median = 4 hours	Involvement hours per week in primary organization	Median = 3 hours
Sport type			
Team	60%		
Individual	40%		

subscale ($M = 5.31$, SD $= 1.46$), friends subscale ($M = 5.50$, SD $= 1.25$) and significant other subscale ($M = 5.94$, SD $= 1.34$).[55] In a study of 222 urban, mostly African-American adolescents, Canty-Mitchell and Zimet reported the following similar results: overall scale ($M = 5.55$, SD $= 1.20$), family subscale ($M = 5.33$, SD $= 1.48$), friends subscale ($M = 5.42$, SD $= 1.42$) and significant other subscale ($M = 5.9$, SD $= 1.30$),[56] while Zimet et al. reported the following results from a study of 275 American undergraduate university students: overall scale ($M = 5.80$, SD $= 0.86$), family subscale ($M = 5.80$, SD $= 1.12$), friends subscale ($M = 5.85$, SD $= 0.94$) and significant other subscale ($M = 5.74$, SD $= 1.25$).[57]

In the present study, the MSPSS scale had a very good internal consistency with a Cronbach's α coefficient of 0.95. The internal consistency for the subscales was also indicated as very good with all three subscales (significant other, friends, family) achieving scores of 0.95.

Multivariate

As illustrated in Table 3, the multiple regression reveals that for the overall MSPSS five variables had a significant predictive effect: having a partner ($\beta = 0.182$, $p \leq 0.001$),

Table 3. Hierarchical regression of involvement types and demographic variables on the overall MSPSS.

Model	B	Std. error	B	Sig.
(Constant)	4.886	0.093		0.000
Sport involved	0.136	0.061	0.055	0.026
Other involved	0.155	0.064	0.061	0.015
Partner	0.475	0.065	0.182	0.000
Full time Employment	−0.037	0.063	−0.015	0.557
Religious attendance	0.059	0.060	0.024	0.327
Gender	0.215	0.062	0.089	0.000
Birthplace	0.274	0.068	0.100	0.000
Education	−0.096	0.066	−0.035	0.149

Note: $R^2 = 0.050$ ($p < 0.001$); $N = 1700$.

being born in Australia ($\beta = 0.100$, $p \leq 0.001$), being female ($\beta = 0.089$, $p \leq 0.001$), involvement in a non-sport community organization ($\beta = 0.061$, $p = 0.015$) and involvement in a community sport organization ($\beta = 0.055$, $p = 0.026$). The model explained 5.0% of the variance in the overall scale.

As illustrated in Table 4, the multiple regression reveals that for the 'significant other' subscale of the MSPSS, having a partner had the most significant predictive effect ($\beta = 0.258$, $p \leq 0.001$), followed by being born in Australia ($\beta = 0.104$, $p \leq 0.001$), being female ($\beta = 0.079$, $p = 0.001$), being involved in a non-sport community organization ($\beta = 0.053$, $p = 0.028$) and being involved in a community sport organization ($\beta = 0.051$, $p = 0.033$). None of the other predictors had a significant effect. Unsurprisingly, having a partner provided the single most powerful predictive effect on the significant other subscale. Similarly, being female was likely to indicate the independent existence of a close relationship. The result associated with being born in Australia is largely unexplained within the confines of the present study. The model explained 7.9% of the variance in the significant other subscale.

As illustrated in Table 5, the multiple regression reveals that for the 'family' subscale of the MSPSS, having a partner ($\beta = 0.160$, $p \leq 0.001$) and being born in Australia ($\beta = 0.052$, $p = 0.038$) were the only two predictors that had a significant effect within the model. It is reasonable to expect that having a partner may extend familial networks in many cases, while family members of those people not born in Australia might still be located in the person's country of birth. In this respect, the person might be isolated from a

Table 4. Hierarchical regression of involvement types and demographic variables on the 'Significant Other' subscale.

Model	B	Std. error	B	Sig.
(Constant)	4.896	0.103		0.000
Sport involved	0.146	0.069	0.051	0.033
Other involved	0.157	0.072	0.053	0.028
Partner	0.779	0.072	0.258	0.000
Full time Employment	−0.031	0.070	−0.011	0.654
Religious attendance	−0.016	0.068	−0.006	0.809
Gender	0.220	0.069	0.079	0.001
Birthplace	0.327	0.076	0.104	0.000
Education	−0.126	0.075	−0.040	0.091

Note: $R^2 = 0.079$ ($p < 0.001$); $N = 1764$.

Table 5. Hierarchical regression of involvement types and demographic variables on the 'Family' subscale.

Model	B	Std. error	B	Sig.
(Constant)	5.000	0.110		0.000
Sport involved	0.074	0.073	0.025	0.307
Other involved	0.060	0.076	0.020	0.430
Partner	0.499	0.077	0.160	0.000
Full time Employment	−0.098	0.075	−0.034	0.189
Religious attendance	0.134	0.072	0.046	0.063
Gender	0.102	0.074	0.036	0.164
Birthplace	0.169	0.081	0.052	0.038
Education	−0.147	0.080	−0.045	0.065

Note: $R^2 = 0.028$ ($p < 0.001$); $N = 1751$.

Table 6. Hierarchical regression of involvement types and demographic variables on the 'Friends' subscale.

Model	B	Std. error	B	Sig.
(Constant)	4.676	0.098		0.000
Sport involved	0.183	0.065	0.068	0.005
Other involved	0.248	0.068	0.089	0.000
Partner	0.122	0.069	0.043	0.076
Full time Employment	0.028	0.067	0.011	0.670
Religious attendance	0.046	0.064	0.018	0.470
Gender	0.374	0.065	0.143	0.000
Birthplace	0.395	0.072	0.133	0.000
Education	−0.022	0.071	−0.007	0.760

Note: $R^2 = 0.052$ ($p < 0.001$); $N = 1771$.

family support network. The lack of other significant predictors may be seen as largely to be expected, for none of the other variables are likely to influence the perception of social support from family. The model explained 2.8% of the variance in the family subscale.

As illustrated in Table 6, the multiple regression reveals that for the 'friends' subscale of the MSPSS, being female had the most significant predictive effect ($\beta = 0.143, p \leq 0.001$), followed by being born in Australia ($\beta = 0.133, p \leq 0.001$), being involved in a non-sport community organization ($\beta = 0.089, p \leq 0.001$) and being involved in a community sport organization ($\beta = 0.068, p = 0.005$). None of the other predictors had a significant effect in the model. The model explained 5.2% of the variance in the friends subscale.

Finally, there were no significant associations between the MSPSS or its subscales and a range of involvement measures: the number of sport organizations a person was involved with, the number of years of involvement in a sport organization, the number of hours spent in involvement in the sport organization, the type of sport organization (traditional club, fitness business or recreational), the type of involvement (player, coach, administrator or other volunteer) and whether the person was involved in team-based sport organizations versus those involved in sport organizations that facilitated individual competition.

Discussion

Involvement in sport and non-sport community organizations each had a small but significant predictive effect on the overall scale, as well as on the significant other and friends subscales. Arguably, the results indicate that social networks developed through voluntary associations not only are important in developing the breadth of a person's social network, but also contribute to its depth. In other words, the social networks developed through these associations contain people who can be relied upon to provide social support when things go wrong, when a person has problems or needs to make decisions or when they need someone with whom to share their joys and sorrows. It is possible that the social interactions facilitated by these voluntary groups and associations in turn facilitate the development of social support, or at least are conducive to people perceiving that they have greater levels of social support. Given that full-time work did not have a significant predictive effect on perceived social support, it is possible that the voluntary nature of the association is central to the development of social support, either real or perceived. In other words, those social relationships that are entered into freely or voluntarily and are based on common interests and needs might be more useful than those that are created and maintained through the world of work. In many respects, this finding is counter-intuitive, given that it might be expected that the amount of time spent at work might lead to the development of the depth of a social network, particularly among selected individuals, not just its breadth.

Perhaps most importantly for an examination of the specific impact of sport in developing social support, the results from this research, the first to explore the relationship between involvement in sport (and other) organizations to perceived social support, do not support the contention that there is something special about involvement in sport organizations relative to other non-sport community organizations. The differences in the results between these two categories are not significant enough to draw comparisons between them. Rather, we can say that involvement in sport and non-sport community organizations are on a par in terms of their relationship to perceived social support. This finding contradicts much of the policy rhetoric that seeks to claim a special or exalted place for sport and its ability to bind and strengthen communities.[58] This research suggests that sport is not inherently special; the context and environment of sport organizations facilitate social support no more than other types of voluntary community organizations.

The results of this study revealed that having a partner was the variable with the most significant predictive effect for the overall scale, as well as for the family and significant other subscales. This finding supports a consensus within the broader literature that social support is often derived from a significant other, particularly a partner, a family member or a close friend. It is reasonable to expect that a partner would be regarded as a significant other in many cases so the finding that having a partner had a significant predictive effect on the significant other subscale was not surprising. For example, Weiss posited that relationships in which people gain attachment, defined in part as a sense of security and place, are likely to be of central importance in developing an individual's adequate life organization.[59] In most cases, suggested Weiss, this relationship is likely to be within marriage or a stable cross-sex relationship. Thus, the notion that a single important relationship provides significant social support is not particularly new.

The findings also demonstrate that being born in Australia was the only variable that had a significant predictive effect in the overall scale and all three subscales. It is not within the remit or capacity of this paper to speculate on this result with any degree of certainty; however, it is possible that people born in Australia have more well-developed social networks relative to people who have recently migrated to Australia. Those people born in Australia are likely to be living in the same country as their immediate family and friends, thus linking them to close social networks. By contrast, people who have migrated to Australia may have left behind significant social networks centred on family and friends in their country of origin. Furthermore, it is likely that it takes time to develop social networks of sufficient size and importance to provide support. As noted above, it is not within the remit of this paper to examine this issue more completely; this is made more difficult by the fact that much of the research in this area examines the utility of social capital and social networks within specific immigrant populations. There is little research that examines the social capital, networks or support evident within indigenous and immigrant populations. In this respect, the research reported within this paper related to the perceived social support of Australian and non-Australian born individuals suggests the need for further research in this area.

Being female had a significant predictive effect on the overall perceived social support scale, as well as on the friends and significant other subscales. As with the findings related to individuals being Australian born, it is not within the ambit of this paper to comment in detail on the implications of the finding that women are more likely to have higher levels of perceived social support than men. It is possible that women have close friends in whom they can trust and confide who in turn provide greater social support than that which is afforded to males by their close friends.

Finally and somewhat surprisingly, being employed full time, attending church and being more highly educated had no bearing on perceived social support. The lack of correlation between education and perceived social support is the least surprising, in part because a person's level of education should not determine the breadth or depth of his or her social network. The resources available through the network of a more highly educated person might be greater, particularly in economic terms, but as the perceived social support scale does not examine this phenomenon it is not relevant to the findings reported within this paper. By contrast, both church attendance and employment are likely to enhance the breadth of a person's social network. In her definition of social support, Thoits referred to the 'functions performed for the individual by significant others, such as family members, friends and coworkers'.[60] Arguably, the results reported here suggest that the breadth of an individual's social network is less important than the depth of the network or its utility in terms of perceived social support. Based on the findings of this study, it is reasonable to suggest that social networks and connections established elsewhere are more important in providing social support than those developed in the workplace or through religious attendance. These findings are somewhat contentious and it remains to be determined what special features other social settings, such as sport or non-sport community organizations, have that might facilitate a greater depth of social relationships and networks.

Conclusion

The results reported within this paper could be used, with caution, to suggest that involvement in community organizations is a potential prescription for people suffering social isolation or who have low levels of perceived social support. However, the barriers to accessing or entering community organizations for particular groups, especially those suffering isolation, need to be explicated. This lies outside the scope of this paper; the barriers to participation within the specific context of social exclusion and disadvantage warrant further research. Many of the variables in this study that were associated with higher levels of perceived social support are ascribed and not amenable to change, or can only be changed with great difficulty, for example gender and birthplace. By contrast, the results of the study point to membership of community organizations as an achievement that could potentially allow a route to greater social support.

Despite claims that sport is social glue, which has a range of prescriptive and restorative powers, the results of this study show that it is not associated with higher levels of perceived social support than other non-sport community organizations. Although these findings are the result of applying only one scale and are part of a broader research project, they do attempt to address the issue of what resources, albeit broadly defined, are made available to people via the social networks that they have access to. In this way, the research attempted to test the validity of the claim that because people are involved in sport they necessarily enjoy more social support and therefore have access to a range of unspecified benefits. It appears that sport involvement does provide a resource upon which people can draw, often at times of need, yet it appears that it is no more important than other community settings in which people voluntarily come together for mutual benefit.

The results do suggest that both sport and non-sport community organizations may be better at fostering the provision of social support than other established social institutions such as the workplace and religious congregations. This in turn suggests that there might be something special about the social networks and the friendships that are developed through voluntary associations. Importantly, they appear to be more associated with perceived social support measures than associations formed at work or through religious attendance. It remains for further research to explore these themes in more depth and it is likely that a qualitative approach will be required. Qualitative research may enable researchers to more fully explore the specific ways in which networks and relationships formed in different social settings are more or less useful in providing social support. This is largely because interview data will enable researchers to examine an individual's social network in far greater depth, particularly the way in which it was formed and developed, as well as delivered specific benefits. The historical or longitudinal dimension will be particularly important, while qualitative interviews might also enable researchers to more adequately disentangle the myriad of activities and organizational associations through which an individual develops a useful social network.

Like Kay and Bradbury,[61] we too are prepared to suggest that the results of this study mean that sport researchers can be less tentative about claims that sport yields social benefits. However, to return to points made earlier in this paper regarding the relationship between sport and social capital, we are also mindful that both the causes and utility of increased perceived social support are contingent. The design of the present study does not allow us to delve more deeply into the conditions under which perceived social support is more or less intense for particular sport participants in particular types of settings.

An important caveat for this research, and use of the MSPSS in attempting to discern whether particular organizations or community structures are more or less important in contributing to perceived social support, is the way in which friendship is conceptualized within the scale. The questions that form the friends subscale are as follows: 'my friends really try to help me'; 'I can count on my friends when things go wrong'; 'I have friends with who I can share my joys and sorrows' and 'I can talk about my problems with my friends'. In the first question, the use of the word 'really' suggests a level of intensity of help that could be associated with close friendship. In each of the other questions, a reference is made to the individual experiencing difficulty or hard times: things going wrong, sorrow and problems. While this conceptualization of friendship is useful for ascertaining whether perceived social support acts as a buffer in times of stress or difficulty and therefore mediates or ameliorates negative mental or physical health effects, it is not as useful for assessing perceived social support across different friendship types. Questions that refer to times of difficulty or hardship lend themselves to a conceptualization of friendship as close friendship, thereby potentially excluding other less intense or intimate friendships. This is of particular importance for examining community groups such as sporting clubs and associations. In this respect, the results of this study might be interpreted as particularly revealing given the conceptualization of friendship. If a broader and more inclusive conceptualization of friendship was used, the perceived social support from involvement in voluntary community organizations such as sporting clubs might be more pronounced.

Directly related to the discussion about the nature of friendship within the scale is the conceptualization of relationships more generally within the MSPSS. As Granovetter proposed, the strength of an interpersonal tie is a combination of the amount of time, emotional intensity, intimacy and reciprocal services.[62] The MSPSS subscales of significant other, family and friends all examine strong ties, or those relationships that are time intensive, have significant emotional intensity, as well as high levels of intimacy and reciprocity. By contrast, the scale does not examine, to use Granovetter's words, the 'strength of weak ties' in delivering perceived social support. These weak ties are likely present in a range of social networks that exist outside the more intimate relationships of partners, family and close friends. These social networks might include those formed within voluntary community settings such as sporting clubs, as well as other more formal settings such as the workplace. The strength of weak ties and their relationship to perceived social support remains largely uncaptured by the MSPSS.

An important limitation of the research reported within this paper also relates to the 'direction' of the findings and the capacity to attribute causality. While the findings demonstrated that involvement in sport and non-sport community organizations had a small but significant predictive effect on the overall perceived social support scale and selected subscales, we are unable to determine whether people who are involved in these organizations and activities receive greater social support as a result of their involvement, or whether people with greater levels of social support are more likely to participate in community organizations. The results that revealed no correlation between perceived social support and either intensity of involvement or tenure of involvement cast further doubt on the direction of the findings and the possibility of attributing causality. These results could be used to suggest that perceived social support is almost instantaneously created or developed by involvement. Further research that adopts a longitudinal methodology is likely to be able to tease out the issue of causality more completely, while qualitative research might also provide a valuable perspective, particularly if research participants were able to articulate the benefits they received from involvement at the point they joined the organization, as well as the benefit they are currently receiving.

Acknowledgements

The authors wish to acknowledge the financial support of the Australian Research Council and the Victorian Health Promotion Foundation (VicHealth) for this project.

Notes

1. See, for example, Commission on the European Communities, *White Paper on Sport*; Commonwealth of Australia, *Backing Australia's Sporting Ability*; Commonwealth of Australia, *Australian Sport*; Sport Canada, *Canadian Sport Policy*; and Sport England, *National Framework for Sport*.
2. Skille, 'Meaning of Social Context', 367–68.
3. Long and Sanderson, 'Social Benefits of Sport'.
4. Coalter, *Wider Social Role*.
5. Putnam, *Bowling Alone*.

6. Ibid., 411
7. Stolle, 'Bowling Together, Bowling Alone'.
8. Thoits, 'Stress'.
9. Veiel and Baumann, 'Many Meanings'.
10. House, Landis and Umberson, 'Social Relationships and Health'.
11. Uchino, Cacioppo and Kiecolt-Glaser, 'Relationship between Social Support'.
12. Cohen and Wills, 'Stress'.
13. Thoits, 'Social Support'.
14. Thoits, 'Stress'.
15. Albrecht and Adelman, *Communicating Social Support*.
16. Shumaker and Brownell, 'Toward a Theory'.
17. Sarason, Sarason and Pierce, 'Social Support'.
18. Putnam, *Bowling Alone*, 18–19.
19. Bourdieu, 'Forms of Capital', 248.
20. Coleman, 'Social Capital', S98.
21. Portes, 'Social Capital', 6.
22. Bourdieu, 'Forms of Capital'.
23. Portes and Landolt, 'Downside of Social Capital'; 'Social Capital'.
24. Woolcock, 'Social Capital'.
25. Putnam, *Bowling Alone*, 19.
26. Putnam, 'Bowling Alone', 67.
27. Thoits, 'Stress'.
28. Shumaker and Brownell, 'Toward a Theory'.
29. Zimet et al., 'Multidimensional Scale'.
30. Dahlem, Zimet and Walker, 'Multidimensional Scale'; Thoits, 'Stress'; and Zimet et al., 'Multidimensional Scale'.
31. Bourdieu, 'Forms of Capital'.
32. Portes and Landolt, 'Downside of Social Capital'; 'Social Capital'.
33. Blackshaw and Long, 'What's the Big Idea?'; Brown, 'Position of Australian Community'; Coalter, *Wider Social Role*; Coalter, 'Sports Clubs, Social Capital'; Collins, *Sport and Social Exclusion*; Collins, 'Voluntary Sports Clubs'; Dyreson, 'Maybe it's Better'; Harvey, Levesque and Donnelly, 'Sport Volunteerism'; Jarvie, 'Communitarism'; Nicholson and Hoye, *Sport and Social Capital*; Seippel, 'Sport and Social Capital'; Sharpe, '"It's Not Fun Anymore"'; Sharpe, 'Resources at the Grassroots'; and Tonts, 'Competitive Sport'.
34. See, for example, Bradbury and Kay, 'Stepping into Community?'; Brown, 'Community Sport/ Recreation Members'; Hylton, 'Race Equality'; Kay and Bradbury, 'Youth Sport Volunteering'; Long, 'Sport's Ambiguous Relationship'; and Walseth, 'Bridging and Bonding'.
35. Putnam, *Bowling Alone*.
36. Nicholson and Hoye, *Sport and Social Capital*, 9.
37. Ibid.
38. Barefield and McCallister, 'Social Support'; Bianco, 'Social Support and Recovery'; Hardy, Richman and Rosenfeld, 'Role of Social Support'; Junge, 'Influence of Psychological Factors'; Malinauskas, 'College Athletes' Perceptions'; Petrie, 'Moderating Effects'; Rees, Smith and Sparkes, 'Influence of Social Support'; and Robbins and Rosenfeld, 'Athletes' Perceptions'.
39. Hardy, Richman and Rosenfeld, 'Role of Social Support'; Noblet, Rodwell and McWilliams, 'Predictors of the Strain'; Petrie, 'Moderating Effects'; Smith, Smoll and Barnett, 'Reduction of Children's Sport'; Woodman and Hardy, 'Case Study'; and Rees and Hardy, 'Matching Social Support'.
40. Rees and Hardy, 'Investigation'; Rees, Ingledew and Hardy, 'Social Support Dimensions'.
41. Zimet et al., 'Multidimensional Scale'; Dahlem, Zimet and Walker, 'Multidimensional Scale'.
42. Dillman, *Mail and Internet Surveys*, 3–31.
43. Kaplowitz, Hadlock and Levine, 'Comparison of Web and Mail', 98.
44. ABS, *2006 Census of Population*.
45. ABS, *2015 3235.2.55.001 – Population*.
46. ABS, *2006 Census of Population*.
47. ABS, *3201.0 – Population*.
48. ABS, *2006 Census of Population*.
49. Ibid.

50. Groves and Couper, *Non-Response in Household*.
51. Dillman, *Mail and Internet Surveys*.
52. ABS, *2006 Census of Population*.
53. Ibid.
54. ABS, *2015 3235.2.55.001 – Population*.
55. Dahlem, Zimet and Walker, 'Multidimensional Scale'.
56. Canty-Mitchell and Zimet, 'Psychometric Properties'.
57. Zimet et al., 'Multidimensional Scale'.
58. See, for example, Commission on the European Communities, *White Paper on Sport*; Commonwealth of Australia, *Backing Australia's Sporting Ability*; Commonwealth of Australia, *Australian Sport*; Sport Canada, *Canadian Sport Policy*; and Sport England, *National Framework for Sport*.
59. Weiss, 'Provisions of Social Relationships'.
60. Thoits, 'Stress', 64.
61. Kay and Bradbury, 'Youth Sport Volunteering'.
62. Granovetter, 'Strength of Weak Ties'.

References

ABS (Australian Bureau of Statistics). *2015 3235.2.55.001 – Population by Age and Sex, Victoria, June 2004*. Canberra: ABS, 2005.

ABS. *2006 Census of Population by Age and Sex, Victoria*. Canberra: ABS, 2007.

ABS. *3201.0 – Population by Age and Sex, Australian States and Territories, June 2009*. Canberra: ABS, 2009.

Albrecht, T., and M. Adelman. *Communicating Social Support*. Thousand Oaks, CA: Sage, 1987.

Barefield, S., and S. McCallister. 'Social Support in the Athletic Training Room: Athletes' Expectations of Staff and Student Athletic Trainers'. *Journal of Athletic Training* 32 (1997): 333–8.

Bianco, T. 'Social Support and Recovery from Sport Injury: Elite Skiers Share Their Experiences'. *Research Quarterly for Exercise and Sport* 72 (2001): 376–88.

Blackshaw, T., and J. Long. 'What's the Big Idea? A Critical Exploration of the Concept of Social Capital and its Incorporation into Leisure Policy Discourse'. *Leisure Studies* 24 (2005): 239–58.

Bourdieu, P. 'The Forms of Capital'. In *Handbook of Theory and Research for the Sociology of Education*, ed. J. Richardson, 241–58. New York: Greenwood, 1986.

Bradbury, S., and T. Kay. 'Stepping into Community? The Impact of Youth Sport Volunteering on Young People's Social Capital'. In *Sport and Social Capital*, ed. M. Nicholson and R. Hoye, 285–316. Oxford: Butterworth-Heinemann, 2008.

Brown, K. 'Community Sport/Recreation Members and Social Capital Measures in Sweden and Australia'. In *Sport and Social Capital*, ed. M. Nicholson and R. Hoye, 165–86. Oxford: Butterworth-Heinemann, 2008.

Brown, K. 'The Position of Australian Community Sporting Organisations in the Third Sector: Membership Profiles, Characteristics and Attitudes'. *Third Sector Review* 12 (2006): 17–39.

Canty-Mitchell, J., and G. Zimet. 'Psychometric Properties of the Multidimensional Scale of Perceived Social Support in Urban Adolescents'. *American Journal of Community Psychology* 28 (2000): 391–400.

Coalter, F. 'Sports Clubs, Social Capital and Social Regeneration: "Ill-Defined Interventions with Hard to Follow Outcomes"?' *Sport in Society* 10 (2007): 537–59.

Coalter, F. *A Wider Social Role For Sport: Who's Keeping Score?* London: Routledge, 2007.

Cohen, S., and T. Wills. 'Stress, Social Support, and the Buffering Hypothesis'. *Psychological Bulletin* 98 (1985): 310–57.

Coleman, J. 'Social Capital in the Creation of Human Capital'. *American Journal of Sociology* 94 (1988): S95–S120.

Collins, M. *Sport and Social Exclusion*. London: Routledge, 2003.

Collins, M. 'Voluntary Sports Clubs and Social Capital'. In *Volunteers in Sports Clubs*, ed. G. Nichols and M. Collins, 105–18. Eastbourne: LSA, 2005.

Commonwealth of Australia. *Australian Sport: Emerging Challenges, New Directions*. Canberra: Commonwealth of Australia, 2008.

Commonwealth of Australia. *Backing Australia's Sporting Ability*. Canberra: Commonwealth of Australia, 2001.

Commission on the European Communities. *White Paper on Sport*. Brussels: Commission on the European Communities, 2007.

Dahlem, N., G. Zimet, and R. Walker. 'The Multidimensional Scale of Perceived Social Support: A Confirmation Study'. *Journal of Clinical Psychology* 47 (1991): 756–61.

Dillman, D.A. *Mail and Internet Surveys: The Tailored Design Method*. New York: Wiley, 2000.

Dyreson, M. 'Maybe it's Better to Bowl Alone: Sport, Community and Democracy in American Thought'. *Sport in Society* 4 (2001): 19–30.

Granovetter, M. 'The Strength of Weak Ties'. *American Journal of Sociology* 78 (1973): 1360–80.

Groves, R.M., and M.P. Couper. *Non-Response in Household Interviews*. New York: Wiley, 1998.

Hardy, C., J. Richman, and L. Rosenfeld. 'The Role of Social Support in the Life Stress/Injury Relationship'. *The Sport Psychologist* 5 (1991): 128–39.

Harvey, J., M. Levesque, and P. Donnelly. 'Sport Volunteerism and Social Capital'. *Sociology of Sport Journal* 24 (2007): 206–23.

House, J., K. Landis, and D. Umberson. 'Social Relationships and Health'. *Science* 241 (1988): 540–5.

Hylton, K. 'Race Equality and Sport Networks: Social Capital Links'. In *Sport and Social Capital*, ed. M. Nicholson and R. Hoye, 257–84. Oxford: Butterworth-Heinemann, 2008.

Jarvie, G. 'Communitarism, Sport and Social Capital'. *International Review for the Sociology of Sport* 38 (2003): 139–53.

Junge, A. 'The Influence of Psychological Factors on Sports Injuries'. *The American Journal of Sports Medicine* 28 (2000): S10–S15.

Kaplowitz, M.D., T.D. Hadlock, and R. Levine. 'A Comparison of Web and Mail Survey Response'. *Public Opinion Quarterly* 68 (2004): 94–101.

Kay, T., and S. Bradbury. 'Youth Sport Volunteering: Developing Social Capital?' *Sport, Education and Society* 14 (2009): 121–40.

Long, J. 'Sport's Ambiguous Relationship with Social Capital: The Contribution of National Governing Bodies of Sport'. In *Sport and Social Capital*, ed. M. Nicholson and R. Hoye, 207–32. Oxford: Butterworth-Heinemann, 2008.

Long, J., and I. Sanderson. 'The Social Benefits of Sport: Where's the Proof?' In *Sport in the City*, ed. C. Gratton and I. Henry, 187–203. London: Routledge, 2001.

Malinauskas, R. 'College Athletes' Perceptions of Social Support Provided by Their Head Coach before Injury and after it'. *Journal of Sports Medicine and Physical Fitness* 48 (2008): 107–12.

Nicholson, M. and R. Hoye, eds. *Sport and Social Capital*. Oxford: Butterworth-Heinemann, 2008.

Noblet, A., H. Rodwell, and J. McWilliams. 'Predictors of the Strain Experienced by Professional Australian Footballers'. *Journal of Applied Sport Psychology* 15 (2003): 184–94.

Petrie, T. 'The Moderating Effects of Social Support and Playing Status on the Life Stress-Injury Relationship'. *Journal of Applied Sport Psychology* 5 (1993): 1–16.

Portes, A. 'Social Capital: Its Origins and Applications in Modern Sociology'. *Annual Review of Sociology* 24 (1998): 1–24.

Portes, A., and P. Landolt. 'The Downside of Social Capital'. *American Prospect* 26 (1996): 18–21, 94.

Portes, A., and P. Landolt. 'Social Capital: Promise and Pitfalls of its Role in Development'. *Journal of Latin American Studies* 32 (2000): 529–47.

Putnam, R.D. 'Bowling Alone: America's Declining Social Capital'. *Journal of Democracy* 6 (1995): 65–78.

Putnam, R.D. *Bowling Alone: The Collapse and Revival of American Community*. New York: Simon & Schuster, 2000.

Rees, T., and L. Hardy. 'An Investigation of the Social Support Experiences of High-Level Sports Performers'. *The Sport Psychologist* 14 (2000): 327–47.

Rees, T., and L. Hardy. 'Matching Social Support with Stressors: Effects on Factors Underlying Performance in Tennis'. *Psychology of Sport and Exercise* 5 (2004): 319–37.

Rees, T., D. Ingledew, and L. Hardy. 'Social Support Dimensions and Components of Performance in Tennis'. *Journal of Sports Sciences* 17 (1999): 421–9.

Rees, T., B. Smith, and A. Sparkes. 'The Influence of Social Support on the Lived Experiences of Spinal Cord Injured Sportsmen'. *The Sport Psychologist* 17 (2003): 135–56.

Robbins, J., and L. Rosenfeld. 'Athletes' Perceptions of Social Support Provided by Their Head Coach, Assistant Coach, and Athlete Trainer, Pre-Injury and during Rehabilitation'. *Journal of Sport Behavior* 24 (2001): 277–97.

Sarason, I., B. Sarason, and G. Pierce. 'Social Support, Personality and Performance'. *Journal of Applied Sport Psychology* 2 (1990): 117–27.

Seippel, Ø. 'Sport and Social Capital'. *Acta Sociologica* 49 (2006): 169–83.

Sharpe, E. '"It's Not Fun Anymore": A Case Study of Organizing a Contemporary Grassroots Recreation Association'. *Society and Leisure* 26 (2003): 431–52.

Sharpe, E. 'Resources at the Grassroots of Recreation: Organizational Capacity and Quality of Experience in a Community Sport Organization'. *Leisure Sciences* 28 (2006): 385–401.

Shumaker, S., and A. Brownell. 'Toward a Theory of Social Support: Closing Conceptual Gaps'. *Journal of Social Issues* 40 (1984): 11–36.

Skille, E. 'The Meaning of Social Context: Experiences of and Educational Outcomes of Participation in Two Different Sports Contexts'. *Sport, Education and Society* 12 (2007): 367–82.

Smith, R., F. Smoll, and N. Barnett. 'Reduction of Children's Sport Performance Anxiety through Social Support and Stress-reduction Training for Coaches'. *Journal of Applied Developmental Psychology* 16 (1995): 125–42.

Sport Canada. *The Canadian Sport Policy*. Canada: Canadian Heritage, 2002.

Sport England. *National Framework for Sport*. London: Sport England, 2004.

Stolle, D. 'Bowling Together, Bowling Alone: The Development of Generalized Trust in Voluntary Associations'. *Political Psychology* 19 (1998): 497–525.

Thoits, P. 'Social Support as Coping Assistance'. *Journal of Consulting and Clinical Psychology* 54 (1986): 416–23.

Thoits, P. 'Stress, Coping, and Social Support Processes: Where Are We? What Next?' Extra issue, *Journal of Health and Social Behavior* 35 (1995): 53–79.

Tonts, M. 'Competitive Sport and Social Capital in Rural Australia'. *Journal of Rural Studies* 21 (2005): 137–49.

Uchino, B., J. Cacioppo, and J. Kiecolt-Glaser. 'The Relationship between Social Support and Physiological Processes: A Review with Emphasis on Underlying Mechanisms and Implications for Health'. *Psychological Bulletin* 119 (1996): 488–531.

Veiel, H. and U. Baumann, eds. 'The Many Meanings of Social Support'. *The Meaning and Measurement of Social Support*, 1–7. New York: Hemisphere Publishing, 1992.

Walseth, K. 'Bridging and Bonding Social Capital in Sport – Experiences of Young Women with an Immigrant Background'. *Sport, Education and Society* 13 (2008): 1–17.

Woodman, T., and L. Hardy. 'A Case Study of Organizational Stress in Elite Sport'. *Journal of Applied Sport Psychology* 13 (2001): 207–38.

Woolcock, M. 'Social Capital and Economic Development: Toward a Theoretical Synthesis and Policy Framework'. *Theory and Society* 27 (1998): 151–208.

Weiss, R. 'The Provisions of Social Relationships'. In *Doing Unto Others*, ed. R. Zick, 17–26. Englewood Cliffs, NJ: Prentice Hall, 1974.

Zimet, G., N. Dahlem, S. Zimet, and G. Farley. 'The Multidimensional Scale of Perceived Social Support'. *Journal of Personality Assessment* 52 (1988): 30–41.

How do youth sports facilitate the creation of parental social ties?

Sean F. Brown*

Department of Sociology and Anthropology, Northeastern University, Boston, MA, USA

This article explores the mechanisms by which youth sports leagues facilitate the creation and mobilization of parental social ties and social capital. Through a qualitative examination of a youth baseball league in the Southwestern USA, I witnessed how organizational structures provided parents with opportunities to socialize and form ties with one another. In addition, I explore how players also influence the specific tie formation of their parents. The role of children in the social capital process has thus far been largely limited to that of passive recipient. Within this piece, I seek to alter this vision by repositioning children as active social agents with roles to play in the social capital formation of their parents.

Introduction

In this article, I examine the role that children play in the creation of social capital for their parents. While social capital theorists have noted the benefits children can accrue through their parents and their parents' social connections, little work has been done tracing the reciprocal flow of said benefits through children's activities and connections. Through an ethnographic examination of the Valley City Little League (VCLL), a child-centred voluntary organization, I show how children can serve as a source of social capital for their parents, both indirectly and directly. Parents bring their children to ostensibly play baseball, learn life skills and acquire valuable socialization skills. Along the way, they embed themselves in an environment populated by people with similar aspirations for their own children. This both changes parents' attitudes towards strangers within the league and facilitates acquaintances and relationships between parents through various league mechanisms. Such contacts can ease and spur the sharing of certain resources, explored below.

Social capital

Before unpacking these mechanisms, it is worth the time to examine the concept of social capital, an increasingly difficult task as scholars continue to grapple with it. Karl Marx's work is generally acknowledged as the origin of the concept 'capital' as accumulated labour. Alternative models of capital have emerged since Marx's work, including human capital,[1] cultural capital[2] and social capital theories.[3] Lin refers to these alternative theories as neo-capital theories.[4] The difference between these and conventional capital theory, according to Lin, is in the numbers and types of people who can accumulate surplus labour from their investment (i.e. profit). He writes, ' . . . the laborers, workers, or masses can now invest, and thus acquire certain capital of their own ... they can now generate surplus value in trading their labor or work in the production and consumption markets'.[5] Ronald Burt, meanwhile, notes that social capital is the contextual counterpart

---

*Current affiliation: Department of Sociology, University of Chicago, Chicago, IL, USA.

to human capital theory, which takes the position that '... people who do better are more able individuals; they are more intelligent, more attractive, more articulate, more skilled'.[6] Social capital theorists emphasize the role of context and relations in the production of goods.[7]

While the widespread use of the term 'social capital' is of fairly recent vintage, the concept behind the term is not. In fact, contained within this idea are some of the basic tenets of sociology's classical thinkers:

> That involvement and participation in groups can have positive consequences for the individual and the community is a staple notion, dating back to Durkheim's emphasis on group life as an antidote to anomie and self-destruction and to Marx's distinction between an atomized class-in-itself and a mobilized and effective class-for-itself.[8]

The underlying mechanism by which social capital can function is reciprocity, though the specific form of reciprocity invoked changes depending on the theoretical predilection of the scholar. For those who emphasize a homo economicus view of human action, social capital is derived from the accumulation of specific obligations based on particular favours past.[9] Other scholars, especially those who view social capital as a resource of communities and larger units, prefer the idea of generalized reciprocity. Putnam, for instance, claims, 'The touchstone of social capital is the principle of generalized reciprocity – I'll do this for you now, without expecting anything immediately in return and perhaps without even knowing you, confident that down the road you or someone else will return the favor'.[10] These communal understandings of social capital have grown up alongside network versions of social capital, complicating the matter exponentially. The two versions should not necessarily be thought of as competing, however, as Nicholson and Hoye explain in their pioneering volume on the connection between sport and social capital.[11] In this study, however, I have focused – and believe sports sociologists in general should pay more attention to – individual conceptions of social capital. In essence, participation in sport – at whatever level – can enhance an individual's networks and act as a conduit for the building of network resources.

Sport and social capital

As early as 1993, calls were being made for an investigation of sport that focused on networks and structure, counter to the then current trend, whereby researchers' interest in sport focused on the interpretive meanings of sport to its participants, 'Sport sociology could benefit from relatively more attention to the stripped-down level of social interaction and underlying social structures'.[12] The rationale for Nixon's plea typified the reaction against the 'overpsychologized' treatment of the small group within sporting contexts,[13] even as acknowledgement was made that individual psychology was a relevant element operating within said groups.[14] Nixon specifically cited ethnographies of sporting subcultures to suggest that an understanding of networks within the larger study of sport was a worthwhile endeavour in expanding scholars' understanding of the ways in which groups of people in a sporting context operate.[15] While Nixon was not referring specifically to social capital, his recommendations are noteworthy for establishing the need for both network studies within sport sociology as well as research committed to uncovering structures operating within the sporting realm.

The explicit connection between sport and social capital was given conceptual and visual boost by *Bowling Alone*.[16] Putnam's employment of the decline of bowling leagues as a metaphor for – and a symptom of – the decline of civil society in the USA was a boon to sports scholars, who jumped at the opportunity to show that sport was in fact the next great hope for saving social capital in the USA. Some claimed that Putnam's work had barely scratched the surface of the sport and social capital connection:

> The idea that sport produces public virtue is just a little younger than Jeffersonian agrarianism and somewhat older than American faith in science or confidence in the brand of modern liberalism which insists that government can manage corporate capitalism ... I would argue that Putnam understated the case for sport. Along with perhaps national faith in public education, many Americans have considered sport the most important tool for making social capital. What other antebellum reform movements besides sports still have such cultural power at the end of the twentieth century.[17]

It is critical to note, however, that perhaps largely because of Putnam's explicit connection between the sport and social capital, it is the 'Putnamian' conception of social capital that has dominated the discourse on its relation to sport, and the trope of the lone bowler has been employed as a starting point for much work attempting to uncover the exact nature of the connection between the two.

Linking sport and social capital is appealing to sport scholars and policy-makers alike, 'The general argument put forth is that sport participation creates social connections between people that, in turn, build trust within a community, thereby helping establish the foundation for an active and engaged citizenry who are likely to serve broader community interests'.[18] Furthermore, because the 'community' ideal has appeal across the political spectrum, any tool which might facilitate the building of community (however measured) attracts hordes of policy ideas and private initiatives.[19] Such initiatives have included innovative ideas such as midnight basketball, youth soccer and church softball leagues.[20] These initiatives and the policy-makers responsible for them ignore the common sense understanding of sport as merely a vehicle for either positive or negative externalities. Sport sociology writings, both empirical and conceptual, have largely dealt with social capital in sport within the realm of policy, which has hampered a concrete understanding of how sport can produce or limit social capital formation for its participants.

Children and social capital

The sociological investigation of children and social capital is characterized largely by the flow of capital from parents and significant others to children,[21] but it also predates the modern conception of social capital.[22] This is not without warrant. Children in the USA are rarely in a position to benefit their parents materially. This has not always been the case; the decreased economic utility of children has been noted in the family demography literature, and is largely the result of the removal of children from the regular labour market.[23] Consequently, sociologists have spent the majority of their research efforts detailing the benefits that parental networks and time can and do have for children.

James Coleman's seminal article 'Social Capital in the Creation of Human Capital' represented a crucial moment not only in the definition of social capital, but also in its application as well, particularly where children are concerned.[24] Coleman clearly and explicitly positioned children as passive beneficiaries of the social capital provided them by their parents, either through the parent–child relationship or the parent–parent relationship that characterizes closure. Whether Coleman set a precedent for this particular application of social capital between the generations or if he was simply the first to exploit this natural fit, sociologists have largely followed his lead.[25] While some sociologists and demographers have begun to acknowledge the impact children can have on both their own social capital and their parents, very few studies have explored this link in any meaningful way.

While scholars have been investigating the social networks of children in various contexts,[26] 'social capital' did not enter the lexicon of childhood and adolescent researchers until approximately 1999. Since that time, scholars of childhood and adolescence have become increasingly interested in how children structure their own networks as independent social agents. Virginia Morrow began her discussion of children and social capital by noting that social capital as then characterized and applied was ill-suited to provide a better understanding of the lived experience of children and adolescents.[27] Of particular concern to Morrow was that children were being ignored as active social agents with agendas that extended past their parents' purview:

> A more 'active' conceptualisation of children, drawing on the sociology of childhood would explore how children themselves actively generate, draw on, or negotiate their own social capital, or indeed make links for their parents, or even provide active support for parents. In other words, children's agency, constrained though it may be, is downplayed in US research and children appear as passive burdens on adults' time.[28]

The idea that children should be thought of as active and independent social agents provided researchers with a new avenue to explore the relationship between children and social capital, and laid the foundation for later research exploring the role of children in their parents' social capital.

Research that began with this assumption often dealt with the same issues that the dominant strain of social capital research engaged, such as employment,[29] education transitions and outcomes,[30] neighbourhood ties[31] and recreation opportunities.[32] In these analyses, the social lives of children were explored as important in their own right and not as a by-product of the adult social world. As socialization progresses away from the family and to the peer group as children grow up and mature, it follows logically that their social networks will outgrow the constraints that their limited geographic mobility and social skills place on them in early childhood. While the resources available to youth and adolescents may be of a different order than that accessible by adults – it is primarily emotional support[33] – and fungibility may also be an issue in classifying youth relationships as social capital,[34] these scholars established that youth were not merely the 'passive recipients of the benefits of parental social capital' but were, in fact, 'active producers and consumers in their own right'.[35] The idea of children acting as social agents implies the possibility that children could be benefactors in their family's stock of social capital, and scholars such as Morrow acknowledged this as such. However, sociologists have only within the last decade began engaging the question seriously, and the work that has done so has been general and ambiguous.[36]

The present study is an attempt to address some of the major gaps in the literature at two levels: first, the literature dealing with the intersection of sport and social capital is active, but overall not well developed or helpful. It is lacking in well-grounded, empirical studies of social capital *in situ*, and the ways in which different populations may or may not benefit from whatever social capital is to be built or utilized within sports organizations. Second, this research has largely taken a Putnamian conception of social capital, leaving the network-level understanding of the concept understudied and undertheorized in the sporting context. Less substantially, research on sport and social capital within the context of the USA has been virtually non-existent. The vast majority of works in this area have taken place in Canada, the UK or Australia. To the extent that sport provision is different in the USA than in these other locales, their work may be of limited utility when studying in the USA. Within the more general social capital literature, this study addresses a significant gap. Social capital research has been largely silent on the role of children. While some works are beginning to make the connection between social capital and child-centred contexts,[37] the explicit connection between children and social capital formation is still woefully underdeveloped.

Methods

Valley City is a small (population *c*.15,000) suburban/rural town situated in the Rio Grande Valley of New Mexico, less than an hour from a mid-sized metropolitan area. This site offers a bimodal population, with a fairly even ethnic split between Latinos and whites and an emerging diversity in class composition, as new housing stock slowly turns the west side of town into a fairly prototypical, middle-class southwestern suburb. Valley City offers the standard array of team sporting opportunities (American football, basketball, soccer and baseball) for a wide range of ages. The VCLL offers opportunities for children beginning at the age of 4 and continuing up through the age of 18.

The Valley City Little League

The league is divided up by age and (beginning at the age of 5) gender. Children begin by playing tee-ball, where the main goal is to teach children to hit a stationary ball off of a tee, and to run to the proper base once the ball is hit. Children in the field are taught to throw and catch baseballs. At the age of 7, children are moved to the Pee-Wee division, where kids begin to hit 'live' pitching from a machine designed to adjust to their relative skill levels.[38] Children begin pitching to one another at the age of 9 in the Minor division. At 11 years of age, players move to the Major division. Both the Major and Minor divisions are highly competitive, partly because they are the first leagues to have an All-Star team put together at the end of the regular season to represent the community in tournaments at the local, state, regional and (if they are good enough) the national level. While the youngest teams are sex-integrated, teams beginning at the age of 5 are segregated by sex, and by the age of 7 boys and girls no longer have any on-field contact.

Data gathering

Data were gathered from March 2010 through August of 2011. During that time, I observed four teams over two seasons in the VCLL. The Twins were a team of 4-year-old boys and girls playing in the league for the first time. The Wildcats were softball, a team of 11–12-year-old girls, most of whom had extensive experience in the league. The Mariners were an All-Star team of 11and 12-year-old boys, and the Cubs were a baseball team consisting of 9- and 10-year-old boys with varying levels of experience. I spent many hours observing and speaking with parents during games and practices about their experiences in youth sports and the relationships they had formed in their time at the VCLL. I became a member of and subsequently attended Board of Directors meetings of the league. These observations taught me much about the contexts in which parent conversations take place as well as the meaning and backdrop of those conversations. I also conducted 35 in-depth interviews with city officials, league presidents and parents. In these interviews, I explored league issues, personal and backgrounds, social networks and league experiences. All names used herein are pseudonyms as an attempt to protect the identity of the participants. All interview participants signed informed consent documents. However, not everyone in attendance at practices and games were aware of my involvement with the league. I did not keep notes during practices and games, preferring instead to type detailed fieldnotes upon returning home. I also participated at various levels during practices and games, from retrieving wayward baseballs to helping out with practices. During games, I occasionally acted as an umpire when scheduled officials failed to show up for their assignments. All interviews were recorded, transcribed and coded using Atlas.ti.[39] Because the explicit aims of the project involved uncovering and detailing parental relationships, the coding of the data is biased towards those particular instances. At the same time, I have attempted to be very sensitive to other readings and interpretations of the data.

Mechanisms for social capital creation

When a parent signed a child up in the VCLL, they were placing both their child and themselves in a setting with hundreds of other parents similarly committed to their child's participation in the league. This commonality, though shallow, was very salient for the participating parents, as it altered their orientation to the presence of 'strangers' in the league.[40] While strangers were still strangers in the conventional sense, there was a sense among parents that the common values that brought together the group of children in the league indicated a similar value orientation between themselves and the other parents within the league. This allowed parents in the league to be slightly less guarded with each other when first meeting other parents, and provided a sliver of positive affect that characterized first meetings between parents. There were several mechanisms operating within the league that facilitated the creation and mobilization of social capital: indirectly (through the team creation process, team practices, games, All Star participation and participation on the Board of Directors) and directly (through the relationships that children formed among themselves, which affected the friendship choices of their parents as well). By mere participation in these activities, parents embedded themselves in a setting rich in social capital potential, even as the mobilization of such resources tended to be both setting-dependent and sporadic. While both the indirect and direct forms of children's influence were interesting and important, I have chosen to focus largely on the direct influence of children's networks on those of their parents.

Indirect influence of children – team creation, practices and games, all-star participation and the Board of Directors

Social capital was mobilized at perhaps its greatest rate in the process of team creation. In the lower age divisions, where parents' requests for coaches were honoured (in full or in part), parents and coaches both could leverage their previous interactions and relationships to facilitate a desirable outcome. Parents could request a coach they have had in the past, or coaches with good reputations in the league. Likewise, coaches could ask parents to request them in the event that they wanted a particular player, either for his or her ability or because the families have *a prior* relationship. The process was less formal and more complex in the older age divisions, where all players participated in the tryout process and were then drafted onto teams. Coaches often found themselves attempting to balance the sometimes-contradictory goals of fielding a competitive team with choosing players that also provided him or her with cooperative parents. Existing social relationships and reputations that permeate a small community like Valley City further complicated the situation for coaches:

> When [Nicholas' son] came up to hit, after already blowing the grounders and fly balls portion of the tryout (and showing off a poor arm to boot), the coaches remarked that they wouldn't draft him under any circumstances because of Nicholas. I remarked that I knew Nicholas, and

he wasn't such a bad guy … just a bit 'type A'. I told Lawrence (a coach in the division) that as a police officer, he should understand working with those types. He chuckled and just nodded. At any rate, Nicholas had already asked Brent (another coach in the division) to pick his kid, and this eventually happened. Their wives are apparently good friends, and they have known each other since childhood. (Fieldnotes)

Despite these pressures, coaches tended to find ways to draft teams that they felt would be competitive in the league and that satisfied whatever social obligations they had. In the event that one had to be sacrificed to save the other, coaches usually erred on the side of competitiveness.

Once teams were chosen, parents' potential resource-sharing partners were largely limited to the other parents on their child's team. The main areas for the development of relationships within these groups of parents were during team practices and games. While each form of participation was suited to certain forms of interaction between parents (and the way a parent choose to participate in the social life of the team in these contexts influenced their potential to form closer relationships with other parents), their child's mere inclusion on the team entitled them to certain access to the resources possessed by other parents on the team. Whether practices or games were more important for relationship building depended on the age division in which a team played. For younger teams like the Twins, practices were more conducive to relationship building. First, practices were both mandatory and short for parents as well as children. Second, the action on the field was of little concern to the parents in the bleachers, and they were free to chat away as their children learned the game. Conversely, for older children, practices were long and parent attendance, while encouraged, was not strictly required. Parents often used the 2-hour practice windows to run other errands or accomplish any other chores around the house that might otherwise have been put off. Thus, for the Wildcats team, very few parents stayed for practice times, and there was little opportunity for relationships to develop in that context. Interestingly, games worked in the opposite way. In the younger divisions, games were not conducive to the development of social relationships between parents, owing mainly to the presence of much extended family at these events. Interactions in the stands tended to be intra-familial. In the older age divisions, extended families were largely absent, allowing parents to focus on one another during games. While the action on the field was often intense, the natural breaks that baseball affords left them with much time to converse and interact.

All-Star teams were chosen from among the best players in each eligible age division of the league. They were chosen and announced in mid-June, with practices often beginning the day the teams were announced. Once a child committed, they could count on at least five practices a week leading up to the District Tournament, which featured teams from the area competing for a chance to go to the State Tournament. This 'ramped up' level of both competition and commitment meant that parents found themselves spending more time together in a more emotionally involved setting, as winning fully replaced fun and enjoyment as goals of the games. In addition to practices and games, All-Star parents coordinated fundraising activities, including a car wash and a food sale outside of a local store. After the team won the District Tournament, they also spent several days together at the State Tournament 3 hours from Valley City. While there, they stayed in the same motel, took many of their meals with other parents and waited together as an August downpour cost the team two full days of game play. These events provided several opportunities for the team parents to establish relationships with each other and create bonds of trust that facilitated the development of social capital.

Participation on the Board of Directors represented the ultimate commitment to the smooth operation of the league. The Board ran all aspects of the league except for the coaching of the teams (and many Board members were coaches as well). The Board formulated and implemented league policy and ensured that the league adhered to Little League International rules, mandates and by-laws. This was a significant undertaking. The list of skills needed to successfully run a league on a year-to-year basis was substantial and wholly dependent on the donated time and skills of its members. Thus, the Board of Directors was both the site of social capital building and social capital consumption, as the members of the Board brought their own time, expertise and connections to the benefit of the other members and the league as a whole, such as a local accountant agreeing to serve as Treasurer for the league, or when a contractor on the Board took an off-the-books job to renovate a dilapidated piece of the clubhouse for a much lower price than other estimates from outside companies.

Direct influence of children on parents' social networks

In addition to the baseline relationships that grew between parents on a given team, which were characterized at the minimum by a friendly exchange of greetings, closer relationships did form on most teams. Most of these relationships were described by parents as 'acquaintances', but some of them moved beyond this and into the realm of friendship. The homophily principle would suggest that parent relationships form on the basis of the elective affinities people share with one another.[41] In contexts such as Little League, where there was a diverse array of life circumstances and characteristics on any given team, parent networks could form on the basis of many different characteristics, whether they are ethnic, political, religious or some other characteristic. That is, homophily was expressed at the status or value level.[42] However, in the youth sport context, it was not strictly parent affinities and similarities that drove relationship formation. It was instead often driven by the friendship networks the children created among themselves. This is because children can play a crucial role in the relationships that formed between their parents. In this particular context, kids played the primary role in facilitating the creation, dissolution and closeness of parent relationships. The evidence that children's networks could either augment or subvert homophily lies in the tendency of parents to emphasize the differences between themselves and their close sport friends as much as they emphasize their similarities. In addition, they also often attributed primacy to the relationship of the children. This condition arises partially because of the importance to the vast majority of parents of intergenerational closure[43]:

> I make it my cause to know all of my kids' friends' parents. Cause I want to know who my children associate themselves with. Maybe the kids are really good kids, but maybe the parents aren't that, and that's it. So that way I know who they're around and everything. I make it a point to know who they are. 'Cause whether my kids enjoy that or not, I still do that. (Leanne, mother of four children, ranging in age from 4 to 15, in Little League)

This does not mean that they sought friendships with their children's friends' parents. In most cases, they did not. But they did seek closure within these networks, and for much the same reason as Coleman noted, particularly monitoring. Again, as Leanne says:

> It's funny how when they do try and think they're gonna be sneaky, they forget that the parents talk (laughs) so we kind of like always seem to stop their little plans that they think they're making. That's fine, you know. We all thought we were smarter than our parents, but whatever. I think that that helps because sometimes I'll call up the mom or whatever. I'm like 'You know what?' Or I'll just text the mom, and I'm like 'Hey you know what? This is what's going on'. She's like 'Oh no, that's not what they told me'. And so I think it helps.

However, the network benefits of getting to know one's children's friends did not end with social control. In some cases, the children's friendship spurred the development of closer relationships between the parents. It is important to note that, in all of the cases I encountered of close sport relationships between parents, the children's friendship preceded that of the parents. While here the principle of homophily does operate, because parents generally had options for which of their children's friends they create close ties with, parents were equally likely when I interviewed them to point out the ways in which they were different from their close friends. They tended to attribute the closeness of their relationship merely to the 'niceness' or 'friendliness' of the other party involved:

> I'd say she was very friendly, very friendly, very nice and open and um … Also, different political views and I'm not anywhere near as religious as she is. I guess, it's probably more of a, you know, [we] probably got to know each other more because of the kids at first …. (Ruth, mother of a Wildcats player, describing a close friendship developed when her child was playing basketball)

When people described their close friends, they were talking about people for whom they would go out of their way, both socially and economically. The relationships created in youth sports were not seen as any different in that respect from relationships developed in other contexts. These were friends for whom my respondents would loan money, give a place to stay, take their kids for a time if necessary and in general do anything (within reason) necessary to see their friends through tough times:

> Yeah. I mean, this one family, it's crazy. We were coming back from Pueblo, Colorado, just last March actually. And the roads were snowy and icy. We actually all got snowed in back in Raton (Colorado). Well, this family decided to leave early. And then they ended up getting into an accident. And … they lived in their fifth-wheel that they were pulling when they got into the accident. So we found them a place to live, bought them all groceries. We took care of them. (Arlene, board member)

These close relationships did not form often, and they usually did not form over the course of one season. Consequently, I did not witness first hand the formation of close friendships taking place within the youth sport context. However, nearly every parent I spoke with had at least one close friend that they had met through baseball or softball, and they tended to speak of the formation of those relationships in terms of time spent with each other over multiple seasons:

> It's a progression, yeah. 'Cause I've known Jack since … his son is the same age as Miguel, so we coached Pee Wee, I mean tee-ball together. That's where I got to first know him. And then we coached, you know, a fall ball team together. And then we didn't coach together for a few years, but we're still kinda general friends. But this year, actually, we've actually become real good friends, where we're doing things together. In fact, we're going out with them tonight, so (laughs). So it's a progression thing. It's not an overnight thing, you know? (Scott, board member and coach)

The kids involved not only played a role in friendship formation, but they also played a role in relationship dissolution. In some cases, parents pre-empted the end of the kids' relationships by avoiding investment in the relationship. This was done with the explicit knowledge that the end of the children's relationship meant the end of the parents' relationship. As an example, Rita and Maria served as co-team mothers for the Mariners during their season.[44] The coordination of an All-Star team in terms of fundraising and tournament travel was immense, and the women spent a great deal of time in contact with one another during the season. During my interview with Rita, she was either called or text messaged by Maria no fewer than six times. They began to develop what I thought to be a close bond. I was certain that their relationship would continue at the conclusion of the season. However, when I asked Rita about it, she was quite certain that it would not:

> Interviewer: Do you see yourself continuing any sort of relationship with Maria past the end of the season? You know, you two have been interacting so intensely for a while.
>
> Rita: Mmmm ... Probably not, because the kids go to different schools and there aren't any other common bonds between the boys after the season ends.

The effects of children's sometimes roller-coaster type relationships on parental relationships extended outside of the youth sport context as well. Leanne detailed this process when talking about a tumultuous relationship her daughter shared with one of her friends:

> Recently, they had a falling out, were mad at each other, and you try and not let it affect how you speak to the person but it kind of made it a little awkward for the time, because we both said we knew the girls were mad at each other, so we kind of um ... still talked, but it made the relationship slightly awkward at the time, until the girls decided they were done being girls and made up. And they were fine, and so me and her started to talk again normal. So I think that sometimes when there's a falling out with the kids, if your relationship's based solely off of ... you became friends because your kids were friends, I think that it tests that or messes with that a little bit like, you're not real sure where you stand, if you should stay being really good friends, even if your kids hate each other (laughs). Or if maybe your relationship should end because their relationship ended.

While sometimes parents attempted to keep a relationship going when their children have a falling out, it was extremely difficult to do so, and the relationship status of the children had a significant impact on the relationship status of the parents.

Discussion

When kids participate in Little League (and other sports and extracurricular activities as well), in most cases, their parents participate as well, although the extent to which they participate varied widely. Outside of All-Stars, there was very little in terms of commitment that a parent needed to make outside of registration fees, fundraising obligations and making sure their child arrived at practices and games on time. There was not a sense of obligation to socialize with the other parents on a child's team, even if niceties were regularly observed between nearly all sets of parents. Even within these spaces, however, there was a sense that the parents whose children played on the same team constituted some sort of group, with benefits and privileges accorded to its members. To the outside observer, the patterns of interactions between all of the parents on these teams probably would not look like relations upon which one could depend on a bind. In other words, it did not appear to me during my first season – in which I was observing the Twins and Wildcats – that parents viewed each other as much more than strangers, and that social capital creation lay only in the close relationships that I had heard formed, but had not actually witnessed forming in the three and a half months I had spent with the teams. My interviews, however, revealed a very different process within the parent group. The ties that parents were forming were, in some cases, weaker than Granovetter's (1973) 'weak ties,' but they served similar purposes. While parents were very much in agreement with my observations that they did not interact very much, they still visualized themselves as a coherent group. They identified with each other and seemed quite willing to help each other out in the event that it was warranted. What emerged in my analysis was the view that there was a baseline level of social trust, cooperation and willingness to help (indicators of social capital within a relationship) that existed even within a group of relative (or even actual) strangers whose kids played baseball or softball together. While there did not often seem to be any all-inclusive groups of parents forming on a youth sports team – there were always specific networks, groups within groups, cliques within a team, etc. – this did not preclude the willingness to offer help to other parents on the team, even those whose relationship was hardly any stronger than strangers (i.e. even weaker than the 'nodding' relationship described by Granovetter). While the demand for much of the helping behaviour described in these relationships was created by the participation in youth sport (such as ferrying kids back and forth and child care), there was nothing precluding the expansion of such helping behaviour beyond the sporting context, and parents often indicated that this was the case.

In *Unanticipated Gains*, Mario Small argued that tie formation between parents in the context of urban day care centres was facilitated by the opportunity to interact, a focus for the interaction, and when the interaction involves cooperative rather than competitive processes. The VCLL offered, through its structure, all three of these elements. First, the rigid scheduling of league events, particularly practices and games, offered plenty of opportunities for parents to interact. Once there, the children became the focus of the event and a natural starting point for conversations and relationships, as league Treasurer Marilyn explained to me:

> You all start when they're little. So, you see this really super cute moments, and you're like, 'Ah, he's so cute'. And to a mom, when somebody says they're so cute, you're like instantly like 'Thank you, your son's cute too. What's your name?' Like it starts a whole conversation. You know, or you do one thing for somebody's kid, and the other mom feels totally inclined to pay you back. Like if you stayed with somebody's kid and the coach left, and you stayed till his mom came, and ... I don't know. In baseball, it's like you're friends after that. You just are. 'You remember her? She stayed with Tommy that day, remember?' (laughing). It's weird.

Further, the entire process of running a team requires significant amounts of cooperation between parents. Parents organize snack schedules, arrange transportation among themselves, prepare the fields, officiate the games and organize the end-of-season team parties, among other things. The coordination and cooperation involved are substantial. While obviously the competitive process is integral to sport (and the VCLL is certainly no exception), competition can actually encourage relationships formation among parents on the same team. The emotionally heightened circumstances that surround competitive games (especially All-Star games) facilitate more intense parental involvement, both with the game and with each other. Many parents reiterated that more competitive leagues around town (such as the local American football league) and more competitive baseball leagues (such as travelling or 'select' teams) would have offered me a greater opportunity to witness parental relationships because parents feel like there is far more at stake in those environments. For these reasons in particular, sport may be seen as a particularly fruitful site for social capital creation.

The league mechanisms for bringing parents together can also be viewed in the light of general theories of network formation. Broadly, research on network formation has taken a few major directions. In one strain, rational actors develop networks in accordance with their own needs and desires as well as the constraints of the social context.[45] The principle of homophily, as mentioned earlier, posits that people are simply more likely to create relationships with those who are 'like' them on some critical variable.[46] Still another strain of research offers that in order for people to form relationships, they must first meet, and that for any given individual, their dispositions, routines and patterns of behaviour mean that they are more likely to meet some and less likely to meet others, known as the principles of meeting and mating.[47] Once meeting has occurred, Feld noted that ties are more likely to form in social contexts where action is focused.[48]

Within the VCLL, there were multiple sets of actors engaging in the process of both meeting and mating, and multiple factors converging to facilitate or constrain relationship formation. In this setting – and likely in most others – these processes illustrated a mishmash of these various network formation theories at work. Underlying all of these processes, however, is the focused nature of the activity. Feld defined a focus as, ' . . . a social, psychological, legal, or physical entity around which joined activities are organized (e.g. workplaces, voluntary organizations, hangouts, families, etc.)'.[49] Little League, through its mission as an organization dedicated to serving children, is assuredly a focused organization. That focus allowed parents to have a natural starting point for conversations, as well as a trait in common. As there was also an attribution of value similarity between many parents in Little League – the idea that parents whose children participate in Little League had similar or at least compatible values to their own – it allowed even strangers to start from a position of amiability rather than suspicion, which eased the process of moving from strangers to acquaintances.

However, because the players themselves had a significant impact on the potential relationship partners for their parents in this context, parents sometimes found themselves with what they might consider less-than-ideal choices to move from acquaintance to friend. Children on sports teams may not base their friendships on the same criteria as their parents might; they instead create a hierarchy based largely around playing ability.[50] My own conversations with parents revealed not only that their children significantly impacted the social networks they formed in the league, but that they could also form close friendships with people they were apt to describe as 'different' from them as much as they were 'similar'. To the extent that Little League drew a diverse cross-section of a given population, it may be that it is a productive site for the construction of 'bridging' social capital.[51]

In this article, I have sought to bring light to several processes operating at the intersection between social capital and sport, particularly youth sport. On the one hand, I have provided a look at the mechanisms by which social capital can be formed and consumed in a youth sport setting, such as through team creation, practices and games, All-Star participation and participation on the Board of Directors. Further, I have shown how children's networks have a direct bearing on the networks of their parents. This work shows how sport participation may fit into the larger question of the connection between sport and social capital. However, it should in no way be inferred that this should be considered more than merely a starting point for future research. Many questions remain, and this study suffers from several limitations. First, there is an obvious selection problem, in that one cannot establish whether sport participation causes parents to interact in different ways that facilitate social capital formation, or if parents who are more likely to cooperate and build relationships with others are more likely to participate in sport. There is also the significant question as to whether or not sport is unique (or even exceptional) in its ability to build social capital among its participants. Other work in this volume (see Nicholson) suggests this may not be the case. However, by framing this work in terms of other child-centred studies (Small, in particular), we can see a way forward, at least theoretically. It may be that sport which provides best for opportunity, focus and cooperation may be best for social capital formation. It may be fruitful for future work to explore sport and social capital creation in those terms. What both Nicholson's work and this work show, however, is that sport is a site for the creation for social support and social capital. Its precise place, however, remains to be properly seen.

Notes

1. Becker, *Human Capital.*
2. Bourdieu, 'The Forms of Capital' and Bourdieu and Passeron, 'Cultural Reproduction'.
3. Bourdieu, 'Social Space'; Coleman, 'Social Capital', in *Foundations of Social Theory*; Putnam, *Making Democracy Work*, Putnam, 'Bowling Alone' and Putnam, *Bowling Alone.*
4. Lin, 'Building a Network Theory'.
5. Ibid., 6.
6. Burt, 'Social Capital of Structural Holes', 32.
7. Goods here can take many forms, which is part of the challenge of constructing good social capital theory. Goods can be tangible or intangible, physical, mental, emotional or spiritual. The list has become virtually inexhaustible.
8. Portes, 'Social Capital', 2.
9. Ibid.
10. Putnam, 'Bowling Alone', 134.
11. Nicholson and Hoye, *Sport and Social Capital.*
12. Nixon, 'Social Network Analysis of Sport', 315.
13. Lüschen, 'On Small Groups and Sport'.
14. Melnick, 'Small Group Research in Sport'.
15. Particularly Klein, 'Pumping Irony'.
16. Putnam, 'Bowling Alone'.
17. Dyreson, 'Maybe It's Better to Bowl Alone', 24.
18. Perks, 'Does Sport Foster Social Capital?', 381.
19. Jarvie, 'Communitarianism, Sport, and Social Capital'.
20. Dyreson, 'Maybe It's Better to Bowl Alone'.
21. For a notable exception, see Small, *Unanticipated Gains.*
22. Cochran and Brassard, 'Child Development'.
23. Caldwell, *Theory of Fertility Decline*; Handwerker, 'Culture and Reproduction' and Hoffman, Thornton, and Manis, 'Value of Children to Parents'.
24. Coleman, 'Social Capital in the Creation of Human Capital'.
25. For a useful review, see Dika and Singh, 'Applications of Social Capital'.
26. See Belle, *Children's Social Networks* for a useful review.
27. Morrow, 'Conceptualizing Social Capital'.
28. Ibid., 751.
29. Raffo and Reeves, 'Youth Transitions and Social Exclusion'.
30. Schaefer-McDaniel, 'Conceptualizing Social Capital' and Weller, 'Sticking with Your Mates?'
31. Holland, Reynolds, and Weller, 'Transitions, Networks and Communities'; Hossain et al., 'Social Capital, Ethnicity' and Leonard, 'Children, Childhood and Social Capital'.
32. Morrow, "No Ball Games" and Weller, 'Skateboarding Alone?'
33. Weller, 'Sticking With Your Mates?'
34. Leonard, 'Children, Childhood and Social Capital'.
35. Holland, Reynolds, and Weller, 'Transitions, Networks, and Communities', 97.
36. But see Engelberg, Skinner, and Zakus within this volume.
37. Small, *Unanticipated Gains.*
38. In some leagues, coaches pitch to their teams instead of a pitching machine.
39. Using the method advocated by Emerson, Fretz, and Shaw, *Writing Ethnographic Fieldnotes.*
40. See also Calhoun, 'Community Without Propinquity Revisited'.
41. McPherson, Smith-Lovin, and Cook, 'Birds of a Feather'.
42. Lazarsfeld and Merton, 'Friendship as a Social Process'.
43. Coleman, 'Social Capital in the Creation of Human Capital'.
44. Officially known as team parents – but colloquially known as 'team mom', as it is nearly always taken on by a mother, the team parent is responsible for many administrative and 'off-the-field' tasks necessary to run a team. They collect funds, coordinate snack schedules and plan the end-of-season team party, among other things. Some people within the league estimate that the team parent is a more demanding job than coaching the team.
45. See Snijders, van de Bunt, and Steglich, 'Introduction to Stochastic Actor-Based Models' for a recent example of the balance between rationality and exogenous factors in network structure.
46. McPherson, Smith-Lovin, and Cook, 'Birds of a Feather'.
47. Verbrugge, 'Structure of Adult Friendship Choices'.

48.   Feld, 'Focused Organization of Social Ties'.
49.   Ibid., 1016.
50.   Fine, *With the Boys*.
51.   Putnam, *Bowling Alone*.

References

Becker, Gary S. *Human Capital: A Theoretical and Empirical Analysis With Special Reference to Education*. New York: Columbia University Press, 1964.

Belle, Deborah, ed. *Children's Social Networks and Social Supports*. New York: John Wiley & Sons, 1989.

Bourdieu, Pierre. 'The Forms of Capital'. In *Handbook for Theory and Research for the Sociology of Education*, ed. J. Richardson, 241–58. New York: Greenwood, 1985.

Bourdieu, Pierre. 'The Social Space and the Genesis of Groups'. *Theory and Society* 14 (1985): 723–44.

Bourdieu, Pierre, and Jean-Claude Passeron. 'Cultural Reproduction and Social Reproduction'. *Knowledge Education and Cultural Change Papers in the Sociology of Education* 10 (1973): 71–112.

Burt, Ronald S. 'The Social Capital of Structural Holes'. In *New Directions in Economic Sociology*, ed. M. F. Guillen, R. Collins, P. England, and M. Meyer. New York: Russel Sage Foundation, 2001.

Caldwell, John C. *Theory of Fertility Decline*. London: Academic Press, 1982.

Calhoun, Craig. 'Community Without Propinquity Revisited: Communications Technology and the Transformation of the Urban Public Sphere'. *Sociological Inquiry* 68 (1998): 373–97.

Cochran, Moncrieff M., and Jane Anthony Brassard. 'Child Development and Personal Social Networks'. *Child Development* 50 (1979): 601–16.

Coleman, James S. 'Social Capital in the Creation of Human Capital'. *American Journal of Sociology* 94 (1988): S95.

Coleman, James S. *Foundations of Social Theory*. Cambridge, MA: Belknap Press, 1990.

Dika, Sandra L., and Kusum Singh. 'Applications of Social Capital in Educational Literature: A Critical Synthesis'. *Review of Educational Research* 72 (2002): 31.

Dyreson, Mark. 'Maybe It's Better to Bowl Alone: Sport, Community and Democracy in American Thought'. *Sport in Society* 4 (2001): 19–30.

Emerson, Robert M., Rachel L. Fretz, and Linda L. Shaw. *Writing Ethnographic Fieldnotes*. Chicago, IL: University of Chicago Press, 1995.

Feld, Scott L. 'The Focused Organization of Social Ties'. *American Journal of Sociology* 86 (1981): 1015–35.

Fine, Gary Alan. *With the Boys: Little League Baseball and Preadolescent Culture*. Chicago: University of Chicago Press, 1987.

Handwerker, W. Penn. 'Culture and Reproduction: Exploring Micro/Macro Linkages'. In *Culture and Reproduction*, ed. W. P. Handwerker, 1–28. Boulder, CO: Westview Press, 1986.

Hoffman, Lois Wladis, Arland Thornton, and Jean Denby Manis. 'The Value of Children to Parents in the United States'. *Journal of Population* 1 (1978): 91–131.

Holland, Janet, Tracey Reynolds, and Susie Weller. 'Transitions, Networks and Communities: The Significance of Social Capital in the Lives of Children and Young People'. *Journal of Youth Studies* 10 (2007): 97–116.

Hossain, Rosa, Charles Watters, Rupert Brown, Lindsey Cameron, Anick Landau, Dominique LeTouze, Dennis Nigbur, and Adam Rutland. 'Social Capital, Ethnicity and Children's Well-Being: Aspects of Social Capital in the Everyday Lives of British Punjabi Children'. *International Journal of Migration, Health, and Social Care* 3 (2007): 4–21.

Jarvie, Grant. 'Communitarianism, Sport and Social Capital: Neighbourly Insights into Scottish Sport'. *International Review for the Sociology of Sport* 38 (2003): 139.

Klein, Alan. 'Pumping Irony: Crisis and Contradiction in Bodybuilding'. *Sociology of Sport Journal* 3 (1986): 112–33.

Lazarsfeld, Paul F., and Robert K. Merton. 'Friendship as a Social Process: A Substantive and Methodological Analysis'. In *Freedom and Control in Modern Society*, ed. M. Berger, T. Abel, and C. Page, 18–66. New York: Van Nostrand, 1954.

Leonard, Madeleine. 'Children, Childhood and Social Capital: Exploring the Links'. *Sociology* 39 (2005): 605–22.

Lin, Nan. 'Building a Network Theory of Social Capital'. In *Social Capital: Theory and Research*, ed. N. Lin, K. S. Cook, and R. S. Burt, 3–29. New Brunswick, CT: AldineTransaction, 2001.

Lüschen, Günther. 'On Small Groups and Sport: Methodological Reflections With Reference to Structural-Functional Approaches'. In *Sport and Social Theory*, ed. C. R. Rees and A. W. Miracle, 149–57. Champaign, IL: Human Kinetics, 1986.

McPherson, Miller, Lynn Smith-Lovin, and James M. Cook. 'Birds of a Feather: Homophily in Social Networks'. *Annual Review of Sociology* 27 (2001): 415–44.

Melnick, Merrill J. 'Small Group Research in Sport – Theory and Method: A Response to Luschen, Fine, and Widmeyer'. In *Sport and Social Theory*, ed. C. R. Rees and A. Miracle, 189–97. Champaign, IL: Human Kinetics, 1986.

Morrow, Virginia. 'Conceptualizing Social Capital in Relation to the Well-Being of Children and Young People'. *Sociological Review* 47 (1999): 744–66.

Morrow, Virginia. 'No Ball Games'. In *Child Space: An Anthropological Exploration of Young People's Use of Space*, ed. K. Malone, 70–93. New Delhi: Concept Publishing Company, 2007.

Nicholson, Matthew and Russell Hoye, eds. *Sport and Social Capital*. Amsterdam: Butterworth-Heinemann, 2008.

Nixon, Howard L., II. 'Social Network Analysis of Sport: Emphasizing Social Structure in Sport Sociology'. *Sociology of Sport Journal* 10 (1993): 315–21.

Perks, Thomas. 'Does Sport Foster Social Capital? The Contribution of Sport to a Lifestyle of Community Participation'. *Sociology of Sport Journal* 24 (2007): 378–401.

Portes, Alejandro. 'Social Capital: Its Origins and Applications in Modern Sociology'. *Annual Reviews in Sociology* 24 (1998): 1–24.

Putnam, Robert D. 'Bowling Alone: America's Declining Social Capital'. *Journal of Democracy* 6 (1995): 65–78.

Putnam, Robert D. *Bowling Alone: The Collapse and Revival of American Community*. New York: Simon and Schuster, 2000.

Putnam, Robert D. *Making Democracy Work: Civic Traditions in Modern Italy*. Princeton, NJ: Princeton University Press, 1993.

Raffo, Carlo, and Michelle Reeves. 'Youth Transitions and Social Exclusion: Developments in Social Capital Theory'. *Journal of Youth Studies* 3 (2000): 147–66.

Schaefer-McDaniel, Nicole. 'Conceptualizing Social Capital Among Young People: Towards a New Theory'. *Children, Youth, and Environment* 14 (2004): 153–72.

Small, Mario Luis. *Unanticipated Gains: Origins of Network Inequality in Everyday Life*. New York: Oxford University Press, 2009.

Snijders, Tom A. B., Gerhard van de Bunt, and Christian E.G. Steglich. 'Introduction to Stochastic Actor-Based Models for Network Dynamics'. *Social Networks* 32 (2010): 44–60.

Verbrugge, Lois M. 'The Structure of Adult Friendship Choices'. *Social Forces* 56 (1977): 576–97.

Weller, Susie. 'Skateboarding Alone? Making Social Capital Discourse Relevant to Teenagers' Lives'. *Journal of Youth Studies* 9 (2006): 557–74.

Weller, Susie. '"Sticking with Your Mates?" Children's Friendship Trajectories During the Transition From Primary to Secondary School'. *Children and Society* 21 (2007): 339–51.

Working together through sport? Local authority provision for ethnic minorities in the UK

Jamie A. Cleland

Department of Sport and Exercise, Staffordshire University, Leek Road, Stoke-on-Trent ST4 2DF, UK

Ethnic minority participation in sport or physical activity has been the subject of recent sociological debate but has received relatively limited empirical analysis. This article assesses the extent to which two local authorities in the UK, Stoke-on-Trent City Council and East Staffordshire Borough Council, had developed strategies to increase participation rates for ethnic minorities. It draws on 16 semi-structured interviews with ethnic minority community leaders, local authority employees and a selection of active ethnic minority participants involved in projects in both areas. The results highlight projects established by both local authorities to engage with ethnic minorities and although this is acknowledged as a step forward, racial inequalities and other barriers to participation remain. The article concludes by suggesting that there are still many opportunities for local authorities to work more closely with ethnic minorities to reduce racial inequalities and barriers to participation.

Introduction

Ethnic minority participation in sport or physical activity in the UK is of growing interest. It has been helped by the increasing focus of the national government and local authorities in establishing strategies and projects to improve participation. At the same time, it has also created opportunities for evaluative research to be undertaken to assess how effective these strategies and subsequent projects are in achieving their objectives. Studies have examined ethnic minority participation in various British sports, including cricket and football, but there is a dearth of material which examines local authority leisure provision.[1] For example, it has been suggested that local authority provision can present confused ideas regarding equal opportunity and race equality and this often leads to inconsistent interpretations of policy.[2]

This article empirically analyses local authority provision for ethnic minorities in two areas of the UK: Stoke-on-Trent and Burton-on-Trent. It has two objectives: (a) to assess each local authority's level of provision in sport or physical activity for ethnic minorities and (b) to identify whether racial inequalities continue to detrimentally affect participation for ethnic minorities. Before it addresses these two objectives, the article first engages with the relevant literature on the changes in policy and the academic attention paid to them as well as participation levels and the reported barriers facing ethnic minorities. It then analyses the data collected from 16 in-depth interviews with ethnic minority community leaders, local authority employees and some active ethnic minority participants to offer some explanations on each local authority's level of provision.

Within sociology, the term 'race' is complex as there is a large amount of disagreement over its exact meaning. Burdsey states how some authors place 'race' in inverted commas 'to demonstrate that it is the *idea* of race that is being referred to and the fact that it has no biological validity'.[3] For Miles and Brown, 'race' is a meaningless term that reflects class exploitation more than anything else.[4] Similarly, Garner states that trying to provide a definition of 'race' is impossible as nobody is actually 'white' or 'black' and instead these terms have social meanings rather than biological ones.[5] Garner argues that there is no consensus regarding dividing lines between different 'races' and by dividing people into 'races' has 'very serious and measurable impacts on people'.[6] For example, Swinney and Horne state that how membership of an ethnic group is not related to the 'colour of skin', as Irish people living in Scotland would be seen as an ethnic minority.[7] Indeed, these difficulties also affect the gathering of data on sports participation. A survey of sports participation by ethnic group in England, for example, found that a number of respondents did not identify with any of the ethnic categories in the survey.[8]

In terms of the ethnic demographics of both Stoke-on-Trent and Burton-on-Trent, the 2001 Census data outlined that for East Staffordshire (where Burton-on-Trent is located), the total population was 103,770 with 92% White British and 4.5% Asian or Asian British. In assessing the wards in Burton-on-Trent where the data was collected, in Anglesey, the total number of residents was 5835 with 72% White British and 24% Asian or Asian British. In Shobnall, out of a total of 6132 residents, 75% were White British with nearly 22% Asian or Asian British. Finally, in Stoke-on-Trent, out of a total number of 240,636 residents, 95% were White British with 3.5% Asian or Asian British. In the Burslem South ward of Stoke-on-Trent where the data was also collected, out of 12,071 residents, 85.5% were White British with nearly 8% Asian or Asian British.

To put the importance of this article in context, in East Staffordshire, the number of people taking part in 30 min of moderately intense sport and active participation at least 3 days a week had slightly increased from 22.8% in 2005–2006 to 23.0% in 2007–2008 (the national average was 21.3%).[9] However, in Stoke-on-Trent, in 2005–2006 the figure was 15.8% but had dropped to 14.4% in 2007–2008. In terms of participation levels for what Sport England term 'non-white adults', the survey highlighted how this had decreased from 18.6% in 2005–2006 to just 17.6% in 2007–2008 (for 'white adults', it had increased from 21.2% to 21.7% over the same period).[10] Similarly, for some ethnic minorities across the country, less than one in five people are participating just once a month in some form of physical activity.[11] In fact, it is not just participation levels where ethnic minorities fall behind 'whites'; it is also the case in the levels of volunteering, club membership, tuition and organized competition.[12]

The importance of determining strategies for ethnic minorities is also evidenced by other data produced by the 2001 Census. For example, it illustrated how the ethnic minority population grew by 53% from 3.0 million in 1991 to 4.6 million in 2001 (totalling 7.6% of the population). Half of the ethnic minority population were Asians of Indian, Pakistani, Bangladeshi or other Asian origin with a further quarter listed as Black (Black Caribbean, Black African or Other Black). The 2001 Census data also helped to highlight that a greater number of children from ethnic minority groups are more likely to live in deprived areas than white children and thus support the need for specific, more inclusive, strategies focusing on ethnic minorities to engage them in sport or physical activity. This, therefore, challenges sports organizations and local authorities to work more closely with ethnic minorities in their own communities. However, as the 'Changes in policy' section highlights, there is some difference between the discourse emanating from sports organizations/local authorities and the actual implementation of racial equality policies.

Changes in policy

Sports policy in the 1970s tended to concentrate on the development of local leisure centres rather than active participation. Despite the creation of *Sport for All* during this period, 'race' and ethnicity were not identified as areas requiring specific governmental intervention. Things started to change slightly in the 1980s when the Sports Council, as part of its strategic policy *Sport in the Community: The Next Ten Years*, targeted specific groups in society where it was felt policy interventions were needed. Here, and somewhat influenced by the political environment at the time (such as the aftermath of the Toxteth and Brixton riots in the early 1980s), black (male) urban youths were prioritized as a disruptive group that needed urgent strategic attention. Despite this, it was not until 1994 when the Sports Council produced a policy document titled *Black and Ethnic Minorities and Sport* that any specific attention was given to the ethnic minority population. However, no sooner had this document been published than the Conservative government at the time outlined a policy titled *Sport: Raising the Game*, which focused on the development of excellence in the UK's traditional team sports at the expense of more community-based initiatives.[13]

To try and force a change in policy, during the 1990s, some non-governmental agencies such as governing bodies, fan groups and voluntary organizations all contributed in shaping an awareness of the inequalities faced by ethnic minorities. By way of illustration, in 1993, a successful partnership between football fan groups, the Professional Footballers' Association and Commission for Racial Equality (CRE), led to the establishment of 'Let's Kick Racism Out of Football' (in 1997 this became Kick it Out). This particular campaign moved the debate away from 'race' and ethnicity to more of an emphasis on the perpetrators of racism and how the relevant authorities should act in trying to eliminate it. Its immediate impact began to encourage campaigns in other sports such as 'Hit Racism for Six' in cricket and 'Tackle It – Tackle Racism in Rugby League' (both established in 1996).

From a strategic viewpoint, the UK witnessed the establishment of the Department of Culture, Media and Sport (DCMS), UK Sport, Sporting Equals and Sport Councils like Sport England in the latter part of the 1990s. As part of their wider remit, there has been an increase in policy and strategy with regard to ethnic minorities. Part of this stems from the creation of Sporting Equals in 1998 by Sport England and the CRE to work closely with sport governing bodies and public sector local authorities to develop policies on racial equality. Not long after it was created, Sporting Equals surveyed 62 sport governing bodies to analyse how each one approached the importance of achieving racial equality in their organization.[14] The results were worrying with half not responding at all, whilst half of those that did stated that racial inequalities were not present in their organization. In addressing this, in 2000, Sporting Equals published *Achieving Racial Equality: A Standard for Sport* with the aim of encouraging sports organizations and governing bodies to develop Race Equality Action Plans.[15] By monitoring the demographics of their participants (such as ethnic origin, age and gender), it provided an opportunity for each organization to show how it was working towards racial equality objectives (in particular as funding was often attached to it). The aim was to begin the process where racial equality became a recognized component of sporting policy. In implementing this, three areas of action were covered:[16]

- commitment, policy and planning;
- participation and public image;
- administration and management.

Within each area were three levels of achievement – preliminary, intermediate and advanced. At the lower preliminary level, all that organizations were asked to do was publicly commit to achieving equality, undertake ethnic monitoring and develop policies and procedures. At the higher advanced level, organizations were expected to produce equality training, promote role models and liaise with ethnic minority groups.

Since the introduction of the Equality Standard, equality and diversity in sport has become a key and changing area of sports policy. In 2004, the Sports Equality Standard was introduced, this time also including gender and disability. This was formed through the co-operation of UK Sport and the four UK Sports Councils, the English Federation of Disability Sport, Sporting Equals and the Women's Sport Foundation to highlight a significant commitment towards equality development work for sport providers. Furthermore, in 2007, the Commission for Racial and Human Rights was established through the dissolution of the CRE, the Equal Opportunities Commission and the Disability Rights Commission. This strategy was aimed towards achieving equality, in particular focusing on the commitment of public organizations towards the implementation of policies and practices. Moreover, in 2010, just before Labour lost power, a new Equality Act was approved, although at the time of writing this is yet to be officially implemented by the new coalition government.

Indeed, Coalter states that the previous Labour government started two broad approaches in seeking to generate greater social inclusion through policy: first, to increase sports participation through area-based targeted programmes in socially deprived areas and, second, to emphasize the contribution which sports volunteering can make to 'active citizenship'.[17] These projects focused on community initiatives such as improving the health and participation rates amongst different groups of people and backgrounds and tackling drugs, crime and anti-social behaviour. This emphasis on social inclusion led to Sport England establishing an Active Communities programme aimed at providing opportunities for increased participation and coaching in areas of social deprivation. Here, volunteering and the promotion of role models helped local authorities develop a number of projects with particular target groups in mind (like ethnic minorities).

The emphasis on equality and inclusion has brought about many changes in a short space of time, but the extent to which racial equality policies have actually been implemented has become a focal point for academic research. In reviewing this area, a consistent theme emerges across many different studies between what sports organizations and local authorities say and what they actually do.[18] In the research conducted by Long et al., for example, racial inequalities existed and policies in this area were not viewed as a high priority if they were faced with other resource demands.[19] In later work, Long et al. argued that there was an increased recognition within sports organizations to develop better links with ethnic minorities.[20] However, whilst they found that 62% of sport organizations monitored ethnic minority participants and staff members, only 8 (out of 45 organizations) managed to achieve the preliminary level of the original standard by June 2003.[21] In fact, Spracklen et al. drew similar conclusions about the implementation of racial equality policies as nearly all of the governing bodies they researched stated that little had changed in their approach to equity in the preceding 12 months.[22]

In assessing the implementation of equal opportunity policies, Horne and Swinney and Horne examined local authority providers of sport and leisure for black and ethnic minorities in Scotland.[23] Horne looked to distinguish between those which had a formal written equal opportunities policy and those local authorities which did not.[24] To help address this, he developed three types of local authority providers in terms of the importance placed on achieving equality:

- *Gestural.* Organizations which had a policy or policy statement but did not go any further than that.

- *Reactive*. Organizations which were likely to have equality policies in place but would not adequately monitor it and could sometimes be complacent in its approach to equality.
- *Proactive*. Organizations which were likely to be active in challenging racism and sought to achieve its goals regarding equality.

Horne found that one-third of local authorities in Scotland had not adopted any formal equal opportunity policy and as such only a few local authorities were placed in the proactive category.[25] This was found to be the case for the more urban communities in Scotland that had a higher number of black and ethnic minorities. Similar uneven findings between rhetoric and implementation were also found by Swinney and Horne in their follow-up research in Scotland.[26] Whilst most local authority respondents indicated that work in the area of racial equality was in progress or planned for the near future, 18 out of the 32 respondents had yet to conduct any research on the sport and leisure requirements of black and ethnic minorities. With findings similar to those of Horne, the authorities viewed as proactive were located in urban areas which were more highly populated by black and ethnic minorities. This led to Swinney and Horne concluding that only minor change had occurred since 1995.[27] In fact, they described some local authorities as gestural in dealing with ethnic minorities (usually those in more rural areas with very low numbers of black and ethnic minorities). However, the majority of councils did demonstrate an intention towards achieving equality and thus were classified as proactive and reactive.

As well as examining local authorities and sports organizations regarding racial equality policies, there has also been an increasing focus on the power and interests of 'whiteness' and how this is found to prevent managerial intervention to effect change and diversity in society.[28] The issue of 'race' and its understanding in sport and leisure has been examined elsewhere, but a significant recent contribution has been the development of critical race theory (CRT).[29] Although it originated in North America, Hylton has made a strong case for CRT to be applied more specifically to sport and leisure policy to promote racial equality more effectively.[30] Hylton argues that 'race' has been marginalized and that by adopting a CRT approach it 'challenges traditional dominant ideologies around objectivity, meritocracy, colour blindness, race neutrality and equal opportunity'.[31] For Long and Hylton, it is important to now challenge the power and influence of 'whiteness' when seeking to achieve greater racial equality within sport.[32]

Ethnic minority participation in sport

Ethnic minorities do not necessarily all share similar lifestyles or cultures, and until recently, there was very little survey work which analysed their patterns of participation in sport or physical activity. *Sports Participation and Ethnicity in England National Survey 1999/2000* was the first ever large-scale quantitative survey (consisting of 3000 ethnic minority participants) to begin to address this issue.[33] Highlighting some racial inequalities, the survey helped to illustrate the diverse nature of participation levels for men and women from different ethnic minorities. It found that the overall participation rates for ethnic minority groups in sport were 40% compared with a national average of 46%. At a national level, the gap in participation between men and women was 15% but for Bangladeshis it was 27%, for Black Africans it was 26% and for Pakistanis it was 20%. It also indicated how Black African men had a higher participation rate than the national average for all men, while Bangladeshi women had participation rates well below the national average for women.

In seeking to encourage greater levels of participation, sports organizations and local authorities are often faced with many diverse barriers which prevent ethnic minorities from taking part in some form of sport or physical activity. In research conducted by Sport England, a lack of money was cited by 25% of Black Caribbean and Black Other as preventing them for participating in sport.[34] Similarly, 40% of Afro-Caribbean and Indian and over 80% of Pakistani and Bangladeshi (compared with 28% of the total population) were estimated to live in households with below average income.[35]

In other research, the perceived barriers to low participation for ethnic minorities were culture, gender, age, access to facilities, language and actual racism or fear of racism.[36] When asked about sports provision and their access to it, the location of the facility to their home and a lack of appropriate transport were cited as being crucial as to whether they participated.[37] In similar work, it was stated how Pakistani and Bangladeshi women reported a fear of going out alone due to the risk of actual or potential racist abuse.[38] This, therefore, can lead to low motivation rates and helps to explain some of the participation findings discussed above.

Most of the research on the barriers to participation tends to focus on girls and women from various Asian cultures. Collins and Kay, for example, found that work, school, childcare and other domestic duties are often stated as preventing ethnic minority women from having sufficient leisure time to participate.[39] Similar results were also found in the *Sports Participation and Ethnicity in England National Survey 1999/2000*.[40] Here it was reported that over 40% of Indian, Pakistani, Black Caribbean and Black African women felt home and family responsibilities prevented them from participating in some form of physical exercise. In comparison to males, Asian parents may put their daughters under greater pressure to care for siblings and help with household tasks such as meal preparation and general cleaning duties.

For some Muslim girls and women, there are other cultural and religious challenges which prevent them from participating in any form of sporting activity. Self-image has been found to play a crucial role as some respondents had stopped attending due to increased internal negative feelings of being seen by other women when getting changed and by men when exercising or attending a particular location.[41] However, whilst most of the literature on this is applied to Muslim women, it is important to state that this barrier is not just confined to one particular ethnic minority group and that every woman and man interprets their religious requirements differently.

In terms of trying to increase participation rates amongst ethnic minorities, there are many recommendations.[42] In summarizing their research, Carroll et al. recommended using instructors from the ethnic minority group participating, providing free sessions held at the local community centre, having access to a crèche and an extensive local promotion to ensure that the local community was kept informed of physical activities.[43] Similar recommendations have also been proposed elsewhere on how ethnic minorities can be incorporated better into physical activity initiatives, including better provision provided by local authorities.[44]

Method

To address the two research objectives, 16 semi-structured interviews were carried out from February 2009 to May 2009 with individuals in both Stoke-on-Trent and Burton-on-Trent. The aim was to split the participants into three groups and this ultimately proved successful: (1) those involved in the community, such as community leaders or managers of specific ethnic minority centres; (2) those employed by the local authorities to engage with the local community and develop projects to improve sports participation and physical activity levels and (3) some ethnic minority participants actually involved in the projects in operation.

To help in recruiting participants into Group 1, a list of names that were known to the County Sports Partnership 'Sport Across Staffordshire and Stoke-on-Trent' (SASSOT) was provided and they were subsequently contacted. Initial contact was made by telephone where the research objectives as well as the confidential nature of their response and their right of withdrawal were explained. It was also explained that the researcher was white and although access within particular ethnic minority groups proved problematic, enough individuals gave their support for the research to be carried out. Snowball sampling certainly helped and once a face-to-face meeting had taken place the participants were willing to pass on the contact details of other individuals they felt would strengthen the research objectives.[45] SASSOT also provided the relevant contact details for those individuals in Group 2 and again a telephone call and subsequent face-to-face interview was carried out with representatives of both local authorities. This also helped recruit participants for Group 3, where permission was given to attend projects directed towards ethnic minorities in both areas. Here, participants were asked whether they were willing to participate in the research and those who gave their permission were asked some general questions on the project in which they were involved and their thoughts on local authority provision for ethnic minorities.

As suggested by Carrington and McDonald, although an investigation of this type can be quantitative in nature, 'understanding the subjective experiences of individuals in sports demands a theoretically informed interpretative approach'.[46] Supporting the need for an in-depth qualitative investigation, there is the increasing need for research to analyse how social and cultural factors, including racial ideologies, create and perpetuate differences in society. In doing this, 14 interviews were carried out face-to-face but the club secretary of Grange Park Rangers (an Asian Sunday league football team in Cobridge, Stoke-on-Trent) and a contact at Madina (an Asian sports club in Burton-on-Trent) both had to be interviewed over the telephone due to work commitments. This was agreed upon to maintain the collection of key data.

On analysing all of the interview data, a manual form of content analysis was adopted. Although content analysis can be used quantitatively to count themes in numerical terms, for this article, the interview data was themed into categories addressing the two research objectives. Once completed the analysis then began to identify 'patterns and processes, commonalities and differences' within the collected data.[47] Whilst the findings cannot be deemed representative of all ethnic minorities in Stoke-on-Trent and Burton-on-Trent, they do provide empirical evidence regarding how some ethnic minorities felt about the local projects currently in existence. In fact, many of the responses were similar, thus suggesting some commonality across different ethnic minority groups.

Results

As recognized by Coalter, one of the priorities within community-based initiatives is the need to engage more widely with ethnic minorities.[48] Taking a more proactive approach to ethnic minority provision (as identified by Horne), some of the programmes occurring in Burton-on-Trent included those specifically targeting Asian women and in the 2008 summer holidays, a project was successfully organized, using Asian coaches, between two local communities (one with a low and one with a high representation of ethnic minorities) to try and encourage the mixing of different cultures.[49]

Another recent initiative is the implementation of the 'Streets Ahead' project taking place in the Victoria and Angelsey wards in Burton-on-Trent. As highlighted earlier, both of these areas are populated by a number of ethnic minorities and by taking the projects into these communities it is felt by local authority employees to prevent the barriers identified by Collins from being used as a reason for non-participation.[50] The project was awarded £40,000 over 2 years by the Staffordshire Children's Fund and is free to all those eligible to take part. The aim of this project is to provide physical activities to young people aged 6–16 years with good access to high-quality leisure, cultural and sporting experiences. It is delivered during the evenings with the aim of providing a safe environment as well as encouraging greater use of children's time. Activities are adapted to the street and include football, cricket, basketball, hockey and handball and street dance.

Again concurring with the thoughts of Coalter, with a similar proactive approach, in Stoke-on-Trent, a more national project 'StreetGames' is being delivered to lots of different wards in the city including those with a high number of ethnic minorities. This was established in 2006 to promote participation in sport for young people living in the most disadvantaged communities. The project is aimed at the 7–25 age group with a target to get nearly 3000 engaged in regular positive activity. Other objectives within the project include attracting 320 new volunteers aged over 16 years, 320 people benefiting from access to nationally accredited leadership training and a further 40 gaining employment as sports coaches/leaders.[51] In fact, the first phase was so successful that the second phase of the project began at the end of 2008. In addressing one of its objectives, due to high levels of attendance by those not eligible to take part (i.e. they are too old), such as mothers, fathers, brothers and sisters, the next stage is to encourage these individuals to become trained up to the Community Sports Leader Award (Level 2), so that they can voluntarily assist in the local community.

Understandably, those employed by the local authorities stressed a more proactive picture of local engagement with ethnic minorities. Concurring with the findings of Long et al., both authorities monitored participation rates by ethnic minorities with the sports development officer for managing 'StreetGames' at Stoke-on-Trent City Council stating:

> it's important we get ethnic minorities involved in sport in this city. Statistics carried out nationally paint a worrying picture of physical activity levels in Stoke-on-Trent and as a local provider we need to keep this momentum going. It's hard, especially with the media painting this city as racist after the British National Party targeted it as a place to win votes politically, but we owe it to the ethnic minorities that they are welcome in this city and this type of project goes some way towards that.

However, both local authority employees did recognize that as well as low participation rates there remained a dearth of coaches from ethnic minority groups across both areas. Both local authorities only employed ethnic minority coaches on a casual basis, so it was not surprising for them to acknowledge how this hampered the opportunity for the development of role models for younger ethnic minorities.[52] Each local authority employee stressed the importance of racial equality and how policies and projects were reflecting this approach, but with no full-time roles for ethnic minority coaches it is unclear how effective the racial equality policies and objectives to begin increasing participation will be.[53]

To begin evaluating the actual impact of the projects across both areas, a small number of participants from Group 3 were asked about the importance of them for ethnic minorities. In fact, all of the participants stated that the projects in operation were an important part of integrating ethnic minorities into sport with one participant involved in the 'Streets Ahead' project stating:

in the past I did not engage with physical activity on a regular basis due to a lack of free time and motivational laziness. However, now that different projects seem to be coming into our neighbourhoods it has given me an incentive to become physically active again.

With regard to how the local authorities could engage with ethnic minorities better, three participants from Group 3 stressed the need for greater communication between the local authorities and ethnic minorities so that everyone knows how to get involved. For example, an active participant involved in the 'Streets Ahead' project suggested the need for

a central advice centre or newsletters or e-mail contact with representatives of different groups within the local community. This would be a start in attempting to engage with ethnic minorities...ethnic minorities need to be better informed of activities and events than they are at present.

Moreover, another participant involved in the 'StreetGames' project outlined the need to

make facilities more accessible for ethnic minorities, provide more information, reduce the cost of some activities where possible and encourage the community to make better use of local parks as they are free to use if parks were maintained better, were kept dog free and were patrolled better by the local authorities this would encourage more families to spend time in a local park and would encourage more people to actively exercise.

From a different perspective, another participant involved in the 'Streets Ahead' project stated:

there is the interest there from a number of different ethnic minorities. For me it's one of two things. Local authorities need to get into particular areas more and develop a way of letting people know what is going on. For some communities sport or physical activity is a sign of racial inequality and whilst I get the impression they would like to take part a large number still remain reluctant. A bit more encouragement and opportunity to take part might do the trick.

Supporting the literature discussed earlier by Collins, a participant in the 'Streets Ahead' project stated that although he could see more ethnic minorities taking part in sport, the same barriers preventing participation such as culture, cost, a lack of information and access to facilities remain a prohibitive factor.[54] Similarly, a member of the Afghan society in Burton-on-Trent stated that whilst some community members had an interest in sport or physical activity, it did not appear high on the list of their priorities. Here, he stated how

parents view education and religion as more important to the development of their children and these are unfortunately viewed as a higher priority than sport is... I also presume a number of them do not want to place their children in a position where inequalities are prevalent.

Although there has been an increasing focus given to generating greater levels of participation for ethnic minorities, a number of studies have recommended the need for better lines of communication and for more transparency regarding equality.[55] Unfortunately, some of the participants in Group 1 felt that a more inclusive strategy remained crucial if participation rates were to be improved. For example, when probed about the local authority's provision for ethnic minorities in a wider sense, a senior member of the Pakistani Community Centre in Burton-on-Trent was quite vocal in his views. This particular individual felt that there was a lack of engagement with local ethnic minorities, despite the fact that there were facilities which the local authority could utilize better. In fact, after a visit to this particular centre, the opportunity for engagement was evident. It is home to youth clubs, women's groups, welfare associations, health initiatives, luncheon clubs, community education, sports clubs, drop-in facilities, and information and advice centres. In response to a lack of suitable provision for young people, a Central Youth Club was established and has quickly become popular as it attracts dozens of young people who attend on a regular basis. The aim is to provide a safe environment where young people can gain informal education and enjoy social activities whilst supervised by adults. Young people get the opportunity to play computer games, pool, badminton, table tennis, hockey, football, cricket, darts and basketball and there are plans in place to build a sports centre on the same site. There is also an Asian Girls Group in a culturally appropriate environment where issues affecting Asian girls are discussed and support is given (as recommended by Wray).[56]

Indeed, these views were not just applicable to Burton-on-Trent as a senior member of the Pakistani community in Stoke-on-Trent felt that

> whilst I have to recognise the efforts of the local authority in attempting to engage with the Pakistani community, better lines of communication and engagement in activities within these communities would lead to greater levels of participation and activity.

Likewise, a lack of communication between ethnic minority groups and the local authority was also raised by a representative of the Queen Street Community Club in Burton-on-Trent. This, she claimed, was having a detrimental effect on the number of local residents (a) hearing about activities taking place and (b) then actually taking part in them. One of the centre's limitations is a lack of physical activity-based classes, although they do run a Socatots session on a Saturday morning and it is involved in the 'Streets Ahead' project run by the local authority. Two out of the four sessions currently run by the 'Streets Ahead' project team are held at the Queen Street Community Centre, which is situated right in the heart of a ward heavily populated by ethnic minorities (Shobnall).

With similar views, although the Pakistani Community Centre in Burton-on-Trent tried to cover a number of sports that appealed to the local community, a senior member felt that a lack of available facilities in the wider community detracted in persuading more to participate. Again supporting the literature discussed earlier, a lack of communication and promotion of activities was raised with a lack of provision for Asian sport (the opposite to Birmingham it was suggested) and limited material available regarding racial equality.[57] Interestingly, this participant also stated the difficulty in gaining access to funds, which could further eliminate the Asian community from active sports participation.

Encouragingly, those who worked in the Pakistan Community Centres in both Burton-on-Trent and Stoke-on-Trent were all volunteers. However, for other ethnic minorities, the need for more funding and the worryingly low number of active volunteers were raised during some interviews.[58] A senior member of the Indian community in Stoke-on-Trent stated how this undermined the opportunities for the Indian community to take part in physical activity as the lack of Indian volunteers meant a lack of role models for youngsters to aspire to. Adding to this is the greater demand now placed upon coaches and administrators involved in volunteering to demonstrate high levels of professionalism, knowledge and skills. Despite the efforts of the local authorities discussed earlier, in particular communities which sport is not of high cultural value, this seriously undermines the opportunities to recruit ethnic minority volunteers.

With regards to evidence of racial inequalities in a managerial sense, a representative from the Queen Street Community Centre in Burton-on-Trent illustrated the level of ethnic minority representation in the organization. Only 1 out of 12 board members came from an ethnic minority and could support her comment that 'it is seen as a white centre'. Thus, as recommended by Hylton, the continued significance of 'whiteness' in the power structure of organizations and community centres gives further weight to the need for CRT to be treated seriously.[59] To begin combating racist ideologies and inequalities, ethnic minorities need to be incorporated into senior, more powerful, positions within sports organizations and local authorities have a significant role to play in this.

As well as the two main projects being run in particular wards in both Burton-on-Trent and Stoke-on-Trent, there are other examples of success. These include the establishment of Madina, an Asian sports club in Burton-on-Trent, and Grange Park Rangers, an Asian football club in Stoke-on-Trent. Research has suggested that many ethnic minorities established their own teams to protect themselves from racism.[60] However, representatives of both clubs suggest the breaking down of perceived barriers facing Asians in sport and state that the amount of racist acts they have witnessed has dramatically fallen over the years. Both clubs now feel more accepted in the wider sporting community and see themselves as good examples of how Asians can get involved and realize the personal benefits that engaging in sport or physical activity can bring to their lives.

Conclusion

Based on the research findings, a number of conclusions can be drawn from this study. From a policy perspective, it has highlighted how two local authorities in the UK have started to be proactive by developing strategies and projects to engage with ethnic minorities. These include the 'StreetGames' project currently being run in Stoke-on-Trent and the 'Streets Ahead' project currently being run in Burton-on-Trent. These two initiatives are needed in both areas as active participation in sport and physical activity for ethnic minorities remain low. Although at an early stage of development, by taking sport and physical activities into wards which are populated by a large number of ethnic minorities, this negates the common barriers of travelling and cost becoming factors for non-participation. This might encourage more of the local community to become involved in voluntary work and possible future training; each of which assists the local authorities in meeting its objectives.

Although there has been progress in mixing participation between ethnic minorities and whites, this does not mean that the problems of racial inequalities and discrimination have been eliminated. The in-depth interviews with those involved in the ethnic minority community proved this. Thus, although there are policies in place and progress has been made, local authorities in particular still need to tackle racial inequalities better than they do at present and begin to fully understand the impact of social exclusion on ethnic minorities.

Overall, this article has illustrated how sport is facing a tough challenge of releasing the shackles of a discriminatory historic past. Through this, individual views and beliefs were shaped in ways which have allowed racial inequalities to remain at the forefront of society for a long time and for which certain institutions (such as sport) have found difficult to eradicate. If greater changes are to occur, it will need local authorities to proactively seek new ways of engaging with ethnic minorities through more inclusive projects and equality policies. Future research can continue to assess whether these are being achieved and how successful they are in meeting their objectives.

Acknowledgements

I would like to thank the two anonymous reviewers for their insightful and helpful thoughts on an earlier draft of this article.

Notes

1. See, for example, Carrington and McDonald, 'Whose Game is it Anyway?'; King, *Offside Racism*; Burdsey, *British Asians and Football*.
2. Baglihole, *Equal Opportunities and Social Policy*.
3. Burdsey, *British Asians and Football*, 11.
4. Miles and Brown, *Racism*.
5. Garner, *Racisms*.
6. Ibid., 17.
7. Swinney and Horne, 'Race Equality and Leisure Policy Discourses'.
8. See Rowe and Champion, *Sports Participation and Ethnicity in England*.
9. Sport England, *Active People 2 Survey*.
10. Ibid.
11. Sporting Equals, *Briefing Paper*.
12. Sport England, *Active People 2 Survey*.
13. Department of National Heritage, *Sport: Raising the Game*.
14. Sporting Equals, *Findings from the Racial Equality Survey*.
15. Sporting Equals, *Achieving Racial Equality*.
16. Long, Robinson and Spracklen, 'Promoting Racial Equality'.
17. Coalter, *A Wider Social Role for Sport*.
18. Horne, 'Local Authority Leisure Policies'; Swinney and Horne, 'Race Equality and Leisure Policy Discourses'; Carrington and McDonald, 'Whose Game is it Anyway?'; Long, Robinson and Welch, *Raising the Standard*; Long, Robinson and Spracklen, 'Promoting Racial Equality'; Spracklen, Hylton and Long, 'Managing and Monitoring Equality and Diversity'.
19. Long, Robinson and Welch, *Raising the Standard*.
20. Long, Robinson and Spracklen, 'Promoting Racial Equality'.
21. Ibid.
22. Spracklen, Hylton and Long, 'Managing and Monitoring Equality and Diversity'.
23. Horne, 'Local Authority Leisure Policies'; Swinney and Horne, 'Race Equality and Leisure Policy Discourses'.
24. Horne, 'Local Authority Leisure Policies'.
25. Ibid.
26. Swinney and Horne, 'Race Equality and Leisure Policy Discourses'.
27. Ibid.
28. Spracklen, Hylton and Long, 'Managing and Monitoring Equality and Diversity'; King, *Offside Racism*; Long and Hylton, 'Shades of White'.
29. See King, *Offside Racism*; Burdsey, *British Asians and Football*; Carrington, 'Sport, Masculinity and BlackCultural Resistance'.
30. Hylton, '"Race", Sport and Leisure'.
31. Ibid.
32. Long and Hylton, 'Shades of White'.
33. Rowe and Champion, *Sports Participation and Ethnicity in England*.
34. Sport England, 'The Use and Management of Sports'.
35. Cabinet Office, 'Minority Ethnic Issuers in Social Exclusion'.
36. Carroll, Ali and Azam, 'Promoting Physical Activity in South Asian Women'; Collins and Kay, *Sport and Social Exclusion*.
37. Carroll, Ali and Azam, 'Promoting Physical Activity in South Asian Women'.
38. Johnson, 'Perceptions of Barriers to Healthy Physical Activity'.
39. Collins and Kay, *Sport and Social Exclusion*.
40. Rowe and Champion, *Sports Participation and Ethnicity in England*.
41. Wray, 'Connecting Ethnicity, Gender and Physicality'.
42. Carroll, Ali and Azam, 'Promoting Physical Activity in South Asian Women'; Duval, Sampson and Boote, *Perceptions of Local Women about Physical Exercise*; Sporting Equals, *Briefing Paper*.
43. Carroll, Ali and Azam, 'Promoting Physical Activity in South Asian Women'.
44. Duval, Sampson and Boote, *Perceptions of Local Women about Physical Exercise*; Sporting Equals, *Briefing Paper*.
45. Gratton and Jones, *Research Methods for Sports Studies*.
46. Carrington and McDonald, 'The Politics of "Race" and Sports Policy', 242.

47. Miles and Huberman, *Qualitative Data Analysis*, 9.
48. Coalter, *A Wider Social Role for Sport*.
49. Horne, 'Local Authority Leisure Policies'.
50. Coalter, *A Wider Social Role for Sport*; Collins and Kay, *Sport and Social Exclusion*.
51. Coalter, *A Wider Social Role for Sport*.
52. Long, Robinson and Welch, *Raising the Standard*.
53. As suggested by Carroll, Ali and Azam, 'Promoting Physical Activity in South Asian Women '.
54. Collins and Kay, *Sport and Social Exclusion*.
55. See Long, Robinson and Welch, *Raising the Standard*; Long, Robinson and Spracklen, 'Promoting Racial Equality'; Horne, 'Local Authority Leisure Policies'; Swinney and Horne, 'Race Equality and Leisure Policy Discourses'; Spracklen, Hylton and Long, 'Managing and Monitoring Equality and Diversity'.
56. Wray, 'Connecting Ethnicity, Gender and Physicality'.
57. Ibid.
58. As identified by Sport England, *Active People 2 Survey*.
59. Hylton, '"Race", Sport and Leisure'.
60. See Johal, 'Playing Their Own Game'; Carrington and McDonald, 'Whose Game is it Anyway?'.

References

Baglihole, B. *Equal Opportunities and Social Policy: Issues of Gender, Race and Disability*. London: Longman, 1997.
Burdsey, D. *British Asians and Football: Culture, Identity, Exclusion*. London: Routledge, 2007.
Cabinet Office (2000) 'Minority Ethnic Issues in Social Exclusion and Neighbourhood Renewal'. In *Sport and Social Exclusion*, edited by M. Collins and T. Kay, 127–132. London: Routledge, 2003.
Carrington, B. 'Sport, Masculinity and Black Cultural Resistance'. In *The Sport Studies Reader*, edited by A. Tomlinson, 298–303. London: Routledge, 2007.
Carrington, B. and McDonald, I. 'Whose Game is it Anyway? Racism in Local League Cricket'. In *'Race', Sport and British Society*, edited by B. Carrington and I. McDonald, 50–69. London: Routledge, 2001.
Carrington, B. and McDonald, I. 'The Politics of 'Race' and Sports Policy in the United Kingdom'. In *Sport and Society: A Student Introduction*, 2nd Edition, edited by B. Houlihan. 230–254. London: Sage, 2008.
Carroll, R., N. Ali, and N. Azam. 'Promoting Physical Activity in South Asian Women through "Exercise on Prescription"'. *Health Technology Assessment* 6, no. 8 (2002): 1–99.
Coalter, F. *A Wider Social Role for Sport*. London: Routledge, 2007.
Collins, M., and T. Kay. *Sport and Social Exclusion*. London: Routledge, 2003.
Department of National Heritage. *Sport: Raising the Game*. London: HMSO, 1995.
Duval, L., J. Sampson, and E. Boote. *Perceptions of Local Women about Physical Exercise Provision in Shelton, Tunstall, Burslem and Longton*. Stoke-on-Trent: Staffordshire University, 2004.
Garner, S. *Racisms: An Introduction*. London: Sage, 2009.
Gratton, C., and I. Jones. *Research Methods for Sports Studies*. London: Routledge, 2004.
Horne, J. 'Local Authority Leisure Policies for Black and Ethnic Minority Provision in Scotland'. In *Policy and Politics in Sport, Physical Education and Leisure*, edited by S Fleming, M Talbot, and A Tomlinson, 159–76. Eastbourne: LSA publication no. 55, 1995.
Hylton, K. '"Race", Sport and Leisure: Lessons from Critical Race Theory'. *Leisure Studies* 24, no. 1 (2005): 81–98.
Johal, S. 'Playing Their Own Game: A South Asian Football Experience'. In *'Race', Sport and British Society*, edited by B. Carrington and I. McDonald, 153–169. London: Routledge, 2001.
Johnson, M.R. 'Perceptions of Barriers to Healthy Physical Activity among Asian Communities'. *Sport, Education and Society* 51, no. 1 (2000): 51–70.
King, C. *Offside Racism: Playing the White Man*. Oxford: Berg, 2004.
Long, J, and K Hylton. 'Shades of White: An Examination of Whiteness in Sport'. *Leisure Studies* 21, no. 2 (2002): 87–103.

Long, J., P. Robinson, and K. Spracklen. 'Promoting Racial Equality within Sports Organisations'. *Journal of Sport and Social Issues* 29 (2005): 41–59.

Long, J.A., P. Robinson, and M. Welch. *Raising the Standard: An Evaluation of Progress*. Leeds: Coachwise, 2003.

Miles, M.B., and M.A. Huberman. *Qualitative Data Analysis*. London: Sage, 1984.

Miles, R., and M. Brown. *Racism*. 2nd ed. London: Routledge, 1993.

Rowe, N., and R. Champion. *Sports Participation and Ethnicity in England: National Survey 1999/2000*. London: Sport England, 2000.

Sport England. *Active People 2 Survey*. Sport England: London, 2008.

Sport England (2000). 'The use and management of sports halls and swimming pools in England 1997'. In *Sport and Social Exclusion*, edited by M. Collins and T. Kay, 127–132. London: Routledge, 2003.

Sporting Equals. *Findings from the Racial Equality Survey of National Governing Bodies*. Sport England: London, 1999.

Sporting Equals. *Achieving Racial Equality: A Standard for Sport*. Sport England: London, 2000.

Sporting Equals. 'Briefing Paper – Ethnic Minorities and Physical Activity in the East Midlands'. Available at: http://www.sportingequals.org.uk/DynamicContent/Documents/BriefingPapers/East_Midlands_briefing_paper.pdf (accessed April 15, 2009) 2007.

Spracklen, K., K. Hylton, and J. Long. 'Managing and Monitoring Equality and Diversity in UK Sport: An Evaluation of the Sporting Equals Racial Equality Standard and its Impact on Organisational Change'. *Journal of Sport and Social Issues* 30, no. 3 (2006): 289–305.

Swinney, A., and J. Horne. 'Race Equality and Leisure Policy Discourses in Scottish Local Authorities'. *Leisure Studies* 24, no. 3 (2005): 271–89.

Wray, S. 'Connecting Ethnicity, Gender and Physicality'. In *Gender and Sport: A Reader*, edited by S. Scraton and A. Flintoff. 141–155. London: Routledge, 2002.

What does commitment mean to volunteers in youth sport organizations?

Terry Engelberg[a], James Skinner[b] and Dwight Zakus[b]

[a]Department of Tourism, Sport and Hotel Management, Griffith Business School, Griffith University, Southport, Australia; [b]Department of Tourism, Leisure, Hotel and Sport Management, Griffith Business School, Griffith University, Gold Coast, Southport, Australia

Youth sport is heavily dependent on volunteers to ensure successful delivery of sport programmes. This paper qualitatively investigated motivations and commitments of volunteers at various stages in their careers. Data were gathered through focus group interviews with 34 participants representing five sports and analysed using the *Analysis Method Framework*. Probes included volunteers' motivations for volunteering, views of commitment, views on commitment targets, and views on clashes between different types of volunteers. Statements were classified on two key dimensions: commitment to organisational targets, and status as core or casual volunteers. This classification resulted in the creation of a typology describing four types of volunteeers ('Mums and dads', 'Specialists', 'Über-volunteers task-oriented', and 'Über-volunteers team-oriented'). Future research should focus on the application of the volunteer typology for further understanding of how commitment influences volunteer behaviour.

Introduction

The Australian sport and recreation sector is dependent on volunteers for the everyday functioning and success of their organizations. The number of volunteers in sport, recreation and hobby organizations reached 1.7 million adults (11% of the adult population) in the year 2006.[1] Of these volunteers, over half are involved with delivering and administering programmes for children and young people under 18 (youth sport). Youth sport presents unique challenges in that it is heavily reliant on the work of young athletes' parents and guardians, as without the assistance of these the delivery of sport in Australia would be severely hindered.[2] The organization and delivery of youth sport is very labour intensive and subject to strict legal and risk management requirements (e.g. the need for volunteers to have 'blue cards' or police clearance to be allowed to work with minors). Appeals to involve more parents are a feature of both government and club-level publications, such as *Keep it Fun: Supporting Youth Sport*[3] and *On the Right Track* from the Queensland Little Athletics Association,[4] to name but a few. Despite these appeals, anecdotal evidence suggests that club administrators and committees are at a loss when it comes to getting and keeping more adults involved in all areas of club functioning and management.[5]

One variable that has been found to be critical in the effective organization and delivery of community-based sport is organizational commitment.[6] Organizational commitment can be defined as an attachment to and an identification with the goals of an organization, and has been found to be linked to volunteer retention,[7] satisfaction[8] and performance,[9] and inversely related to adverse consequences, such as burnout.[10] However, despite this progress in our understanding of the concept of commitment, little is known about how volunteers themselves define their commitment. This gap in our knowledge is arguably partly due to a preponderance of quantitative research methods in volunteer commitment research. Qualitative studies of commitment in paid-worker settings suggest that individuals highlight their desire to sacrifice personal concerns for the organization[11] and their concern for being proactive and ready for a challenge.[12] Studies that use qualitative methodologies show that a richer, more in-depth or thicker analysis of commitment emerged when volunteers use their own 'voice'.

The purpose of this research was to explore how volunteers in youth sport viewed their commitment to their organizations (that is, their clubs) and the relationships between commitment and volunteer motivations, and attitudes and perceptions of volunteering, and other volunteers and non-volunteers. In doing so, a volunteer typology, based on volunteers' commitment and motivations, was drawn. The following sections review the key variables addressed in this study, namely: volunteer motivations, commitment, commitment targets, and clashes between different types of volunteers and non-volunteers.

Volunteer motivations

Researchers[13] outlined a sport volunteering model based exclusively on research findings in this context. According to this model, there are three levels of volunteer motives, each having different relative importance. At the top level is the *core motive*, which is said to be to 'help a cause'.[14] This is 'common (and most important) to all volunteers, and reflects the altruism in volunteering'.[15]

In the middle, *primary motives* are identified which are 'personal needs and interests'.[16] It is noted[17] that sport volunteers are more likely than other volunteers to become involved because someone close to them is involved. In the case of youth sport, parents become volunteers because their own children are participants. This is consistent with the findings of the *Voluntary Work Survey*[18] that found that about two-fifths (43%) of volunteers with a sports involvement reported a reason for undertaking the work was due to a personal or family involvement (e.g. their children might play for the club). Another commonly cited reason was personal satisfaction (42% of volunteers). In contrast, helping others in the community was a more significant reason for volunteering in other areas (50% of volunteers in general gave this as a reason, compared with 38% of sports volunteers).

At the bottom level, *secondary motives* are identified.[19] These comprise 'social' and 'personal development' motives.[20] Variations amongst volunteers with respect to these motives have been identified.[21] For example, younger volunteers may be keen to acquire career-related skills and experiences (career function) whilst other volunteers, including parents of young athletes, may view social motives as an attractive bonus of volunteering.

In brief, it is thought that motivations change and evolve over time.[22] As involvement increases and volunteers develop their own experiences of volunteering, motives are also likely to change. Similarly, it is noted[23] that motives may evolve in line with original reasons for volunteering. For example, serving motives have been found to decline after joining. Social motives appear to strengthen with the passing of time[24] not only in youth sport but also in sport organizations in general.

Finally, the furthering of organizational goals appears to strengthen over time, above and over personal interests. This is highlighted where[25] 'sport volunteers tend to get involved for themselves, and tend to stay involved for the organization', a mechanism likely to occur through feeling part of and identifying with the organization, which is congruent with affective organizational commitment.

Finally, it is important to stress that general service motives may be fragile as too many organizations can offer these. Thus, each organization 'must proffer something particular for its own members'.[26] As such, goals have to be specific to the organization. Most importantly, it is thought that although commitment to other individuals (the social rewards) is of crucial importance, the power of volunteers' social environments to bind them to the organization has not received enough attention. In sum, commitment to the people in the organization may ultimately become salient with the passing of time. This study explores the motivations of volunteers at various stages in their volunteering activities and how these are interlinked with their commitment.

The organizational commitment of volunteers

Volunteers may be strongly committed to the goals of the organization, but have weaker ties to the institution itself.[27] For example, volunteers who work for a youth sport organization, because they want to help their own children, might find alternative ways of helping, such as taking them to training sessions or driving them to events.[28] A parent who is committed to the development of the sport may make a monetary or other donation to the club. Theoretically, a distinction is made between attitudinal and behavioural commitment.[29] Attitudinal commitment denotes a mindset. In contrast, the behavioural view suggests that commitment is the process whereby the individual becomes committed to a course of action.[30] Researchers[31] contend that voluntary 'work' is carried out in behaviourally weak environments with low performance expectations. This means that volunteers often perform their work when and how it suits them and are not subject to the same constraints paid employees are (e.g. keeping hours and attending meetings). Volunteers' attitudes, unlike their behaviour, are not situationally constrained. Under such circumstances, the attitudinal view of commitment may be more appropriate.[32]

Some studies[33] have compared volunteers and paid workers with respect to specific attitudes, such as organizational commitment, and found that the attitudes of both types of workers are not that dissimilar. Researchers[34] concluded that despite the differences between paid workers and volunteers, their organizational commitment is similar in nature. This suggests that models developed for paid workers may be successfully translated into the volunteer context. This study examines volunteers' constructions of their commitment as an attitude or mindset.

Targets of commitment

The application of commitment research to sport volunteering has typically extended the commitment conceptualization to the organization as a whole (i.e. the club). However, individuals can become committed to other constituents, targets or domains that are part of that organization.[35] For example, individuals can become committed to their 'occupation' or their work team. These different commitments are believed to interact and shape an individual's overall commitment profile.[36] A study of volunteers in Little Athletics centres[37] found that volunteers could distinguish among different commitment targets, specifically commitment to the centre (the club), commitment to the team of volunteers and commitment to the volunteer role. A follow-up study[38] showed that volunteers could not only distinguish between commitment to their respective organizations and commitment to a volunteer role, but also that each commitment target predicted a different organizational outcome, such as volunteer involvement and performance.

Beyond these studies, little is known about which targets volunteers are committed to and the implications of this commitment to volunteer behaviour. Identifying and assessing suitable targets of work-related commitment would add to the understanding of the commitment of volunteers in the same way it has helped understand the complexities of commitment in paid-worker settings. This study follows-up on findings[39] that volunteers can become attached to their volunteer team and their volunteer role by asking volunteers about their attachment to these organizational targets.

Core and casual volunteering and clashes of motivations

According to researchers,[40] volunteering can be viewed as a leisure and non-coerced activity, and a satisfying and enjoyable experience. There are three forms of volunteering: serious, casual and project-based leisure. Serious volunteers engage in sustained and significant effort, providing benefits for the organization and for them. Serious volunteers are also known as *core* volunteers[41] or systematic volunteers.[42] In contrast, casual volunteering involves less substantial efforts, there is no career to follow as such and the efforts are more 'one-off' than systematic. Volunteers who engage in casual leisure are also known as peripheral volunteers.[43] Many parents in youth sport organizations fit into this category; that is, they want to help their own children but they do not want a high degree of involvement.[44] Finally, project-based leisure[45] is a special category reflecting involvement in 'one-off or occasional, though infrequent, creative undertaking'. Although it has the potential to build community, it is not serious leisure. Sport event volunteering may fall under this category.

According to researchers,[46] core volunteers usually undertake formal roles, for example committee members, and are deeply involved in the running of the organization. In general, they also devote far more time to the organization. Casual and project-based volunteers, in contrast, help occasionally or when it is needed, most likely in informal roles. Interestingly, these volunteers may be moved by a sense of obligation but as indicated,[47] this obligation can provide the volunteer with satisfaction and pleasure. The work of casual or periphery volunteers should not be disregarded as in many organizations tasks have to be shared. It is also important to note that although these types of volunteers have been identified, there are no fixed boundaries as volunteer involvement may change over time. Thus, a heavily involved career volunteer may eventually move to the periphery, whilst a casual volunteer may decide to make a career out of volunteering.

Core and casual volunteers, as well as non-volunteers, do not always interact in harmony and this can contribute to a 'clash of cultures and motivations'.[48] Reviewing research conducted for Sport England[49] discovered that there were conflicts between core volunteers and parents of athletes (non-volunteers). Core volunteers were found to perceive the latter as wanting a child-minding service for their children, whilst parents expected the full service of a privately run organization. It has been suggested[50] that voluntary organizations consist of an activist core and a more inactive periphery and that the core is often perceived as influential, regardless of their position, whilst the periphery, although less involved, can still provide substantial help. Interestingly, whilst the core is frequently overworked, it may be difficult for periphery volunteers to become more involved, due to long-established interpersonal relationships of the core.[51] The core has a general resistance to welcome other volunteers.[52] This situation may have implications for the development of volunteer commitment and may further contribute to the development of these clashes of cultures.

Following from the above research, this study explores how volunteers see themselves in terms of their status as the 'core' or the 'periphery' and how such membership affects their commitment and their views of and interactions with other volunteers.

Methods

Sampling and selection of participants

Access to participants was negotiated with the cooperation of the local sport and recreation government body, Sport and Recreation Queensland (SRQ) Northern Region. SRQ sent an email message requesting participation in this study to registered clubs, organizations and associations that manage youth sport. An initial pool of 86 individuals responded to this call and expressed an interest in participating. From this initial pool, a total of 34 individuals (23 females and 11 males) representing five sports (soccer, water polo, little athletics, disability sport and surf life saving) responded and confirmed their willingness to participate in focus group interviews. Participants were then allocated into groups of between five and seven individuals. Table 1 shows the characteristics of the participants.

Data collection materials

The data collection method consisted of focus group discussions. Focus groups offer diversity in terms of group composition, but at the same time there is a degree of commonality between the participants (all are volunteers in youth sport).

In order to guide the discussion, a topic guide was created. Its purpose was to serve as an interview agenda and to enhance the consistency of the data collection process.[53] Items or probes were worded as issues to be explored rather than as questions to be asked. This procedure encouraged active interviewing and aided the researcher's responsiveness to the actual wording or language used by participants. The topic guide was piloted with an initial group of four volunteers. This exercise was successful and only minor modifications to the wording and order of topics were required.

Data collection procedures

All participants were contacted a few days prior to their scheduled focus group interviews and given an introductory briefing. On the day of the interviews, the researchers provided

Table 1.   Characteristics of focus group participants ($N = 34$).

Background variable	N
Age	
30 or less	2
31–40	14
41–50	15
51 or more	3
Children enrolled	
Yes	29
No	5
Experience (seasons as volunteer)	
First season	3
2–4 seasons	16
5 seasons or more	15
Main role	
Committee member	18
Another role	16
Size of club (number of members)	
Less than 100	13
100 or more	21

participants with an informed consent form describing the aims of the research, the nature of the data collection procedures, and data handling and storage. For those interviews that took place in a clubhouse or other designated place, the researchers arrived half an hour prior to the scheduled start time, met with a club representative, greeted the participants as they arrived and then proceeded as described earlier.

Permission to take digital audio recordings of interviews was requested and granted by all participants in every group. Once consent was obtained from all participants, the sessions began. Discussions lasted between 35 and 50 min.

Data analysis

Digital recordings for all focus group discussions were downloaded into digital audio files. Whenever possible, the recordings were transcribed within 1 or 2 days of each respective focus group discussion. Each focus group transcript included details of each discussion session: date, location, time and duration of the discussion, number of participants and sport (s) represented. Transcripts contained a coded form of the participants' name (female 1, male 1 and so on). Names of clubs, centres, associations and all other identifying details were removed.

The analyses were conducted following the *Analysis Method Framework.*[54] The process of analysis requires two key steps: managing the data and making sense of the evidence through participants' accounts. During the data management stage, initial themes were identified. These themes led to the development of an index with subthemes grouped under four main substantive headings. To facilitate this process, the main headings followed the order of the key topics of the topic guide with the addition of another heading for demographic and other background information. Once the original index was created, it was applied to the raw data and refined further until a final index was achieved. The final thematic index was then applied to the raw data. The main topics of the original index appear as follows:

(1) main reasons for volunteers' initial and current involvement with their respective sport clubs;
(2) volunteers' views of commitment;
(3) volunteers' views of targets of commitment and
(4) clashes between core and casual volunteers.

The final step consisted of sorting the data through thematic charting.[55] Effective thematic charting not only reduces data but also retains participants' key words or terminology. Separate thematic charts were created for each of the focus groups.

Findings

Main reasons for volunteers' initial and current involvement with their respective sport clubs

The findings of this study indicate that having a child involved was the key reason for initial involvement for the majority of parent volunteers, which is seen as a primary motive.[56] The second most cited reason for initial involvement was a feeling of obligation; this constitutes a secondary motive.[57] Conversely, non-parents were more likely to cite prior involvement in the sport and wanting to put something back into the sport as the main reason for their initial involvement. Helping the children and developing their own skills were also important considerations. A feeling of obligation was a less prevalent reason.

Participants were asked whether they considered themselves core or casual volunteers. Just over a third of participants considered themselves core volunteers, as defined in terms of extent and nature of involvement with the organization. All non-parents described themselves core volunteers and considered their volunteering in sport as a serious pursuit. Most parents, however, identified themselves as casual volunteers.

Consistent with research,[58] volunteer motivations change with time and according to the volunteering experience. However, very few volunteers reported an initial involvement for themselves which, with time, turns into remaining involved for the organization.[59] The most prevalent reasons for remaining involved were social, including making friends, fun and enjoyment, and wanting to belong to a social group. The majority of the parents gave these as current reasons for involvement, whilst the remaining parents stated that helping their child was their key motivation. Furthermore, the latter reported that regardless of how much enjoyment they derived from the volunteering activities, once their child or children ceased their involvement with the sport, they too intended to cease volunteering. Only parents who were core volunteers or had a previous involvement with the club or sport did not intend to cease volunteering regardless of their own child's or children's involvement. Non-parents (all of whom were core volunteers) reported fewer changes in motivations: helping the cause remained the key motivation, followed by development of skills, and social motives.

Volunteers' views of commitment

Most participants described commitment as a feeling or a state of mind, a view consistent with attitudinal frameworks of commitment.[60] There was widespread consensus within and between groups that commitment fluctuated with time. However, participants differed in the way they described their own and other volunteers' commitment.

Committee members and other core volunteers were more likely to describe their commitment with terms and phrases such as 'belongingness' and 'being part of something important'. Conversely, other volunteers described their commitment in terms of enjoying the experience of helping, and, for parents, as part of the parenting role. In the words of one mother:

> I am committed because I like helping, being with other like-minded people and being with my kids. Helping here is part of my role as a mother. (Female, parent, soccer)

There was widespread agreement that a feeling of obligation was a necessary component of volunteering. Volunteers with children stated that they felt an obligation to contribute to the sporting development of their own child or children, rather than an obligation to the club or the sport. Volunteers without children, on the other hand, regarded feelings of obligation as a duty to put something back into the sport or the club.

A prevalent view was that commitment fluctuated over time depending on the volunteer experience.[61] Although participants generally reported an increasing level of commitment with the passing of time, temporary declines in commitment often followed from negative experiences. In general, volunteers agreed that non-volunteers lacked organizational commitment and that some volunteers, such as long-serving volunteers, could be too committed.

Other prevalent meanings of commitment included 'putting oneself out', 'doing what is required' and 'caring about other volunteers, the parents and the children'. Some of these meanings are similar to those reported in a qualitative study of managers'[62] organizational commitment.

Volunteers' views of targets of commitment

There was widespread agreement that sport volunteers could become committed to various organizational constituencies, including the volunteer role, other volunteers, the sport itself and the children. Volunteers who disagreed with this distinction belonged to very small clubs where all tasks were shared among everyone. For these volunteers, the distinction amongst targets of commitment was not meaningful.

Commitment to the role was salient particularly with the passing of time. Participants believed that with increasing role-specific experience, competence and self-confidence would also increase, which in turn would result in a stronger commitment to the role undertaken. Committee members felt that this was crucial in fostering commitment to a committee position.

Some gender differences were evident with regard to commitment to a volunteer role. Women were more likely to believe that volunteers should take on any role as needed by the club. This finding is consistent with the construction of the woman's role in sport as that of a support person.[63] Conversely, some male volunteers expressed the view that the volunteer role undertaken was an important consideration and that commitment to the role should take precedence over commitment to the club.

Commitment to other volunteers (or the team of volunteers) was particularly prevalent amongst parents and volunteers with no prior experience in the sport. A handful of committee members agreed that commitment to the team was essential for committee cohesiveness. Their accounts highlighted the importance attached to the social nature of the volunteering experience:

> If you are committed to the other volunteers, this means that you don't want to let them down. (Female, parent, surf life saving)

Participants were also asked whether they could distinguish other targets of commitment. The most prevalent response was 'the children':

> As parents our commitment is to our kids. Clubs, other adults, and roles all come second. The moment my kids decide to quit all other commitments go out of the window. (Female, parent, soccer)

Clashes between core and casual volunteers

The classification[64] of leisure into serious, casual and project-based was applicable to the level of involvement of participants in this study. For example, participants acknowledged that their involvement as volunteers could vary according to their circumstances and interests, with some preferring to help at specific events or for specific projects. Others preferred to lend a hand when required, whilst others preferred the structure and predictability of certain positions. Some of these views are expressed as follows:

> To me, volunteering is about helping at events, to ensure things go smoothly. I am not interested in further involvement. (Male, non-parent, disability sport)

> I am more comfortable with a specific job or role. That way I know exactly what I have to do. (Female, parent, water polo)

Conflicts between different types of volunteers and between volunteer and non-volunteers[65] emerged throughout the group discussions. Both casual and core volunteers expressed their unhappiness with non-volunteers, particularly with parents who never helped or who did not take an interest. In one participant's words:

> What I would really want to know is why there are people who drop their kids, sit themselves on a comfy chair and read the paper throughout the training session, ignoring our requests for help. (Male, non-parent, little athletics)

Clashes of cultures were also evident between core and casual volunteers. For example, core volunteers expressed their unhappiness at the perceived lack of involvement of casual volunteers, whereas casual volunteers generally perceived core volunteers as dogmatic and overly committed. As one casual volunteer noted:

> Clubs cannot move forward with people who are not prepared to change and to let others lead. (Male, parent, soccer)

Overall, however, despite the various motivations, perceptions of other volunteers, and conflicts, most participants declared that they would be willing to continue to volunteer for as long as it was possible or for the entire duration of their child or children's involvement.

Creating a volunteer typology

As a final step in the descriptive analysis, a typology was created to capture how volunteers differed in terms of their commitment. Typologies are usually multi-dimensional classifications; they are systematically created by combining at least two dimensions to achieve a more elaborate picture of a characteristic.[66] The characteristic here is the type of volunteer. The other key aspect of typologies is that individuals can only be assigned to one category, thereby '"dividing" or "sectoring" the social world'.[67]

We took into account two key dimensions in the development of a volunteer typology. The first was strength of participants' commitment to each of the three organizational targets. For example, volunteers whose primary target of commitment is the volunteer team are more socially oriented and less concerned about the role undertaken or the organization. Volunteers whose primary target of commitment is the volunteer role are more task oriented and less concerned about the team of volunteers and the organization.

The second dimension taken into account was participants' status as core or casual volunteers. This dimension is based on a predefined typology, either being a core or a casual volunteer. It is acceptable to use a predefined typology at the analytical stage of research.[68] Once both dimensions are taken into account, a volunteer is further classified as, for example, a socially oriented core volunteer or a socially oriented casual volunteer. This development process led to the construction of four main categories that were tested by looking at individual cases across the sample. The validity of these categories was established by having a second and a third rater independently assess the classification process and the choice of dimensions. The final four categories established were labelled as *mums and dads, specialists, über-volunteers task-oriented* and *über-volunteers team-oriented.*

Type 1: The 'mums and dads'

The primary motivation for volunteering for the *mums and dads* is that they have a child in the club. Their initial commitment is rooted in a feeling of obligation but later may develop into enjoyment. Their key targets of commitment are their child or children (as these volunteers see themselves as parents performing a child-minding role) and the other volunteers. They are drawn to the social aspect of volunteering and usually avoid committee or 'serious' roles. They like helping on an 'as needed' basis and may not have any knowledge of the sport or the club.

Type 2: The specialists

The primary motivation of the *specialists* is that they have a child in the club (if they are parents) or because of previous involvement in the club or the sport. Their key target of commitment is their specific role as coach, official or other. Although they are highly proficient in their roles, they avoid committee positions. They may have been a committee member in the past, but now prefer to help sporadically, such as during an event.

Type 3: Über-volunteers task-oriented

The primary motivation of the *über-volunteers task-oriented* is their history of involvement with the club or the sport. This involvement may have started as an athlete, coach or even as an athlete's parent, although the latter is much less likely. They feel deeply committed and bound to the club. They are usually a committee member or hold a role that is considered necessary for the survival of the club. These volunteers perceive themselves as hardworking and perceive other volunteers and non-volunteers as uncommitted and even incompetent. Their attitudes and behaviour are consistent with one description of 'martyred leaders'.[69]

Type 4: Über-volunteers team-oriented

The *über-volunteer team-oriented* shares similarities with the über-volunteers task-oriented because they take their volunteering as serious leisure. This volunteer, however, is more socially oriented, highly committed to the other volunteers and perceived by other volunteers and non-volunteers alike as friendlier.

Figure 1 maps out the typology and its categories. The horizontal axis divides volunteers into core/serious and casual. The vertical axis divides volunteers into those who are task or role oriented and those who are socially oriented. Core volunteers who are task oriented comprise most of the über-volunteers task-oriented (top left quarter of the circle).

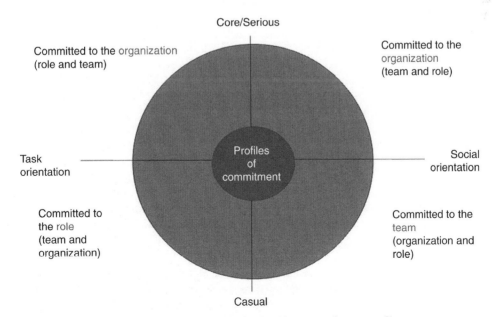

Figure 1.   Representation of volunteer typologies based on commitment profiles.

Their key commitment is to their organizations, followed by a commitment to their role and their team. Core volunteers who have a social orientation include the über-volunteers team-oriented (top right quarter of the circle). Although they are also primarily committed to their respective organizations, they are more committed to their team than to their roles. Casual volunteers can also have a task or a social orientation. Task-oriented casual volunteers include the specialists (bottom left quarter of the circle). They are primarily committed to a role, which they specialize in, but do not volunteer in a systematic fashion, i.e. they do not see themselves as core or serious volunteers. Their secondary targets of commitment are the team and the organization. Socially oriented casual volunteers include the mums and dads. These volunteers enjoy the social aspects of volunteering and are primarily committed to the team. Their secondary targets of commitment are the organization and the role undertaken (bottom right quarter of the circle).

Although this typology and classification provide a useful framework for the understanding of volunteer commitment in youth sport organizations, these classifications are fluid. Volunteers' changing motivations and situation mean that transitions between categories may occur throughout the volunteering experience and over time.

Discussion

The purpose of this study was to explore volunteers' views on their commitment. The main topics explored were motivations for volunteering, views of commitment, views on commitment targets and clashes between different types of volunteers. In sum, this research shed light on the question 'What does commitment mean to volunteers in youth sport organisations?'

Participants gave various motivations for their initial and their current involvement as volunteers. Most parents became involved due to a desire to help their own child or children. However, with the passing of time, many volunteers remained with their respective clubs due to social reasons, making friends, and wanting to be part of a social group.

Participants also recognized that commitment could be directed at organizational targets other than a club as a whole. These targets included the volunteer team and the volunteer role. Other targets of commitment, such as the children and the sport, were also identified but not explored in depth. Commitment to the role was more salient to core volunteers irrespective of role, whereas casual volunteers did not generally feel an attachment to a particular role, preferring to help on an 'as needed' basis and avoiding demanding roles. Commitment to the team was more salient to committee members and casual volunteers, but less central to coaches.

Other issues that emerged during the group discussions included motivations, different types of leisure, culture clashes, non-volunteers' behaviour, and the interrelationship of these variables with commitment. In brief, volunteers were generally satisfied with their experiences but at the same time acknowledged that their motivations fluctuated with the passing of time.[70] The existence of different types of leisure, such as core and casual leisure,[71] also clearly emerged as a key factor, where participants identified themselves as either core or casual volunteers. The existence of a clash of cultures was a prevalent theme throughout the discussions. Volunteers expressed their opinions towards different types of volunteers (e.g. core vs. casual) and towards non-volunteers. One interesting finding in this respect was that casual volunteers felt that many core volunteers could be too committed and that this led to negative consequences for both the organization and for other volunteers. This finding presents a challenge for future research in the organizational behaviour of volunteers where commitment has been widely regarded as a positive attitude.

Limitations of the study

There are some limitations that must be noted. First, participants were likely to include very committed volunteers. Second, for most groups, the participants consisted of volunteers who already knew each other and worked together in the same club and this may have influenced their accounts. Specifically, participants would have been careful not to express strong feelings about each other or other fellow volunteers not present. Despite this, a variety of opinions and explanations for different phenomena were canvassed. Finally, and common to all focus group research, some participants were more dominant than others. However, this limitation was lessened through careful moderating of the discussion where the researcher ensured that the views of all participants were duly canvassed.

Suggestions for future research

There is a need to continue to examine the nature of volunteer commitment. One interesting finding is that although volunteers feel an emotional attachment to their clubs, they also feel an obligation towards the children, the club or the sport. In this respect, an awareness of the nature of psychological contracts,[72] which is a series of beliefs held by individuals and organizations about their reciprocal obligations, may be useful in understanding volunteers' commitments[73] and their organizational behaviour generally.[74]

This research also showed that commitment to organizational targets, such as the volunteer team and the volunteer role, are also worthy of further exploration. Qualitative methods assist in the identification of targets that are salient to volunteers in various sport contexts. It may be the case that organizational commitment is not the most salient target of commitment to volunteers, particularly given the diversity of motivations that drive volunteers once they join an organization. The targets identified in this research may not be as relevant or as distinct in every sport context and this merits further exploration.

The typology constructed here provides a useful platform for the future understanding of how commitment is shaped and its influence on volunteer behaviour. This typology could perhaps be tested quantitatively. For example, are 'mums and dads' more strongly committed to the volunteer team as the typology suggested? Are 'über-volunteers task-oriented' more committed to their roles than to their fellow volunteers? Another suggestion would be to develop similar typologies for volunteers in other sport organizations (organizations with adult athletes exclusively, or with athletes of all ages) to understand whether volunteers can be classified as a function of their various commitments.

Research addressing the motives and commitment of core and casual volunteers needs to be conducted. This has been highlighted[75] as an issue requiring further exploration. For example, why do some parents become core volunteers and continue volunteering even when their own children cease their involvement, whilst others shy away from any involvement?

Conclusion

Youth sport is dependent on the work of volunteers for its successful organization and delivery. Unfortunately, many volunteers feel overburdened and unappreciated. Of greatest concern, volunteers who once had ownership of their organizations are increasingly 'disempowered and frequently relegated to the role of foot soldier',[76] especially under recent policies imposed by governments. These factors do not bode well for sustainable community sport organizations.

Research shows that commitment can fluctuate according to evaluation of the volunteer experience; hence, the importance to actively manage the volunteer experience by volunteer managers or coordinators. There is a pressing need for sport managers and coordinators in community-based sport to understand that the nature of the relationship between volunteers and their organizations is quite complex and that it is undergoing constant change. As such, volunteer commitment will continue to be a fruitful avenue for research.

Notes

1. Australian Bureau of Statistics, *Sports and Physical Recreation*.
2. Kirk et al., 'Time Commitments in Junior Sport'.
3. Western Australia Department of Sport and Recreation, *Keep it Fun*.
4. Queensland Little Athletics Association, *On the Right Track*.
5. Zakus, 'Managing Risk in Community Sport Organizations'.
6. Cuskelly, McIntyre, and Boag, 'Longitudinal Study of the Development'; Doherty, *Community Sport Volunteers*; Engelberg, Skinner, and Zakus, 'Exploring the Relationship Between Commitment' and Hoye, 'Commitment, Involvement and Performance'.
7. Cuskelly and Boag, 'Organisational Commitment as a Predictor'.
8. Dorsch et al., *What Affects a Volunteer's Commitment?*
9. Engelberg, Skinner, and Zakus, 'Exploring the Relationship' and Hoye, 'Commitment, Involvement and Performance'.
10. Engelberg et al., 'Organisational and Occupational Commitment'.
11. Randall, Fedor, and Longenecker, 'Behavioral Expression'.
12. Singh and Vinnicombe, 'What Does Commitment Really Mean?'
13. Doherty, *Community Sport Volunteers*.
14. Ibid., 31.
15. Ibid., 31.
16. Ibid., 31.
17. Ibid.
18. Australian Bureau of Statistics, *Voluntary Work Survey*.
19. Doherty, *Community Sport Volunteers*.
20. Ibid., 31.
21. Ibid.
22. Ibid.
23. Pearce, *Organizational Behavior*.
24. Nichols and King, 'Changing Motivations and Frustration'.
25. Doherty, *Community Sport Volunteers*, 32.
26. Pearce, *The Organizational Behavior*, 82–3.
27. Ibid. Knoke and Prensky, 'What Relevance do Organization Theories'.
28. Kirk et al., 'Time Commitments in Junior Sport'.
29. Mowday, Porter, and Steers, *Organizational Linkages*.
30. Ibid.
31. Pearce, *Organizational Behavior*, 82–3.
32. Cuskelly and Boag, 'Organisational Commitment as a Predictor'.
33. Liao-Troth, 'Attitude Differences'.
34. Ibid.
35. Brooks and Wallace, 'Discursive Examination'; Meyer and Herscovitch, 'Commitment in the Workplace' and Reichers, 'Review and Reconceptualization'.
36. Cohen, *Multiple Commitments in the Workplace*.
37. Engelberg, Skinner, and Zakus, 'Exploring the Commitment of Volunteers'.
38. Engelberg, Skinner, and Zakus, 'Exploring the Relationship'.
39. Ibid.
40. Stebbins, 'Introduction'.
41. Pearce, *Organizational Behavior*.
42. Shibili et al. 'Characteristics of Volunteers'.
43. Cuskelly, Harrington, and Stebbins, 'Changing Levels of Organisational Commitment'.

44. Cuskelly, Hoye, and Auld, *Working with Volunteers in Sport.*
45. Stebbins, 'Introduction', 7.
46. Pearce, *Organizational Behavior.*
47. Stebbins, 'Introduction'.
48. Nichols et al., 'UK Voluntary Sport Sector', 44.
49. Ibid.
50. Pearce, *The Organizational Behavior.*
51. Nichols et al., 'UK Voluntary Sport Sector'.
52. Pearce, *Organizational Behavior.*
53. Arthur and Nazroo, 'Designing Fieldwork Strategies'.
54. Ritchie, Spencer, and O'Connor, 'Carrying Out Qualitative Analysis'.
55. Ibid.
56. Doherty, *Community Sport Volunteers.*
57. Ibid.
58. Ibid. and Pearce, *Organizational Behavior.*
59. Doherty, *Community Sport Volunteers.*
60. Mowday, Porter, and Steers, *Organizational Linkages.*
61. Green and Chalip, 'Paths to Volunteer Commitment'.
62. Singh and Vinnicombe, 'What Does Commitment Really Mean?'
63. Thompson, *Mother's Taxi.*
64. Stebbins, 'Introduction'.
65. Nichols et al., 'UK Voluntary Sport Sector'.
66. Ritchie, Spencer, and O'Connor, 'Carrying Out Qualitative Analysis'.
67. Ibid., 244.
68. Ibid.
69. Pearce, *Organizational Behavior*, 124.
70. Ibid.
71. Stebbins, 'Introduction'.
72. Rousseau, 'Psychological and Implied Contracts'.
73. Liao-Troth, 'Attitude Differences'.
74. Taylor et al., 'Using Psychological Contract Theory'.
75. Doherty, *Community Sport Volunteers.*
76. Cuskelly, 'Volunteer Retention in Community', 63.

References

Arthur, S., and J. Nazroo. 'Designing Fieldwork Strategies and Materials'. In *Qualitative Research Practice: A Guide for Social Science Students and Researchers*, ed. J. Ritchie and J. Lewis, 109–37. London: Sage, 2004.

Australian Bureau of Statistics. *Voluntary Work Survey.* Cat. No. 4441.0. Canberra: Australian Bureau of Statistics, 2000.

Australian Bureau of Statistics. *Sports and Physical Recreation: A Statistical Overview.* Cat No. 4156. Canberra, Australia: Australian Bureau of Statistics, 2010.

Brooks, G.R., and J.P. Wallace. 'A Discursive Examination of the Nature, Determinants and Impact of Organisational Commitment'. *Asia Pacific Journal of Human Resources* 44 (2006): 222–39.

Cohen, A. *Multiple Commitments in the Workplace: An Integrative Approach.* Mahwah, NJ: Lawrence Erlbaum, 2003.

Cuskelly, G. 'Volunteer Retention in Community Sport Organisations'. *European Sport Management Quarterly* 4 (2004): 59–76.

Cuskelly, G., and A. Boag. 'Organisational Commitment as a Predictor of Committee Member Turnover Among Volunteer Sport Administrators: Results of a Time-lagged Study'. *Sport Management Review* 4, no. 1 (2001): 65–86.

Cuskelly, G., M. Harrington, and R.A. Stebbins. 'Changing Levels of Organisational Commitment Amongst Sport Volunteers: A Serious Leisure Approach'. *Society and Leisure/ Loisir et Societé* 27, no. 3/4 (2002/2003): 191–212.

Cuskelly, G., R. Hoye, and C. Auld. *Working with Volunteers in Sport: Theory and Practice.* Routledge: London, 2006.

Cuskelly, G., N. McIntyre, and A. Boag. 'A Longitudinal Study of the Development of Organisational Commitment Amongst Volunteer Sport Administrators'. *Journal of Sport Management* 12, no. 3 (1998): 181–202.

Doherty, A. *A Profile of Community Sport Volunteers.* Toronto: Parks and Recreation Ontario, 2007. http://www.216.13.76.142/PROntario/PDF/reports/finalReport_phaseOne2005.pdf (accessed September 1, 2007).

Dorsch, K.D., H.A. Riemer, V. Sluth, D.M. Paskevich, and P. Chelladurai. *What Affects a Volunteer's Commitment?* Toronto: Canadian Center for Philanthropy, 2002.

Engelberg, T., J. Skinner, and D.H. Zakus. 'Exploring the Commitment of Volunteers in Little Athletics Centres'. *Australian Journal on Volunteering* 11, no. 2 (2006): 57–67.

Engelberg, T., J. Skinner, and D.H. Zakus. 'Exploring the Relationship Between Commitment, Experience, and Self-assessed Performance in Youth Sport Organizations'. *Sport Management Review* 14 (2011): 117–25.

Engelberg, T., C. Stipis, B. Kippin, S. Spillman, and K. Burbidge. 'Organisational and Occupational Commitment as Predictors of Volunteer Coaches' Burnout'. *Australian Journal on Volunteering* 14, no. 1 (2009): 1–9.

Green, B.C., and L. Chalip. 'Paths to Volunteer Commitment: Lessons from the Sydney Olympic Games'. In *Volunteering as Leisure/leisure as Volunteering*, ed. R.A. Stebbins and M. Graham. Wallingford, Oxfordshire: CABI International, 2004.

Hoye, R. 'Commitment, Involvement and Performance of Voluntary Sport Organisation Board Members'. *European Sport Management Quarterly* 7, no. 1 (2007): 109–21.

Kirk, D., A. O'Connor, T. Carlson, P. Burke, K. Davis, and S. Glover. 'Time Commitments in Junior Sport: Social Consequences for Participants and their Families'. *European Journal of Physical Education* 2 (1997): 1–73.

Knoke, D., and D. Prensky. 'What Relevance do Organization Theories have for Voluntary Associations?' *Social Science Quarterly* 65, no. 1 (1984): 3–20.

Liao-Troth, M.A. 'Attitude Differences Between Paid Workers and Volunteers'. *Nonprofit Management and Leadership* 4 (2001): 423–42.

Meyer, J.P., and L. Herscovitch. 'Commitment in the Workplace, Toward a General Model'. *Human Resource Management Review* 11 (2001): 299–326.

Mowday, R.T., L.W. Porter, and R.M. Steers. *Organizational Linkages: The Psychology of Commitment, Absenteeism, and Turnover.* San Diego, CA: Academic Press, 1982.

Nichols, G., and L. King. 'The Changing Motivations and Frustration Facing Volunteers in Youth Programs. A Study of the Guide Association of the United Kingdom'. *Journal of Applied Recreation Research* 23 (1998): 243–62.

Nichols, G., P. Taylor, M. James, K. Holmes, L. King, and R. Garrett. 'Pressures on the UK Voluntary Sport Sector'. *Voluntas: International Journal of Voluntary and Non-profit organisations* 16, no. 1 (2005): 33–50.

Pearce, J. *The Organizational Behavior of Unpaid Workers.* New York: Routledge, Chapman & Hall, 1993.

Queensland Little Athletics Association. *On the Right Track: How to Help at Little Athletics.* Fairfield Gardens, QLD: Queensland Little Athletics Association, 2004.

Randall, D.M., D.B. Fedor, and C.O. Longenecker. 'The Behavioral Expression of Organizational Commitment'. *Journal of Vocational Behavior* 36 (1990): 210–24.

Reichers, A.E. 'A Review and Reconceptualization of Organizational Commitment'. *Academy of Management Review* 10 (1985): 465–76.

Ritchie, J., L. Spencer, and W. O'Connor. 'Carrying Out Qualitative Analysis'. In *Qualitative Research Practice: A Guide for Social Science Students and Researchers*, ed. J. Ritchie and J. Lewis, 219–63. London: Sage, 2004.

Rousseau, D.M. 'Psychological and Implied Contracts in Organizations'. *Employee Responsibilities and Rights Journal* 2 (1989): 121–39.

Shibili, S., P. Taylor, G. Nichols, C. Gratton, and T. Kokolakakis. 'The Characteristics of Volunteers in UK Sports Clubs'. *European Journal for Sport Management*, 6 (1999): 10–27.

Singh, V., and S. Vinnicombe. 'What Does Commitment Really Mean? Views of UK and Swedish Managers'. *Personnel Review* 29, no. 2 (2000): 228–54.

Stebbins, R.A. 'Introduction'. In *Volunteering as Leisure/Leisure as Volunteering: An International Assessment*, ed. R.A. Stebbins and M. Graham, 1–12. Wallingford, Oxfordshire: CABI International, 2004.

Taylor, T., S. Darcy, R. Hoye, and G. Cuskelly. 'Using Psychological Contract Theory to Explore Issues in Effective Volunteer Management'. *European Sport Management Quarterly* 6, no. 2 (2006): 123–47.

Thompson, S. *Mother's Taxi*. New York: SUNY Press, 1999.

Western Australia Department of Sport and Recreation. *Keep it Fun: Supporting Youth Sport*. Perth, WA: Western Australia Department of Sport and Recreation. http://fulltext.ausport.gov.au/fulltext/2003/wa/keepitfun.pdfwww.dsr.wa.gov.au/dsrwr/_assets/main/lib50079/keepitfun.pdf (assessed February 2, 2007).

Zakus, D.H. 'Managing Risk in Community Sport Organizations: Are We Risking Volunteers?'. Paper Presented at the Leisure Studies Association Conference, Canterbury, UK, July 7–9, 2009.

The mobilizing effects and health benefits of proximity sport facilities: urban and environmental analysis of the Bleu, Blanc, Bouge project and Montreal North's outdoor rink

Romain Roult[a], Jean Marc Adjizian[b], Sylvain Lefebvre[b] and Lucie Lapierre[c]

[a]Department of Leisure, Culture and Tourism, Universite du Quebec a Trois-Rivieres, Trois-Rivieres, Quebec, Canada; [b]Department of Geography, Universite du Quebec a Montreal, Montreal, Quebec, Canada; [c]Urbanism Institute of Universite de Montréal, Montreal, Quebec, Canada

Obesity has become a world-recognized problem, largely attributed to a lack of everyday physical activity. Many recent studies show that the built environment can positively influence people to take on healthier lifestyles. In this article, we analyse the impact the implementation of a free outdoor skating rink has on the local population's social identity and physical activity in the Montreal North district. This research, based on a mixed design, demonstrates that the implementation of a proximity sport facility can inspire the population to engage in physical activity and can stimulate territorial appropriation. It also reveals that building a sport facility is not sufficient in itself to attract a mildly active or non-active clientele. In fact, it seems necessary to complement the facility with onsite-organized activities.

Introduction

Canada's latest strategic plan for physical activity depicted an alarming situation,[1] 85% of Canadian adults and 93% of Canadian children and youth do not reach the minimal level of daily physical activity necessary to maintain good health and satisfactory well-being.[2] According to Canada's House of Commons Standing Committee on Health, Canada has one of the highest levels of child obesity in the developed world, ranking 5th among the 34 Organization for Economic Co-operation and Development countries. Recent statistics show that 26% of Canadian children aged between 2 and 17 years are overweight or obese.[3] The Standing Committee on Health seems particularly concerned by the teenage population, which is most affected by obesity issues, as the levels of obesity within this population tripled in the last 30 years. Statistics from 2007 and 2008 show that, in Quebec, 47.5% of boys aged 12–17 and 64.7% of girls in the same age group perform less than 7 h of physical activity each week, putting them at risk of becoming obese. In the last few years, the bulk of institutional reflections and actions were structured around confining, or at least slowing down, this obesity pandemic within Canadian youth.[4] For this reason, and because of the impact of the built environment on the population's motivation to do physical activity, strategies were also applied in a way to enhance the design of both built and natural aspects found in the urban and peri-urban environments.

In this article, we present the results of our research on the implementation of a free outdoor skating rink[5] and underline its impact on the social and identity elements, and on the levels of physical activity among the Montreal North local population. The Bleu, Blanc, Bouge project[6] was launched in January 2009; it is the flagship project of the Montreal Canadiens Children's Foundation, owned by the local professional hockey club, the Montreal Canadiens. This project intends to build five outdoor rinks with official North American hockey dimensions in Montreal's disadvantaged neighbourhoods. The Foundation describes these rinks as 'animated gathering areas for sports and physical activity which will provide youth from these backgrounds the opportunity to discover the advantages of a healthy and physically active lifestyle'.[7] Montreal Canadiens Children's Foundation ensures the success of the Bleu, Blanc, Bouge project in collaboration with the para-governmental organization Québec en Forme (Quebec in Shape) and with the participation of local community groups. Following the 2008 implementation of the first Bleu, Blanc, Bouge outdoor rink in the St-Michel neighbourhood, the Foundation unveiled its second rink at Le Carignan Park in Montreal North, in January 2010. Montreal North's population largely consist of tenants (72.8%), immigrants [33% of the population, mainly from Haïti (30%), Italy (19%) and North Africa (12%)] and less educated individuals (35% of the individuals who are 15 years old and above do not have a High School diploma). This neighbourhood also has a high-density population (7594 inhabitants per square km), a population of 32,845 individuals with an average income of $23,088 (before taxes) and an unemployment rate of 12.5%.[8]

Besides being the only study of its kind conducted in Montreal, this analysis allows us to examine the research problem through the following three specific objectives:

(1) To measure youth physical activity following the installation of the ice rink. Can we observe a significant change in the physical habits of the neighbourhood's youth? Is the younger demographic more active and is the frequency of its activities higher? In addition, are 'non-active' onlookers, witnessing users on the rink, encouraged to use the facility as well?

(2) To measure the added value of the rink to the neighbourhood. Is this equipment becoming a meeting and socializing location?

(3) To measure the appropriation of the equipment by the population and the neighbourhood's actors and to examine whether the ice rink could become an identity referent. Has the neighbourhood residents' appreciation of their environment increased since the installation of the ice rink?

These questions allow us to posit two principal research hypotheses. First, the implementation of a proximity sport facility in a designed urban setting, especially when the facility is representative of the local sport activities through its multisport character and its relation with a major identity referent (professional hockey club, the Montreal Canadiens), greatly influences the population in engaging in physical activity and concomitantly renews different forms of territorial appropriation. In addition, building such a sport facility is not sufficient to attract, on a weekly basis, participants who are mildly active or non-active. In fact, it appears necessary to combine this design to different forms of onsite-organized activities.

Conceptual framework

To set our research problem and to clearly define our key concepts, we based our conceptual framework on recent studies published in the fields of physical activity, territorial planning, urban planning and public health. In the last few years, research attempting to highlight and analyse the different characteristics involved in physical activity showed that individuals make personal lifestyle choices that will influence their physical and mental health, but that these choices can also be significantly conditioned by milieu.[9] Consequently, it is interesting to observe how the built environment[10] can influence the choices and motivations driving people to adopt active lifestyles.[11] There are many ways to define 'built environment'; however, for the purpose of this article, 'built environment' is understood as all the man-made components of the physical environment, such as public spaces, transportation infrastructures and residential spaces.[12] We believe that this definition does not fully outline the physical complexity of some environments. For this reason, we draw on a variety of research that refine this definition. According to some scholars, this notion has three conceptual dimensions: (1) the transportation system, (2) the land occupancy modes and (3) the urban design.[13] These dimensions can also be divided into analytical subdimensions: configuration of the road network, diversity of the urban public facilities and form of the urban fabric. According to several scholars, most of these components affect physical activity in different ways, particularly the ones connected to urban density, to the functional diversity of residential neighbourhoods, to the connectivity of the local transport network and to the design of the pedestrian precinct.[14] However, these understandings of the built environment remain deeply entrenched in an interpretative dialectic that is largely connected to the field of urban planning, which could be difficult to connect to this research. Therefore, we decided to draw on those studies that directly connect the built environment and physical activity. According to these studies, the built environment inspires physical activity by offering three central factors: accessibility, appeal and security.[15] However, these three factors contain both an objective component, related to the physical and technical characteristics of the built environment, and a subjective component, which is related to individual perceptions.[16] In our opinion, these objective and subjective components are essential to adequately interpret the social and territorial dynamics of our case study.

Three types of accessibility to built environment

We believe that these three central factors are at the core of all analytical interpretations linking the built environment to physical activity, particularly within the context of the research problem. Therefore, we decided to construct our conceptual framework around these three notions. Accessibility is the first motivating factor we want to consider. This factor has three principal dimensions: economic accessibility, symbolic and social accessibility and, finally, geographical accessibility.[17] These dimensions refer to the individual's capacity to consume (financial and economic capacity), to reach (proximity in relation to his work place and household) or to benefit from a particular resource (personal appeal and individual perception). As such, this concept of accessibility seems central to a better understanding of how, in the context of our case study, the ice rink is perceived and used by different groups of users and non-users.[18] Within the context of our research, which addresses outdoor sport facilities, various aspects favour the accessibility of activity sites: ease of access to various sport and leisure facilities near residential neighbourhoods, location of the facility in a dense area known for offering a diversity of services, free access to the facility and proximity to public transport services.[19]

However, this definition of accessibility in connection to physical activity remains broad as it fails to consider specific types of users. As our research targets children, teenagers and young adults, we decided to support our conceptual framework with studies that specifically relate to these user groups. Several researchers confirm that these accessibility aspects become more important with children and teenagers. In that regard, Popkin, Duffey and Gordon-Larsen suggest that, in the case of children and teens, the level of physical activity is more likely to increase if the facilities are near their residential and social environments.[20] According to Tucker et al., 'accessibility was extremely important to parents in making decisions about where to bring their children to play.'[21] Accessibility is also fundamental to the attractiveness of these facilities. On the other hand, Ries et al. note that economic accessibility is also central when it comes to children and youth.[22] Indeed, 'cost is an important issue for adolescents who are often limited financially. This issue was most often raised by participants who do not use facilities.'[23] Nevertheless, these studies are not necessarily underlining the correlations between the socio-economic realities of the investigated territories and the usage of those facilities. Yet, this appears fundamental, especially in our research perspective, which is based on the analysis of a proximity sport facility located in an underprivileged neighbourhood. Some studies state that accessibility logistics should be considered differently in the case of disadvantaged neighbourhoods. As Gordon-Larsen et al. and Ries et al. remind us, when a neighbourhood enjoys a high socio-economic status, the number of sport and leisure infrastructures will generally be equally high.[24] Kipke et al.'s research conducted in a disadvantaged neighbourhood of East Los Angeles, with a high percentage of obese children, confirmed these arguments by showing that there were few spaces designed for the practice of physical activities in this territory (0.543 acres per 1000 inhabitants) in comparison with the metropolitan average (4.2 acres per 1000 inhabitants).[25]

The appeal of built environment

The second factor motivating physical activity is the appeal of the built environment (park and sport infrastructure) for potential users.[26] As the ice rink of the Bleu, Blanc, Bouge project promotes itself as a high quality sport facility in comparison with other ice rinks already available in the district, this second factor seems particularly relevant. Therefore, we believe that it is fundamental to understand in what way and how the appeal of this facility influences the behaviour of some active and less-active users. However, to conduct an analysis of this factor, it is necessary to understand its various aspects, such as the aesthetic and cosmetic characteristics of the site, the presence of vegetation, the atmosphere (in relation to lights and spatial configuration), the quality of the street furniture, the cleanliness and efficient maintenance of the space dedicated to physical activity, and the architectural quality and innovation.[27]

As Handy et al. put it, these different characteristics are connected to urban planning and appear as fundamental when one tries to understand the motivations and the perceptions of individuals towards sites planned for physical activity.[28] However, if these studies refer to the appeal of such facilities, they do not consider the distinctions between the different types of clienteles. We, however, believe that it is essential to weight the influence of this factor on the concerned populations, particularly if we are interested in young users. In this regard, Molnar et al. present similar assessments and also note that teenagers are especially attracted to the aesthetics of these sites.[29] Gordon-Larsen's research, based on the observation of 18,000 American teenagers, reinforces these analytical observations by proposing interpretative nuances: 'physical activity was most influenced by environmental factors, inactivity was much more influenced by socio-demographic factors.'[30]

Our research problem also encourages us to approach this appeal factor from a sociological angle, using the concept of territorial appropriation. On this subject, Vieille-Marchiset's work emphasizes Gordon-Larsen's results by showing that the design quality of sport and leisure facilities mostly impacts already active users.[31] As he observed, individuals who are usually less active are more receptive to sociocultural and sociability factors. Research led by Quebec's Ministry of Education, Leisure and Sport in association with Kino-Quebec regarding Quebec youth's level of physical activity also shows that, for children and teenagers, the appeal of a sport facility is largely connected to the opportunity to make contacts and to socialize.[32] These aspects should therefore be considered as true motivating factors in the induction of different physical activity practices. However, in Ries et al.'s opinion, these sociological factors need to be coupled with reflections on organized onsite activities.[33] Indeed, different activities could stimulate the interest and the participation of less-active users: the reinforcement of commercial diversity in the facility's surroundings, therefore increasing its multifunctionality, the introduction of functional dressing rooms, the installation of various recreational programmes, and the organization of training and introduction schedules.[34] However, for Raibaud, this logic of organized activities has different repercussions depending on the targeted public.[35] For example, through his study of teenagers in Bordeaux (France), Raibaud realized that these strategies often bring female users to places largely dominated by a male population. Although Ries et al. also acknowledge the lack of women in such sites, stating that 'young women are seen at outdoor facilities much less frequently than young men,'[36] they neglect to give specific recommendations.[37]

Security as a built environment factor

The third factor motivating physical activity is security. In our opinion, because of the socio-economic particularities of the investigated neighbourhood, this factor is central to our research. Therefore, it seems fundamental to underline some earlier research that links security to the attendance rate at these physical activity sites. In the literature, this aspect is often analysed and treated through the scope of road traffic. Indeed, various traffic-related issues can impact the individuals' choices with respect to transportation, sport facilities and physical activity in itself. For example, adequate road signalization in the area, traffic calming measures and urban design that favours harmony between different modes of transportation (foot, bicycle, bus and car) are all influential factors in choosing a place for physical activities.[38] However, various researchers also argued the importance of planning adequate subsidiary spaces together with the sport facilities in order to reinforce the users' security.[39] As Molnar et al. put it,

> disordered neighbourhoods may inhibit children and adolescents from engaging in physical activity, both because of the lack of safety of playing sports or games in the neighbourhood, and because of their exposure to criminal activity when traveling to or from recreational activities within or outside of the neighbourhood.[40]

Therefore, the feeling of insecurity due to crime is an important dimension of this third motivating factor. It also affects most decisions when it comes to choosing a place for physical activity. Beyond the installation of playground elements limiting risks and injuries, other key actions could reinforce the appeal of diverse sport and leisure sites for the population, such as planning a secure environment, providing convivial atmospheres and insuring a pleasant community through the application of surveillance measures.[41]

To focus our conceptual reflection on the different populations concerned by the Bleu, Blanc, Bouge project, we decided to analyse different studies focusing on security in relation to young users. In their study on Baltimore (Maryland) teenagers, Ries et al. mention that for these teens, the security of sport spaces and facilities is one of the most important factors when they consider practising an activity.[42] This is even more important for younger teens and girls. In fact, girls are not attracted to places where lighting is inefficient, where there is are no crowds and where onsite surveillance is lacking. Ries et al. consider, as the Committee on Environmental Health did, that onsite events, through the planning of organized sport activities, the construction of dressing rooms, the supervision of playgrounds and the installation of adapted lighting onsite and in the vicinities (green areas, parking, streets, etc.), are likely to increase the security of these sites and their attractiveness.[43] Molnar et al. also believe that routes leading to these sites should be secure in order to convince individuals to attend.[44] This becomes even more important in the case of the young female population, which is usually using active or public transports. According to the authors, security as a motivating factor goes largely beyond the perimeter of the facility; it also concerns its entire location area. In the context of our research, this analytical assessment shows the importance and the pertinence of analysing the social and sport dynamics of the ice rink and of its entire location area, in this case, Le Carignan Park.

Research method

Our research has been structured around three phases of data collection: face-to-face electronic surveys, structured observations and semi-structured interviews. In this regard, our face-to-face electronic surveys has a sample of 352 participants from the three targeted groups took part in our study. In this context, 93 participants were part of the 6- to 11-year-old group, 118 participants were between 12 and 17 years old and 141 participants were over 18 years old. For this purpose, we used random sampling. In fact, each data collection phase was randomly determined and each investigated individual was randomly chosen on the ice rink at a regular interval of five participants. As for our complementary observation phases, they took place during the busiest periods of the ice rink, so we can obtain sufficient pertinent information for our research. However, after we decided on four interesting time slots per week, we selected five random time slots during the winter of 2011. Our observation phase has been structured around a mix method analysis, using quantitative and qualitative observations.

With regard to our interviews, we first made an inventory of 20 public and private organizations involved with or concerned by the Bleu, Blanc, Bouge project in the Montreal North district. Afterwards, we interviewed a representative and/or an executive of each of these organizations during the fall of 2010 and the winter of 2011.

Data collection

We first targeted three user groups: 6–11 years old, 12–17 years old and users over 18 years old. Our main fieldwork phase lasted from December 2010 to March 2011 (therefore covering the entire skating season), it was aimed at individuals freely using the facility and it allowed us to acquire a representative sampling of 352 participants within all age groups. To collect our data, we conducted face-to-face electronic surveys using portable microcomputers. This survey was made of 40 multiple-choice questions which were coded. Ce questionnaire, élaboré à partir d'outils issus de la littérature, a été conçu par l'équipe de chercheurs mais approuvé par le comité d'experts qui supervisait cette étude. The questions used allowed us to specifically underline various issues:

- The level and frequency of free users' physical and sport activities.
- The accessibility of the ice rink and of its location area.
- The appeal of the ice rink to reinforce or to create some social bounds.
- The impacts of the construction of the ice rink on physical activity.
- The lifestyle of its different types of users.
- The socio-demographic particularities of these populations.

- The role of families and parents in the practice of some physical and sport activities on the ice rink (this question was asked in this specific form to the 6- to 11-year-old group).
- The appeal of the ice rink at a social level, to create contacts (this question was only asked to 6- to 11-year-old group)
- The reinforcement of family relationship, particularly regarding children, during organized activities on the ice rink (this question was only asked to the adults)

Thus, this methodological tool allowed us to specifically determine the use and appropriation modes of the ice rink and the surrounding areas, to gather different socio-demographic data and to find information on the participants' activity levels and on the social appeal of the site. More specifically, the results obtained through this survey allowed us to answer several central questions of our research problem, notably:

- Can we observe a significant change in the physical habits of the neighbourhood's youths?
- Is the ice rink becoming a meeting and socializing location?
- Has the neighbourhood residents' appreciation of their living space accrued since the installation of the ice rink?

To find answers to our research questions and in addition to these surveys, we led five observation phases using the System for Observing Play and Leisure Activity in Youth grid. Professor Thomas L. McKenzie from Department of Exercise and Nutritional Sciences, San Diego State University, created this observation grid in 2006.[45] Using it for our observations allowed us to highlight and retrace events that happened on the site as well as the users' ways of using the ice rink. For example, while scanning an activity, we were able to depict the users' profile (gender and approximate age), the intensity of their physical activity (light or intense), the type of activity they do (free, organized or competitive skating), the social impact of their activities (exchanges with other individuals), the accessibility of the site, the presence of surveillance, the availability of the equipment, and the aesthetic and the maintenance of the facility. For each 2-h observation session, the investigator would take notes concerning the grid's indicators at 10-min intervals. Between these note-taking periods, investigators could also record their observations with a digital voice recorder, especially when observing unusual situations.

Lastly, we conducted 20 semi-structured interviews (90 min maximum) with representatives of the Bleu, Blanc, Bouge project, members of the Montreal North district and participants of the local chamber of commerce. In addition, we interviewed various actors in the community, associations and sport stakeholders, as well as individuals responsible for public safety and the supervisors of the outdoor rink. These interviews, organized around 45 open questions regarding seven main analytical themes, allowed us to understand how these individuals design, manage, appropriate and perceive this proximity sport facility. These interviews also allowed us to underline more specifically the different factors explaining why mildly active or non-active users are not fully using the ice rink. The main analytical themes used were as follows:

- The operating modes (types of use and operating processes).
- The appropriation types (social, civic and institutional).
- The perceptions of the Bleu, Blanc, Bouge project and of the ice rink (positive and negative impacts, social and identity impacts, changes in regard to behaviours, attitudes and level of physical activities).

- The type of sports, physical activities and health programmes offered at the ice rink (activities, contributions since the opening of the ice rink, impacts on the students and the users as well as the type of supervision and tutoring offered on the ice rink).
- The impacts of the rink on the social mobilization of local stakeholders (mobilization process before the building the rink, motivation related to taking part in these mobilization processes, role of central stakeholders, instauration of new partnerships, creation of new projects connected to the construction of the ice rink, domino effects and types of consultation employed).
- The management strategies of the ice rink (procedures, governance, roles and actions of the management committee).
- The ice rink and its location area planning principles (form, integration and quality of the built and natural environment, security, accessibility and choice of location).

The data we obtained through these interviews allowed us to especially answer the two following sections of our research problematics:

- To measure the added value to the neighbourhood.
- To measure the appropriation of the equipment by the population and the neighbourhood's actors.

Data analysis

For our analysis phase, we treated our survey data with SPSS in a way to highlight the distribution levels by indicators in percentages and in frequencies. In addition, these techniques allowed us to chart some of our results. With regard to our qualitative data, we analysed them through NVivo to underline the textual occurrences related to our research issues and, subsequently, to proceed from the categorization and grouping of this data. These flexible methodological strategies enabled us to use grounded theory in order to conceive a part of our data analysis phase and to test the concepts we proposed in our conceptual framework.[46] Finally, we cross-referenced some of the data we collected with our surveys and interviews in a way to analyse more accurately some of the situations we observed. We decided on the data we cross-referenced based on an extensive review of the literature on the field.

Results and discussions

Results

A place to discover and rediscover a sport

As was reported by stakeholders responsible of the project during their interviews, the initial purpose of establishing the Bleu, Blanc, Bouge project and its ice rink in the underprivileged neighbourhoods of Montreal was to give the population, and notably the youth, access to a sport facility of great quality that would serve to start a new practice: skating. Furthermore, the Le Carignan rink also allowed many former skaters to rediscover the sport. Moreover, during our field observations, we realized that few of the youth, mostly from ethnic minorities, were teaching themselves to skate. While children were usually learning on a smaller ice rink adjoining the main one, older users would learn in the main rink during improvised hockey games. Our observations allowed us to conclude that other than these beginners, many users visit the ice rink, often out of curiosity, in order to try out the ice rink and rediscover the practice of skating.

Be it to discover or to rediscover skating, one thing is certain: more and more people are skating since the construction of the Bleu, Blanc, Bouge rink in Montreal North. This situation can be observed within the three age categories we surveyed during our field-investigation phase. While 61.5% of adult users say that they have increased their skating sessions since the construction of the rink, this percentage reaches 82.6% for children and 77.5% for teenagers. Additionally, this new installation turned skating into the newly favoured winter activity for a lot of its users. Indeed, 55% of children said skating was their favourite activity while 73.5% of teenagers and 71.6% of adults confirmed the same thing.

Thus, by cross-referencing the data collected through different data collection tools, we discovered that this new facility seems to be a learning vector for a new sport practice. The interviews we conducted with the different stakeholders involved with and concerned by the project lead us to believe that the ice rink of the Bleu, Blanc, Bouge project has become a new sport stage for the neighbouring schools and a source of social integration for the different community groups. Indeed, as our survey results show that the ice rink not only encourages the local populations to practise a new winter sport, but also allows them to 'rediscover' their neighbourhood and to acquire new knowledge.

Rise of a new meeting place

It appears that the Bleu, Blanc, Bouge project has become much more than a place for practising sport; it has also become a place of socialization. Indeed, the interviews conducted and the surveys collected on the field seem to indicate that the ice rink is perceived as a meeting place where family members and friends can practise physical activities during the winter. The family sport of skating is mostly practised by children and adults together. Almost 60% of children aged between 7 and 11 years came to the rink with their parents, while a little more than 30% of adults came with their kids of various ages. Even more revealing, 80% of parents brought their kids to the rink to skate with them. Moreover, 79% of these parents said the installation of such a facility allowed them to spend more time with their families.

Nevertheless, the great majority of users prefer to skate with their friends. This is mostly the case with teenagers. Indeed, 70% of teens said that they came to the rink with their friends, while almost half of the adult participants preferred to come with acquaintances other than their family.

In addition, it is interesting to note that the facility has also become a new meeting place for the residents of the neighbourhood. A great majority of the investigated participants said that it is easier to make contacts at the rink. In addition, 65% of teenagers and 53% of children told us that they made new friends onsite. Therefore, although it is a sport facility, the outdoor ice rink became a meeting place where it is easy to socialize. Our field observations validated this hypothesis. Indeed, we frequently observed that users suspend their activity to engage in small conversations without leaving the ice rink. Furthermore, when we asked them why they chose to skate in this facility, the most popular answer for both teenagers and adults was: 'to engage in an activity while having a good time with friends'.

The dynamism and attendance rate (for all age groups) of the outdoor rink seemed to be the engine driving its increasing popularity. The answers to our survey show that for 70% of the children aged between 7 and 11 years, the presence of other children on the ice rink is an incentive for the use of the facility. In parallel, more than 50% of teenagers and 40% of adults say that their desire to practise physical activity was influenced directly by the construction of this ice rink.

By cross-referencing our data, we discovered that this proximity sport facility has become a meeting place and a sport stage that allows individual users to build social relationships with other members of the community. It also appears that the rink became a place for family activities and a ground for intergenerational meeting. That way, the ice rink of the Bleu, Blanc, Bouge project has become a fundamental aspect of social cohesion in the neighbourhood.

Homogenizing effects regarding user categories and types of use

Despite the rink's apparent popularity, there are some reservations to keep in mind. Indeed, although the rink is widely used, we observed that both the users and the type of use are homogeneous. The initial goal of this project in the Montreal North district, as different stakeholders mentioned, was to instigate appropriation by residents, mainly through the students of neighbouring schools. Some of our interviews show that the project was carried out with the belief that if the neighbouring schools were attending the facility, the students and their parents would see an increase in their motivation to use the facility during family or leisure time. Instead, our survey indicates results that are quite different. Indeed, 64% of the children and 75% of the teenagers we met during free skating hours said that they never used the ice rink during school hours. This shows that the actual clientele is quite different than the one originally hoped for.

Based on the users surveyed at the ice rink, we can note that most of them are individuals with an active lifestyle. Within our sample of 352 participants, few individuals can be described as 'passive' in regard to physical activity. Indeed, 61% of children and adult users took part in physical activities at least three times a week, and this percentage increases to 77% with teenagers. For the great majority of children and teenagers, these activities last 1 h or more. We observed that in terms of their physical activity, the main users of the outdoor rink were people with already healthy habits. The less-active children, who were also the targeted audience of the project, were weakly represented in this facility.

Alongside being mostly active, the ice rink users were also mostly men. Among the 352 study participants, only 62 were girls or women. The children age group has the highest female ratio with 28%. This percentage goes down to 15% for teens and 14% for adults. Besides this majority of men, we can also observe a majority of Caucasian ice rink users. In fact, half of the teenagers and 60% of the adult users were Caucasian. Knowing the allophone character of the Montreal North population, it might be surprising to observe that a very low ratio of immigrants is actually using the sport facility.

Based on our observations, we can state that this homogenization of the users is greatly determined by the fact that hockey has monopolized the rink. Indeed, hockey is the most popular activity on Le Carignan Park ice rink. More than half the children and three quarters of the teenagers say that they prefer to play hockey while at the rink, whereas almost 80% of adults say that hockey is their favourite sport activity. Because of this sport's great popularity, the outdoor rink's schedule leaves less room for other activities. Thus, our results suggest that the homogenization of the practices and of the users on the ice rink actually limits the access and the use of the ice rink to a large range of the community population. Consequently, this homogenization slows down the social integration generated by the facility.

Discussions

The goal of this research was to evaluate the impact of the construction of an outdoor ice rink on the physical activity of the children and youth in the area, and to highlight the type of social and spatial appropriations it generated. We did not succeed in corroborating our data with research conducted on similar installations. However, our results allowed us to make connections with other studies conducted in urban parks and diverse exterior sport facilities. Indeed, similar to the studies of Reis et al. and of Roemmich et al.,[47] our research reveals that accessibility, appeal and security have become central analytical indicators when it comes to studying the use of a proximity sport facility such as Le Carignan Park outdoor rink.

Limited accessibility

At first sight, the outdoor rink of the Bleu, Blanc, Bouge project seems quite accessible from the economic, geographical and social angles. Indeed, the project allows Montreal North's residents to use a quality ice rink for free. The rink is also available to the six neighbouring schools for physical education, as well as to other schools in the area for episodic activities.

The site that was chosen for the Bleu, Blanc, Bouge ice rink project meets general approval with the different stakeholders we interviewed. Le Carignan Park is well served by communal transport networks, which is quite rare in Montreal North, and it is close to different roads. The ice rink is located in the district's eastern sector, which has one of Montreal North's highest poverty rates. Le Carignan Park is already well known as a sport and leisure space; it has a basketball court, a baseball court, a soccer field, a swimming pool, a paddling pool, a children's playground and a lower quality outdoor rink (separate from the rink of the Bleu, Blanc, Bouge project). However, this geographic accessibility needs to be nuanced when it goes to the residents West of the district. Indeed, according to our observations and our interviews, the public transportation's routes and connexions from the West are quite long (almost an hour in some cases) and complex (two to three bus transfers are sometimes needed). As residents from that area are not encited to go to the facility, these accessibility limits certainly have an impact on the mildly active and non-active population. These analytical observations corroborate part of our second research hypothesis according to which the simple construction of a sport facility is not sufficient to attract mildly active or non-active users. As De Visscher, Bouverne-De Bie, and Verschelden[48] and Loukaitou-Sideris and Sideris[49] mention in their studies, transportation accessibility to exterior leisure spaces is a central indicator to explain the success or the failure of such sites.

However, Le Carignan Park is already populated by the presence of users who enjoy physical activities. In fact, 1800 teenagers use this park for physical activity, which represent half of the teenagers practising sports in the eastern sector.[50] As the population of disadvantaged neighbourhoods often suffers the most from youth inactivity, it also made sense to implement good quality equipment in this district.[51] Moreover, Le Carignan Park is located at less than 1.5 km of a dozen of schools which bring together a little less than 6000 children and teenagers. The poverty index implemented by the ministry of Education, Leisure and Sport classifies these institutions as some of the worst schools in the province in terms of family revenues. The ice rink therefore allows these schools to benefit from a new sport venue in which they can offer activities, allowing, at the same time, exposure to a new kind of sport and an improvement in the way the young people appropriate this facility.

The rink of the Bleu, Blanc, Bouge project can potentially allow a vast majority of Montreal North's residents to easily access a great quality sport facility. However, as our results imply, only a certain type of user benefits from the facility. Therefore, we can presume that ease of access to this facility is evenly distributed among categories of users. We actually believe that this accessibility issue is mainly related to the cost of the skating equipment. Indeed, for populations living in such precarious environments, skating equipment is probably not a priority. However, the equipment provided by the district is only available to users visiting in an organized context (e.g. schools, sport associations and leagues). Therefore, a great number of residents, including potential users, have no access to the required equipment. Bedimo-Rung, Mowen, and Cohen,[52] propose similar conclusions, stipulating that the design and planning of exterior sites for physical activity need to be supported by public interventions that aim to improve the economic accessibility of these sites.

Consequently, we believe that Le Carignan Park ice rink is geographically accessible to the resident of the facility's neighbourhood, therefore fulfilling an important need for quality proximity sport facilities. In addition, through different forms of appropriation and the creation of new meeting places, our analysis confirms the symbolic and social access of the facility. However, the economic accessibility of this installation should be nuanced. Indeed, the cost of the equipment necessary for ice rink use (such as free skating and hockey) might act as barriers to participation for members of the local community experiencing poverty or economic disadvantage.

An existing but deficient aesthetic appeal

To motivate different populations in using such a proximity sport facility, appeal is as important as accessibility. Pluhar et al. and Reis et al.[53] estimate that appeal is notably central for the clienteles that are less accustomed to these sites, such as girls. As we specified earlier, two main indicators will define this 'appealing' factor: urban design and possible services and social exchanges that include considerations for onsite animation.

The opening of the Bleu, Blanc, Bouge rink gave way to important renovations in Le Carignan Park and its installations. Indeed, the district gave almost a million dollars for a cosmetic enhancement of the park. This included investments in the renovation of the basketball court and the children's playground, the construction of a cabin acting as a dressing room and the installation of better lighting in the park. The ice rink was one of the major aesthetic and structural elements built to motivate a better use of the park. The architectural and technical quality of the rink, together with its privileged relationship to the local hockey club, the Montreal Canadiens, certainly reinforced the attractiveness of this facility and of the entire site. It also increased the appeal of the entire neighbourhood and its surrounding districts. These results tie up with Loukaitou-Sideris and Sideris' conclusions[54]: the choice of an innovative design in the planning of urban parks or in the implementation of multifunctional areas will increase the appeal of these sites. Furthermore, these results allow us to assert that the improvement of the built environment in Montreal North has had an undeniably positive influence on the residents' physical habits, most specifically for the youth demographic.

However, for the mildly active population segment and for the one that does not have sport identity referents, the omnipresence of hockey in the rink diminishes its appeal. This type of monopolization actually restrains other types of users. The users we observed were often sports-inclined Caucasian young men. At first glance, this may seem surprising if we consider that the rink is located in a neighbourhood with a population of mainly immigrants (33%), second-generation immigrants (12%), visible minorities (32%) and women (54%).[55] There seems to be a cleavage, or at least a gap, between the activities offered at the rink and the neighbouring residents' needs and motivations.

In this regard, it is important to understand that although hockey is one of the most popular sports in Canada, according to the actors we met and the interviews we conducted, it is only in third position for the population of Montreal North. In such multicultural neighbourhoods, the young people from ethnic communities will quite commonly be more attracted to basketball or soccer. These disciplines are indeed closer to their identity, cultural and family referents. The equipment needed for these sports is also usually less expensive. These aspects certainly tie up with what Reis et al.[56] state that parks and other exterior sport facilities should be designed according to the population's desires and needs in terms of the physical activity. As Pluhar et al.[57] note, a large gap between the population's needs and the actual design of spaces in terms of sport or leisure facilities could lead to a complete abandonment of these places.

The problem is similar when it applied to female users. As Yves Raibaud and Ries et al. put it, some practices, often tagged as 'models of virility' through contemporary music and urban cultures, are predominantly masculine.[58] Thus, we find gender homogeneity in places designed for such practices. Proximity sport facilities reflect this situation perfectly. Because of their configuration, because they look like hockey rinks (with boards, and lines limiting the field and goals.) and also because of the sport models they bring out, outdoor rinks become symbolic male venues. Moreover, high-quality proximity sport facilities often become meeting places for active individuals who already practise the sport that emanates from the facility. As Vieille-Marchiset puts it in an article about basketball in Besançon, because they look for the best available facility, these active individuals monopolize the space they choose to attend, not because they reject other users, but because their athletic and technical abilities intimidate the less-active participants and other types of users. In those cases, the less-experienced users usually prefer to smaller infrastructures where they can find people equally inexperienced.[59]

To vary the type of rink users, we believe that onsite activities are necessary. According to Loukaitou-Sideris and Sideris,[60] the event indicator is even central to the appeal of different exterior sites for physical activity. They recommend that professionals supervise these events. In some cases, they could even be recurrent. The different district actors we interviewed largely agreed with these research results. In fact, the general consensus was that better supervision is needed to motivate the less- and non-active youngsters in using the rink and in doing the activities that interest them. Everyone also believed that this supervision should imply onsite activities. According to Lemieux and Thibault, organized activities have many qualities likely to generate physical activity among youth, particularly among girls. In fact, the sociability impact plays an important role in girls' choice of activity.[61] The authors found that, 'pairing sport and recreational facilities, as well as organizing social activities as a complement to sport activities, might multiply the users' opportunities to socialize and therefore attract more girls.'[62] In addition, these individuals would certainly visit the outdoor rink more frequently if they have new activities to do with their peers. However, an important question remains: who should be responsible for these events? According to many local associations and schools, the district, which is also the manager of the park, should be in charge of this mission. They could employ activity leaders to manage the schedule of the ice rink onsite, give technical skating advice to new users and organize open-for-all activities. On the other hand, because Montreal North is one of the neighbourhoods with the highest criminal rate in Montreal,[63] the district prefers using its resources towards the surveillance of the park. They believe that the involved associations should take over the facility and organize onsite activities themselves. These results link to some elements mentioned by Cohen et al.[64] in their study. Indeed, they state that the mobilization of local stakeholders is essential to ensure the constant and adapted attractiveness of the physical activity exterior sites. As stated by Bedimo-Rung, Mowen, and Cohen,[65] the management of these spaces should be conducted in partnership and not in a silo, through isolated actions.

Moreover, these results demonstrate that for the users of the Bleu, Blanc, Bouge ice rink, this space is much more than a place to participate in sport. Indeed, it seems that the users first come to the rink because of its appeal, and they come back mainly because of their social experiences. This analytical statement takes us back to the environmental psychology school as presented by Debenedetti and Taylor, Gottfredson, and Brower[66] Indeed, according to our results, we can observe that a functional attachment to the ice rink is forming around factors such as rooting, commitment and identity representation. The ice rink therefore becomes a live environment as well as a meeting place. This certainly has much to do with the concept of experience as explained by Soubrier.[67] For the users observed and questioned during our research, what counts is not only what they do when they go to the ice rink, but also how and with whom they practise their activities.

When the activity is not as safe as the site

The emphasis on safety put in place around the Bleu, Blanc, Bouge rink is no stranger to the desire to facilitate access to sports facilities to the public. As we mentioned earlier, many studies reveal a strong connection between the security of a sport facility and the population's attendance. Once again, this motivating factor mostly impacts teenagers and young girls.[68] The location of the rink as well as the enhancement of the park were decisions made in order to guarantee the security at different spatial levels (the sector, the park and the facility itself).

Security was in fact an important motive for locating the rink of the Bleu, Blanc, Bouge project in Le Carignan Park. Indeed, several characteristics of this park make it a secure place. This mostly has an impact on the sense of security, which has become a major theme in urbanism since Jane Jacobs's Death and Life of Great American Cities.[69] As the author puts it, 'the bedrock attribute of a successful city district is that a person must feel personally safe and secure on the street among all these strangers.'[70] This sense of security is even more important in a neighbourhood such as Montreal North, which has a high rate of criminality and where issues related to street gangs are widespread. However, in the case of the Bleu, Blanc, Bouge rink, the problem is twofold. On the one hand, there is an important need to decrease criminality and to revitalize the spaces taken over by the offenders, on the other hand, the safe use of these spaces by the local population is paramount in order to create and develop spatial dynamism.

The necessity to secure the streets becomes essential to the success of these two objectives. This makes Le Carignan Park a strategic choice. Indeed, its location in a high-density residential area ensures the frequent use of the rink, mainly because of the young families living near the site. It also guarantees better neighbouring surveillance. In fact, besides the guard paid by the district, parent users are also safeguarding the site, handling both their children and those of other users. In addition, because of the proximity between the park and the residences, neighbouring dwellers also often keep an eye on the site.

Other than the residential component, the proximity services offered to the nearby population also reinforce this sense of security. These services help both the citizens' and the neighbourhood's revitalization. In fact, the ice rink's neighbouring area includes a police station, a fire station and a local community centre. All these services in the park's vicinity can be promptly mobilized in the case of trouble. In addition, there are a school, a cultural centre and a commercial strip in the sector, which increase both road and pedestrian traffic in the park's general area, and help break the isolation that usually reinforces a sense of insecurity. Loukaitou-Sideris and Sideris[71] also mentioned these aspects to remind us of the importance of security in the analysis of the attendance and the appeal of urban parks. As Bedimo-Rung, Mowen, and Cohen[72] note, security is more often perceived than actually experienced and this goes both for the children and their parents. The cleanliness of the site, the type of lighting and its integration within the street grid are some of the elements users consider when evaluating the security of a park. These elements obviously add to the more classic indicators relating to different forms of delinquency.

For our case study, all these aspects seem to strengthen the users' sense of security and largely benefit the rink of the Bleu, Blanc, Bouge project. As a matter of fact, the rink is not only extremely popular, but it is also kept in a good condition, which is surprising when we consider the level of vandalism in neighbouring parks. However, our analysis shows that security is also the main factor behind female and passive users' low attendance. Indeed, despite the constant supervision of the park and its surroundings, the security on the ice rink itself seems to be a concern and to discourage these population segments. In fact, as hockey is often considered rude and violent, hockey players' monopolization of the ice rink is at the core of this insecurity. Although they are inclined to use the rink, many residents avoid venturing onto it because they are scared of collisions with pucks, sticks or oncoming players. This ties up with the analysis of Reis et al., which demonstrates that too vigorous sport activities can discourage the female clientele. For the authors, as it is for Loukaitou-Sideris and Sideris,[73] it is essential to regulate the activity programme of these sites by segmenting the schedule in a way to offer more room for female and mildly active users. Thus, the problem is not related to surveillance, but to the privileged activity. As the district acknowledges the popularity of hockey in the outdoor rink, only 16% of the rink's schedule goes to free skating and other activities. To remediate this situation, a lower quality minor ice rink without boards was added to the park. However, only young children – aged 5–8 years – use it.

Once again, as a result, organized activities could be an important tool against insecurity. As a matter of fact, it was observed on the field that both female and 'mildly active' users already participate to the different activities organized onsite by local associations using the rink. Consequently, we can recognize an obvious interest to use the facility, but the actual organized activities remain insufficient. In that sense, a recreational animator, rather than a guard, could most probably serve and supervise the management of the ice rink site as well as organize activities likely to attract a heterogeneous population. These results reflect the work of Williams and Patterson and Williams and Vaske.[74] According to these scholars, the physical and natural characteristics of a site certainly impact its value, but the capacity to maintain activity as well as the users' satisfaction is also essential. Thus, the very meaning of a proximity sport facility for users is based on two fundamental elements: the built and/or physical environment and the interactions between users. In the case of the Bleu, Blanc, Bouge ice rink, it seems obvious that these forms of socialization should be considered further and secured by the managing entity as well as the different organizations that use the facility. This could be done by developing places for interaction, as these are the cornerstone of this facility's success.

Conclusion

Obesity among Canadian children and teenagers has become an significant public health problem. In fact, obesity due to a lack of physical activity is an important problem across

Canada, mainly in disadvantaged neighbourhoods. To counter this phenomenon of juvenile inactivity, many local projects focusing on the improvement of the infrastructure and facilities developed for sport activities were implemented. The Bleu, Blanc, Bouge project is part of these strategies whose objective is to facilitate the access of disadvantaged populations to proximity high-quality sport facilities.

The implementation of such proximity facilities appears to have the potential to attract the local population and inspire them to adopt a healthier lifestyle. To succeed, new sport infrastructures need to take into account the urban tissue in which they are located, but more specifically, they need to provide three motivating factors: accessibility, appeal and security. In that context, especially in the case of disadvantaged neighbourhoods such as Montreal North, it seems crucial to choose a residential and dense location, to offer services free of charge with year-long access, and to allow different types of activities. Our study demonstrates that the popularity of such places rely on the facility's appeal, meaning both the infrastructure's look and the desirability of its services. Therefore, urban design plays an important role in motivating the population to use the facility and this is especially true for the younger segments of the population. Because of its quality and its technical specificity, the outdoor rink built in Montreal North largely attracts a local clientele and also reaches neighbouring districts. Finally, our study shows that when choosing a place to do physical activity, security becomes a central factor for the less-active clientele. However, this security factor does not only concern the site itself (quality of the facility, road traffic around the site and lighting) but also includes the surrounding places. In the case of the Bleu, Blanc, Bouge project, the Montreal North's outdoor rink seems to respond adequately to this security issue. However, our research has found that the lack of organized activities on the rink has permitted both the monopolization of the rink by hockey players and a homogenization of users. Indeed, because of the lack of organized activities and the predominance of hockey, female and less-active teenagers are less inclined to use the facility. These analytical observations led to the conclusion that these clienteles might need activities that are better suited to their needs in order to improve their skating abilities and that they also need to have greater access to different types of activities.

Despite the above, we are cognizant of the fact that our research includes various analytical limits. First, it is important to note that this study needs to be pursued in the medium and the long term in a way to ensure that the results are constantly verified. This interpretative effort could also be coupled with comparative analyses of other outdoor ice rinks established by the Montreal Canadiens Children's Foundation, built in other underprivileged districts of Montreal. Moreover, our conclusions reinforce a longstanding *status quo*: developing a proximity sport facility alone is not enough to attract new mildly active or non-active, as well as female, users. Indeed, this Bleu, Blanc, Bouge ice rink project mainly attracts young Caucasian males who are already skating enthusiasts. Through some cross-referencing of our data, we could offer different recommendations in order to improve this situation. However, interviews with young residents who do not use the ice rink could allow us to better diagnose this issue and help us to advise targeted changes. Moreover, larger series of observations could be planned in a way to better highlight the dynamics and the social interactions present at the Bleu, Blanc, Bouge ice rink.

That being said, we still believe, despite this limit, that our short-term analysis is of major importance. Our results validate our hypotheses, while our observations and interviews explicitly confirm the importance of onsite activities to ensure a complete success and a better heterogeneity of users and practices. Indeed, to guarantee the success of this project, the outdoor rink should provide management and repartition of activities (allowing practices other than hockey), skating classes by gender and/or by age groups, supervisors and access to basic equipment (skates, helmets, etc.). Hence, a more structured onsite animation might have a positive influence on the level of physical activity of the users and encourage mildly active and non-active population to participate.

Acknowledgements

The authors thank all the members of the GREF (Research Group on Festive Spaces, www.gref.ca) for their significant help in this research. They also thank Québec en Forme, Montreal Canadiens Children's Foundation and this study's advisory committee for their financial and scientific support. Special thanks are due to Taïka Baillargeon and Tanya Austini for their linguistic help. Finally, they thank two anonymous reviewers for their judicious and constructive suggestions and recommendations.

Notes

1. Canada Actif 20/20, *Stratégie et un plan*.
2. The most recent studies and Canadian guidelines regarding physical activity, such as Canada Actif 20/20, stipulate that children (5–11 years old) and the teenagers (12–17 years old) should do an average of 60 min of moderate-to-intense physical activity every day. While adults (18–64 years old) and elders (65+ years old) should do an average of 150 min of moderate-to-intense physical activity every week.
3. Merrifield, *Enfants en santé*.
4. INSPQ, *Impact de l'environnement*; Brownson et al., 'Measuring the Built Environment' and Sallis, 'Measuring Physical Activity Environments'.
5. In the context of this analysis, we decided to use the term 'rink' because it is the common term public stakeholders from the field of leisure use in Quebec. For example, the City of Montreal and the ministry of Education, Leisure and Sport use this term. The stakeholders of the project Bleu, Blanc, Bouge also use this term. Moreover, the terminological dictionary of Quebec uses this terminology when referring to this type of exterior sport facility.
6. Molnar et al., 'Unsafe to Play?'.
7. The name of this project, Bleu, Blanc, Bouge (Blue White Move), is not insignificant. It refers to the popular nickname of the professional hockey club the Montreal Canadiens 'le Bleu Blanc Rouge' (Blue White Red). The word 'Rouge' (Red) was changed to 'Bouge' (Move) for their phonetic similitude in French, thereby allowing a pun and making a connection with the objectives of the Montreal Canadiens Children's Foundation.
8. Fondation des Canadiens pour l'enfance, 'Fondations des Canadiens'.
9. Giles-Corti et al., 'Increasing Walking'; Popkin, Duffey, and Gordon-Larsen, 'Environmental Influences on Food Choice' and Sallis et al., 'Environmental and Policy Interventions'.
10. In the context of this analysis, we decided to use the term 'built environment', because it is the term usually used and recognized in the fields of physical activities, urban studies and public health when referring to the elements built or designed by man.
11. Giles-Corti and Donovan, 'Relative Influence of Individual'.
12. Handy et al., 'How the Built Environment Affects'.
13. INSPQ, *Impact de l'environnement*.
14. Tucker et al., 'Environmental Influences on Physical Activity'; Atkinson et al., 'Association of Neighbourhood Design' and Frank et al., 'Linking Objectively Measured Physical Activity'.
15. Day et al., 'Irvine-Minnesota Inventory'.
16. INSPQ, *Impact de l'environnement*' and Sallis et al., 'Ecological Approach to Creating Active'.
17. Frank et al., 'Urban Form Relationships' and Sallis et al., 'Assessing Perceived Physical Environmental'.
18. Pineault and Daveluy, *Planification de la santé*.
19. Motl et al., 'Perceived Physical Environment'; Day et al., 'Irvine-Minnesota Inventory'; Kino-Québec, *Aménageons nos milieux*; Frank, Engelke, and Schmid, *Health and Community Design* and Spence and Lee, 'Toward a Comprehensive Model'.

20. Popkin, Duffey, and Gordon-Larsen, 'Environmental Influences on Food Choice'.
21. Tucker, Gilliland, and Irwin, 'Splashpads, Swings, and Shade' and Tucker et al., 'Environmental Influences on Physical Activity', 358.
22. Ries et al., 'Environment and Urban Adolescents'.
23. Ibid., 48.
24. Ibid.; Gordon-Larsen et al., 'Inequality in the Built Environment Underlies'.
25. Kipke et al., 'Food and Park Environments'.
26. INSPQ, *Impact de l'environnement*.
27. Sallis, 'Measuring Physical Activity Environments'; Day et al., 'Irvine-Minnesota Inventory' and Sallis et al., 'Environmental and Policy Interventions'.
28. Handy et al., 'How the Built Environment Affects'.
29. Molnar et al., 'Unsafe to Play?'.
30. Gordon-Larsen, McMurray, and Popkin, 'Determinants of Adolescent Physical Activity', 7.
31. Vieille-Marchiset, 'La construction sociale des espaces sportifs ouverts dans la ville' and Gordon-Larsen, McMurray, and Popkin, 'Determinants of Adolescent Physical Activity'.
32. MELS and Kino-Québec, *Activité physique, le sport et les jeunes*.
33. Ries et al., 'Environment and Urban Adolescents'.
34. INSPQ, *Impact de l'environnement*; Committee on Environmental Health, 'Built Environment'; Ries et al., 'Environment and Urban Adolescents' and Vieille-Marchiset, 'Construction sociale des espaces sportifs'.
35. Raibaud, *Nouveaux modèles de virilité*.
36. Ries et al., 'Environment and Urban Adolescents'.
37. Ibid., 47.
38. INSPQ, *Impact de l'environnement*.
39. Day et al., 'Irvine-Minnesota Inventory'; Kino-Québec, *Aménageons nos milieux*; Molnar et al., 'Unsafe to Play?' and Leventhal and Brooks-Gunn, 'Neighborhoods They Live In'.
40. Molnar et al. 'Unsafe to Play?' 379.
41. Giles-Corti and Donovan, 'Relative Influence of Individual'.
42. Ries et al., 'Environment and Urban Adolescents'.
43. Ibid. and Committee on Environmental Health, 'Built Environment'.
44. Ville de Montréal, 'Profil sociodémographique Montréal-Nord'.
45. Brownson et al., 'Measuring the Built Environment' and McKenzie, *SOPLAY, System for Observing*.
46. Nvivo and the methodological strategy of grounded theory were used for the qualitative part of our research and especially for the analysis of our interviews.
47. Reis et al., 'Association Between Physical Activity in Parks' and Roemmich et al., 'Association of Access to Parks'.
48. De Visscher, Bouverne-De Bie, and Verschelden, 'Urban Public Space'.
49. Loukaitou-Sideris and Sideris, 'What Brings Children to the Park?'.
50. Arrondissement de Montréal-Nord, *Mise en candidature*, 10.
51. Ries et al., 'Environment and Urban Adolescents'; Kipke et al., 'Food and Park Environments' and Gordon-Larsen et al., 'Inequality in the Built Environment Underlies'.
52. Bedimo-Rung, Mowen, and Cohen, 'Significance of Parks to Physical Activity'.
53. Pluhar et al., 'Representations of the Relationship Among Physical Activity'and Reis et al., 'Association Between Physical Activity in Parks'.
54. Loukaitou-Sideris and Sideris, 'What Brings Children to the Park?'.
55. Arrondissement de Montréal-Nord, *Mise en candidature*.
56. Reis et al., 'Association Between Physical Activity in Parks'.
57. Pluhar et al., 'Representations of the Relationship Among Physical Activity'.
58. Raibaud, *Nouveaux modèles de virilité* and Ries et al., 'Environment and Urban Adolescents'.
59. Vieille-Marchiset, 'Construction sociale des espaces sportifs'.
60. Loukaitou Sideris and Sideris, 'What Brings Children to the Park?'.
61. Lemieux and Thibault, 'Activité physique, sport et les jeunes'.
62. Ibid., 3.
63. Savoie, Bédard, and Collins, *Neighbourhood Characteristics*.
64. Cohen et al., 'Parks and Physical Activity'.
65. Bedimo-Rung, Mowen, and Cohen, 'Significance of Parks to Physical Activity'.

66. Debenedetti, 'Concept de l'attachement au lieu' and Taylor, Gottfredson, and Brower, 'Attachment to Place'.
67. Soubrier, *Planification, aménagement et loisir*.
68. Ries, 'Environment and Urban Adolescents'.
69. Jacobs, *Death and Life of Great American*.
70. Ibid., 30.
71. Loukaitou-Sideris and Sideris, 'What Brings Children to the Park?'.
72. Ibid. and Bedimo-Rung, Mowen, and Cohen, 'Significance of Parks to Physical Activity'.
73. Loukaitou-Sideris and Sideris, 'What Brings Children to the Park?'.
74. Williams and Patterson, 'Snapshots of What, Exactly?' and Williams and Vaske, 'Measurement of Place Attachment'.

References

Arrondissement de Montréal-Nord. *Mise en candidature. Formulaire La Fondation des Canadiens pour l'enfance: Bleu, Blanc, Bouge*. Montreal: Ville de Montreal, 2009.

Atkinson, J.L., J.F. Sallis, B.E. Saelens, K.L. Cain, and J.B. Black. 'The Association of Neighbourhood Design and Recreational Environments with Physical Activity'. *American Journal of Health Promotion* 19 (2005): 304–9.

Bedimo-Rung, A.L., A.J. Mowen, and D.A. Cohen. 'The Significance of Parks to Physical Activity and Public Health. A Conceptual Model'. *American Journal of Preventive Medicine* 28 (2005): 159–68.

Brownson, R.C., C.M. Hoehner, K. Day, A. Forsyth, and J.F. Sallis. 'Measuring the Built Environment for Physical Activity: State of the Science'. *American Journal of Preventive Medicine* 36 (2009): S99–S123.

Canada Actif 20/20. *Une stratégie et un plan de changement pour accroître l'activité physique au Canada*. Montreal: Publications Gouvernementales, 2011.

Cohen, D.A., T. Marsh, S. Williamson, K. Pitkin Derose, H. Martinez, C. Setodji, and L. McKenzie. 'Parks and Physical Activity: Why are Some Parks Used More Than Others?' *Preventive Medicine* 50 (2010): S9–S12.

Committee on Environmental Health, 'The Built Environment: Designing Communities to Promote Physical Activity in Children'. *Pediatrics* 23 (2009): 1591–8.

Day, K., M. Boarnet, M. Alfonzo, and A. Forsyth. 'The Irvine-Minnesota Inventory to Measure Built Environments: Development'. *American Journal of Preventive Medicine* 30 (2006): 144–52.

Debenedetti, A. 'Le concept de l'attachement au lieu: État de l'art et voies de recherche dans le contexte du lieu de loisirs'. *Revue Management et Avenir* 3 (2005): 151–60.

De Visscher, S., M. Bouverne-De Bie, and G. Verschelden. 'Urban Public Space and the Construction of Social Life: A Social-Pedagogical Perspective'. *International Journal of Lifelong Education* 31 (2012): 97–110.

Fondation des Canadiens pour l'enfance. 'La Fondations des Canadiens pour l'enfance inaugure une troisième patinoire Bleu, Blanc, Bouge à Montréal'. http://www.fondation.canadiens.com/fr/programmes-evenements/troisieme-patinoire-communautaire.php

Frank, L.D., P. Engelke, and T. Schmid. *Health and Community Design: The Impact of the Built Environment on Physical Activity*. Washington, DC: Island Press, 2003.

Frank, L.D., J. Kerr, J. Chapman, and J. Sallis. 'Urban Form Relationships with Walk Trip Frequency and Distance Among Youth'. *American Journal of Health Promotion* 21 (2007): 305–11.

Frank, L.D., T.L. Schmidt, J.F. Sallis, J. Chapman, and B.E. Saelens. 'Linking Objectively Measured Physical Activity with Objectively Measured Urban Form: Findings from SMARTRAQ'. *American Journal of Preventive Medicine* 28 (2005): 117–25.

Giles-Corti, B., M.H. Broomhall, M. Knuiman, C. Collins, K. Douglas, K. Ng, A. Lange, and R.J. Donovan. 'Increasing Walking: How Important is Distance to, Attractiveness, and Size of Public Open Space?' *American Journal of Preventive Medicine* 28 (2005): 169–76.

Giles-Corti, B., and R.J. Donovan. 'The Relative Influence of Individual, Social and Physical Environment Determinants of Physical Activity'. *Social Science & Medicine* 54 (2002): 1793–812.

Gordon-Larsen, P., R.G. McMurray, and B.M. Popkin. 'Determinants of Adolescent Physical Activity and Inactivity Patterns'. *Pediatrics* 105 (2000): 83–90.

Gordon-Larsen, P., M.C. Nelson, P. Page, and B.M. Popkin. 'Inequality in the Built Environment Underlies Key Health Disparities in Physical Activity and Obesity'. *Pediatrics* 117 (2006): 417–24.

Handy, S.L., M.G. Boarnet, R. Ewing, and R.E. Killingsworth. 'How the Built Environment Affects Physical Activity: Views from Urban Planning'. *American Journal of Preventive Medicine* 23 (2002): 64–73.

Institut National de Santé Publique du Québec (INSPQ). *L'impact de l'environnement bâti sur l'activité physique, l'alimentation et le poids*. Montreal: Publications Gouvernementales, 2010.

Jacobs, J. *Death and Life of Great American Cities*. New York: Vintage, 1961.

Kino-Québec. *Aménageons nos milieux de vie pour nous donner le goût de bouger pour une meilleure qualité de vie*. Montreal: Publications Gouvernementales, 2005.

Kipke, M.D., E. Iverson, D. Moore, C. Booker, V. Ruelas, A.L. Paters, and F. Kaufman. 'Food and Park Environments: Neighborhood-Level Risks for Childhood Obesity in East Los Angeles'. *Journal of Adolescent Health* 40 (2007): 325–33.

Lemieux, M., and G. Thibault. 'L'activité physique, le sport et les jeunes – savoir et agir'. *Observatoire Québécois du Loisir* 9 (2011): 1–5.

Leventhal, T., and J. Brooks-Gunn. 'The Neighborhoods They Live In: The Effects of Neighbourhood Residence on Child and Adolescent Outcomes'. *Psychological Bulletin* 126 (2000): 309–37.

Loukaitou-Sideris, A., and A. Sideris. 'What Brings Children to the Park? Analysis and Measurement the Variables Affecting Children's Use of Parks'. *Journal of the American Planning Association* 76 (2009): 89–107.

McKenzie, T.L. *SOPLAY, System for Observing Play and Leisure Activity in Youth. Description and Procedures Manuals*. San Diego, CA: San Diego State University, 2006.

Merrifield, R. *Des enfants en santé: Une question de poids. Rapport du comité permanent de la santé*. Ottawa: Chambre des Communes Canada, 2007.

Ministère de l'Éducation, du Loisir et du Sport du Québec (MELS) et Kino-Québec. *L'activité physique, le sport et les jeunes*. Montreal: Publications Gouvernementales, 2011.

Molnar, B.E., S.L. Gortmakerm, F.C. Bull, and S.L. Buka. 'Unsafe to Play? Neighborhood Disorder and Lack of Safety Predict Reduced Physical Activity Among Urban Children and Adolescents'. *American Journal of Health Promotion* 18 (2004): 378–86.

Motl, R.W., R.K. Dishman, D.S. Ward, R.P. Saunders, M. Dowda, G. Felton, and R.R. Pate. 'Perceived Physical Environment and Physical Activity Across One Year Among Adolescent Girls: Self-Efficacy As a Possible Mediator?' *Journal of Adolescent Health* 37 (2005): 4038.

Pineault, R., and C. Daveluy. *La planification de la santé: Concepts, méthodes, stratégies*. Montréal: Éditions Nouvelles, 1995.

Pluhar, Z.F., B.F. Piko, A. Uzzoli, R.M. Page, and A. Dull. 'Representations of the Relationship Among Physical Activity, Health and Perceived Living Environment in Hungarian Urban Children's Images'. *Landscape and Urban Planning* 95 (2010): 151–60.

Popkin, B.M., K. Duffey, and P. Gordon-Larsen. 'Environmental Influences on Food Choice, Physical Activity and Energy Balance'. *Physiology and Behaviour* 86 (2005): 603–13.

Raibaud, Y. 'De nouveaux modèles de virilité: Musiques actuelles et cultures urbaines'. Université de Bordeaux, 2011.

Reis, R.S., A.A. F. Hino, A.A. Florindo, C.R. R. Anez, and M.R. Domingues. 'Association Between Physical Activity in Parks and Perceived Environment: A Study with Adolescents'. *Journal of Physical Activity and Health* 19 (2009): 503–9.

Ries, A.V., J. Gittelsohn, C.C. Voorhees, K.M. Roche, K.J. Clifton, and N.M. Astone. 'The Environment and Urban Adolescents' Use of Recreational Facilities for Physical Activity: A Qualitative Study'. *American Journal of Health Promotion* 23 (2008): 43–50.

Roemmich, J.N., L.H. Epstein, S. Raja, L. Yin, J. Robinson, and D. Winiewicz. 'Association of Access to Parks and Recreational Facilities with the Physical Activity of Young Children'. *Preventive Medicine* 43 (2006): 437–41.

Sallis, J.F. 'Measuring Physical Activity Environments: A Brief History'. *American Journal of Preventive Medicine* 36 (2009): S86–S92.

Sallis, J.F., A. Bauman, and M. Pratt. 'Environmental and Policy Interventions to Promote Physical Activity'. *American Journal of Preventive Medicine* 15 (1998): 379–97.

Sallis, J.F., R.B. Cervero, W. Ascher, K.A. Henderson, M.K. Kraft, and J. Kerr. 'An Ecological Approach to Creating Active Living Communities'. *Annual Review of Public Health* 27 (2006): 297–322.

Sallis, J.F., M.F. Johnson, K.J. Calfas, S. Caparosa, and J.F. Nichols. 'Assessing Perceived Physical Environmental Variables that May Influence Physical Activity'. *Research Quarterly for Exercise and Sport* 68 (1997): 345–51.

Savoie, J., F. Bédard, and K. Collins. *Neighbourhood Characteristics and the Distribution of Crime on the Island of Montréal*. Crime and Justice Research Paper Series. Ottawa: Statistics Canada, 2006.

Soubrier, R. *Planification, aménagement et loisir*. Sainte-Foy: Presses de l'Université du Québec, 2000.

Spence, J.C., and R.E. Lee. 'Toward a Comprehensive Model of Physical Activity'. *Psychology of Sport and Exercise* 4 (2003): 7–24.

Taylor, R.B., S.D. Gottfredson, and S. Brower. 'Attachment to Place: Discriminant Validity, and Impacts of Disorder and Diversity'. *American Journal of Community Psychology* 13 (1985): 525–42.

Tucker, P., J. Gilliland, and J.D. Irwin. 'Splashpads, Swings, and Shade: Parents Preferences for Neighbourhood Parks'. *Canadian Journal of Public Health* 98 (2007): 198–202.

Tucker, P., J.D. Irwin, J. Gilliland, M. He, K. Larsen, and P. Hess. 'Environmental Influences on Physical Activity Levels in Youth'. *Health Place* 15 (2009): 357–63.

Vieille-Marchiset, G. 'La construction sociale des espaces sportifs ouverts dans la ville. Enjeux politiques et liens sociaux en question'. *L'Homme et la Société* 165–6 (2008): 141–59.

Ville de Montréal. 'Profil sociodémographique Montréal-Nord'. http://ville.montreal.qc.ca/portal/page?_pageid=6897,68087658&_dad=portal&_schema=PORTAL

Williams, D.R., and M.E. Patterson. 'Snapshots of What, Exactly? A Comment on Methodological Experiments and Conceptual Foundations in Place Research'. *Society Natural Resources* 20 (2007): 931–7.

Williams, D.R., and J.J. Vaske. 'The Measurement of Place Attachment: Validity and Generalizability of a Psychometric Approach'. *Forest Science* 49 (2003): 830–40.

Sport and community integration in Northern Ireland[1]

David Hassan and Rachael Telford

Ulster Sports Academy, University of Ulster at Jordanstown, Room 15E01E, Shore Road, Newtownabbey, County Antirm, Northern Ireland BT37 0QB, UK

This article addresses the role of sport in Northern Ireland, a country that, despite experiencing 20 years of relative peace, remains deeply divided along ethno-sectarian lines. It locates this analysis amid publication by the Office of the First and Deputy First Minister in Northern Ireland's devolved Assembly of its draft proposals to tackle community divisions in the country. The Programme for Cohesion, Sharing and Integration consultation (2010) document was the local government's attempt to commence dialogue around how decades of division in Northern Ireland could be meaningfully addressed. However, one of its principle failings has been its reluctance to build upon well-established programmes, many of them using sport as a tool to promote social and community cohesion, which have existed in the country for some time. Moreover, these community-based initiatives are typically at their most potent within the so-called hard-to-reach communities where relationships between the minority Catholic and the majority Protestant populations present particularly challenging concerns. Of course, sport cannot offer all the answers and an overselling of its potential in Northern Ireland, specifically when addressing deeply ingrained levels of mistrust in the country, is contained in a detailed critique in this paper.

Introduction

On 2 April 2011 Police Service of Northern Ireland (PSNI) Constable Ronan Kerr was killed when a bomb placed underneath his car exploded as he was setting out on his way to work. His murder, widely attributed to Irish republican terrorists opposed to the ongoing 'peace-process' in Northern Ireland, drew a remarkable level of condemnation from all shades of political opinion in the country.[2] It also presented an opportunity for the Gaelic Athletic Association (GAA), Ireland's largest sporting body, to demonstrate the full extent of its transformation since the signing of the Belfast-Good Friday peace agreement in April 1998. This organization, which for much of its 129-year history has existed as a touchstone for opposition to the British presence in Ireland, was faced with the challenge of having to publically demonstrate its support for the new policing arrangements in Northern Ireland as Ronan Kerr was not alone a member of the PSNI but was also a Gaelic footballer with the Beragh Red Knights GAA club in County Tyrone.[3]

As leading members of the GAA's Ulster Council, in whose jurisdiction the murdered officer had lived, came to terms with the implications of Mr Kerr's murder for their organization, it quickly became clear that the GAA constituency in the northern province, indeed large numbers of the nationalist community living in Northern Ireland, was unequivocal in their opposition to the young police officer's death. During the 4 days spanning Mr Kerr's murder to his funeral in County Tyrone on 6 April, the GAA's public support for the PSNI and particularly GAA members who were employed (or who may wish to be employed) by the PSNI became abundantly clear.[4] The abiding image of the dead constable's funeral therefore was one of members of the Beragh Red Knights GAA club standing shoulder-to-shoulder with serving PSNI officers amid an unprecedented show of unity.

In fact, it was less than 10 years prior to the events following the death of Mr Kerr that the GAA had decided to remove Rule 21 from its official constitution. Its existence had prevented members of the police and army in Northern Ireland from joining what remains both an indigenous and proudly Irish nationalist organization. Instead, the rule was considered a necessary bulwark against British cultural and political influence in Ireland and a reminder that the perceived ills of the past were not to be readily forgotten. Yet, in an apparent desire to demonstrate leadership following the signing of the Belfast-Good Friday agreement and specifically in the light of recommendations arising from an independent review into policing in Northern Ireland, completed in 1999, and which made specific reference to the presence of Rule 21, it was felt that the time had finally arrived for the GAA's central administration to delete the controversial ruling (NIO 1999).

Of course, this was to be a by no means straightforward undertaking as large numbers of GAA followers in Northern Ireland remained implacably opposed to the rule's eradication, citing ongoing allegations of police harassment against the minority nationalist population in Northern Ireland. For many others, it was simply too soon following the changes to policing in Northern Ireland (the PSNI was only established on 4 November 2001) to gauge whether a new dispensation had indeed been established and whether a once partisan police force, in the eyes of many Irish nationalists, had been fully transformed. Thus, all but one of the GAA county boards in Northern Ireland – Down being the exception – voted against the repeal of Rule 21 at a special congress called to debate the matter in November 2001. However, as more than two thirds of the organization's membership held an opposing view, a motion proposing deletion of Rule 21 was passed and serving police officers in Northern Ireland were free, if they so wished, to join the GAA, to establish a PSNI Gaelic football team and compete in GAA-sponsored tournaments at home and abroad (Hassan 2005).

However, despite members of the GAA, a sporting body overwhelmingly patronized by Catholics, now being free to join the PSNI there still remained reluctance on the part of many to actually do so. This was borne out of fear of attack from splinter republican terrorist groups operating in Northern Ireland that disagreed with a policy, publically endorsed by nationalist and republican political parties, to seek a locally agreed settlement concerning the constitutional future of Northern Ireland. Instead such groups, typically referred to as 'dissident republicans', continued to argue in favour of a policy of armed resistance to British rule in Ireland. By targeting Catholic recruits to the PSNI, a strategy designed to strike fear into such individuals and thereby serve as a deterrent against them joining the police service, such groupings believed that they were securing meaningful advancement of their ultimate aims of achieving a united and sovereign Irish nation. This policy, of dissuading the nationalist community in Northern Ireland from becoming overly acquiescent with the new police service there, certainly exercised an effect in certain rural nationalist communities and other strongly republican parts of Northern Ireland where a long-standing reticence to 'break rank' still existed. Nevertheless, some young Catholics continued to join the PSNI in spite of the obvious dangers they faced, content in the knowledge that they enjoyed the overwhelming support of the nationalist community in Northern Ireland and, moreover, could continue to promote their Irish identity and pursue their interest in Gaelic games by retaining their membership of the GAA (Hassan 2005, 64). Thus, the response of the organization to the death of Ronan Kerr, its publically stated support for the PSNI and the rule of law in Northern Ireland, confirmed that the GAA was now unequivocally signed up to the new arrangements in place across the country and there was to be no going back.

In the same week as Ronan Kerr was buried in Northern Ireland came the announcement that as part of the first ever visit to the Republic of Ireland by a serving British Monarch, Queen Elizabeth II would be welcomed to Croke Park, the headquarters of the GAA, and the scene in November 1920 of the murder of 13 unarmed civilians by the Black and Tans, a battalion of the British army. Once again, the symbolism of this development neither can be overstated nor can it be the apparent desire now for the GAA hierarchy to portray its organization as liberal, enlightened and progressive. Quite how it reconciles this modern image of the GAA with its longstanding and remarkably politicized history is too early to say or even to properly consider. However, one thing is beyond doubt – the events of the week spanning 2–9 April 2011 changed the public face of the GAA in Ireland beyond all recognition and in a manner that is certain to have a profound effect on its role in Irish life in the years ahead.

Programme for Cohesion, Sharing and Integration

Only 10 months prior to the unprecedented events of April 2011, in July 2010, the Northern Ireland executive released its draft Programme for Cohesion, Sharing and Integration (CSI) for public consultation (OFMDFM 2010). The long history of Northern Ireland was marked by sustained periods of political and social division, which had ethno-sectarian undertones defined by struggles for legitimacy, supremacy and power. This dispute, between representatives and others from the majority unionist community, the minority nationalist population, British state forces and various paramilitary groupings, manifested itself in all areas of public life, from politics to culture, and served to construct everyday existence in Northern Ireland as essentially being about 'them and us' (Arthur 1990). Thus, division continued to shape almost every part of life there, from schooling, to choices around where people could live and work and even which sports they played and teams they supported. While life there was by no means 'normal' equally for many people growing up in Northern Ireland, a degree of acceptance around their lived experiences eventually took hold and, notwithstanding the often traumatic and public reminders of a conflict between two opposing communities all around them, for many people life carried on in a largely uneventful manner. Yet, the depth of polarity remained ever-present and, with every passing year, it was clear that the task of properly addressing these entrenched divisions would constitute a considerable challenge when the time was considered right to begin such a process (Towards Sustainable Security 2009). Thus, Northern Ireland became accepted internationally as a country of profound dislocations, its leitmotif a deep level of mistrust between Catholics and Protestants, nationalists and unionists, seemingly incapable of living in comparative peace alongside one another in a small part of Ireland, on the periphery of Europe (Community Relations Council 2010).

The long awaited publication of the draft CSI document drew a mixed response from a range of commentators. On the one hand, there was welcome recognition from some that the devolved (from Westminster) Northern Ireland assembly sitting at Stormont had decided to tackle the vexed issue of community division in Northern Ireland, which clearly hampered the ongoing provision of public services – not to mention the negative impact it exercised on the normal development of society – there. On the other hand however, those observers hopeful of a series of novel and inventive responses to such apparently intractable issues were to be disappointed as the executive's proposals amounted to, in the eyes of many, little more than the management of division and a settlement which contained the strong likelihood that its professed aims, of a shared and integrated future for Northern Ireland, were simply unrealizable. A failure to properly contextualize Northern Ireland's violent past, to establish a credible mechanism by which those most adversely affected by the events of this history could seek appropriate 'closure' and the recognition that the country was no longer one populated simply by 'two communities' (Catholics and Protestants) and was now patently multi-ethnic were some of the more obvious shortcomings contained in the draft report. In an overall sense, its architects appeared intent on proposing a model that permitted some form of managed difference to take root than to creatively tackle, respond and overcome long-standing disputes or even properly embrace the full extent of Northern Ireland's diverse population (Community Relations Council 2010).

That said, one of the most compelling parts of the CSI document concerned proposals dealing with the so-called interface areas, which are parts of Northern Ireland where Catholics and Protestants live in close proximity to one another (NI Executive 2008). These are typically in working class, urban areas. Here, when latent resentment and opposition becomes manifest, violence, injury and even death can result. It is a truism that much of this resentment also emerges from the multiple deprivations being experienced by residents of such communities, who are often working class families for whom concerns around unemployment, ever-present financial worries and levels of educational under-attainment predominate (NIMDM 2010). Coupled with the fear of either perceived or real violent attack from 'the other side', the networks of communities living adjacent to the so-called 'peace walls', erected to keep both communities apart, are adversely affected in many different and complex ways. The CSI document did prioritize these matters by promising to tackle concerns around anti-social behaviour in the vicinity of such peace walls not least as the fear of crime, as correctly identified in the response to the draft CSI document by the Northern Ireland Community Relations Council, is directly correlated to levels of poverty throughout many parts of the country (Community Relations Council 2010).

Regrettably however, the CSI document failed to properly reflect the complexities of these communities or, for that matter, accept the role obligated of the executive to adequately promote safety and security for residents living close to such physical divisions irrespective of, and independent from, policies designed to address low-level, persistent incidences of crime within these locales. In some respects, it was typical of government intervention into seemingly intractable cases of community division, i.e. an arms-length response in which the symptoms and not the causes of such divisions are fore grounded. Moreover, beyond rhetoric implicitly suggestive of additional investment within deprived urban locales – for the most part in the country's capital Belfast – there was an absence in the CSI document of any proposals designed to enact the meaningful regeneration of these same areas. It was as if the removal of physical barriers keeping communities apart represented a triumph in itself and/or achieving this would serve as a catalyst for significant inward investment by a host or private and public bodies (2009). Such failings merely confirmed the view that this was a document lacking in proper strategic thought or even a full and nuanced appreciation of the causes of division in Northern Ireland (McEvoy-Levy 2006).

An absence of such foresight, as contained within the draft CSI document, was made evermore apparent when reflecting on the vast networks of community development agencies and bodies already engaged in work right across Northern Ireland, but especially in the so-called flashpoint urban areas such as those in North and East Belfast. It is here that a body of low-level work has been ongoing for many years, often funded by a series of European direct-investment programmes, which have sought to regenerate deprived areas of Northern Ireland while simultaneously advancing cross-community programmes aimed at raising awareness of the cultural differences that exist within Northern Ireland and overcome these. In fact, it is difficult to conceive of that country today without according proper recognition of the role played by community bodies, institutions around which otherwise disparate communities can cohere, project a positive image of the place in which they reside and reaffirm a sense of local pride and identity (Shirlow and Murtagh 2006).[5]

Yet, the CSI document made little explicit reference to the role undertaken by this network of agencies or indeed did it propose to borrow from its experiences, build upon its local knowledge or even refer to its successes. Instead a top-down response to the challenges faced by inner-city communities was proposed in which much of the existing and ongoing work was simply overlooked and a new, largely untested approach was being proposed instead. Its interesting to note amid all of this that the role of sport as a medium for peace building in Northern Ireland was cited as an example of good practice worthy of further encouragement; the Irish Football Association's (IFA) Football for All campaign being a case in point. However, there is little meaningful engagement with the work that has been undertaken to date on this programme or proper account of any such plans for the future contained within the document. As will be seen in the latter part of this paper, the architects of this draft proposal may well be correct in adopting a jaundiced view of sport's capacity to serve as a harbinger of peace and reconciliation in divided societies. Nevertheless, sport clearly does have some role to play in this regard and, properly resourced, can assist in a wider programme of proper understanding and reconciliation between disparate populations. Likewise, sport presents an excellent opportunity for people to meaningfully engage with their communities, to physically invest in their locales through volunteering and social engagement and to create a sense of ownership and collectivistic identity that few other platforms can replicate. As of now, however, division remains manifest throughout many aspects of life in Northern Ireland, including sport. Separate codes, separate teams and separate identities have meant that until relatively recently sport has offered little other than the opportunity to rehearse old divisions. Indeed it is only of late, and again only in certain parts of Northern Ireland, that things have begun to change and those involved with sport have also played their part (Magill, Smith and Hamber 2010).

Indeed, the emergence of a more concerted academic interest in sport and the creation of social capital at the beginning of this century was particularly well received in Ireland, north and south, as it presented an obvious platform upon which to address outstanding levels of deprivation and isolation while simultaneously offering enhanced potential through voluntarism for greater cohesiveness within the society at large. In Northern Ireland, it also had the added potential to assist efforts in bringing together a society divided along ethno-sectarian lines through the establishment of a range of 'cross-community' programmes, many using sport as a useful tool to attract and retain popular levels of interest among often disenfranchised youth. However, as will be seen, these developments have not been without their own problems. In deeply divided societies separate communities are effectively self-perpetuating entities as they retain an ingrained suspicion of any moves that would seek to establish common ground with the 'other'. Under these conditions, the success of programmes designed to underpin forms of 'bridging' social capital is undermined along social, economic and religious lines (Hamber and Kelly 2004). That said, significant progress has been made in this area and in response to those who criticize such schemes because of their perceived short-termism are indications that some of the work undertaken to date is beginning to bear fruit.

Notwithstanding this however, and simply put, up until now there has been little contained within the emergent public policy that has sought to utilize the role of sport in promoting social contact and community involvement among people living in Northern Ireland. Instead, there has been a broad repackaging of activity that was already taking place and some benign suggestions about how more of the same could be facilitated. In certain parts of Northern Ireland, despite the reservations outlined earlier, there was at least a commitment on behalf of some non-state agencies, however belatedly, to recognize their role in achieving these aims for the betterment of the wider society. The Ulster Council of the GAA has a very progressive outreach policy for its volunteers, including cross-community programmes and targeted attempts to encourage Ireland's evolving migrant population to engage with its games. Likewise, the IFA has sought to engage its members in enlightened programmes designed to address reluctance by the minority nationalist community to engage with its activities as well as targeting a series of marginalized and deprived sections of society, among them the homeless, those with disabilities and other ethnic minority groupings. Thus in an Irish context, the most pertinent aspects of the social capital literature are those that stress the role of sport in overcoming division, addressing social isolation, establishing networks and enhancing community identity and association.

Sport, division and grand promises

As such, in recent times, questions have been raised concerning the role of sport in a range of divided societies and, in particular, whether 'sport for good' is considered a cost-effective antidote to a range of engrained social problems (Coalter 2008). In Northern Ireland, there is an additional political interest in sport's potential to transcend the community divide that still exists in that country. As implied, this division is particularly pronounced in the realm of education as the vast majority of schools are founded upon religious difference, which does little to assuage ongoing mistrust and suspicion between the two main ethnic groupings in Northern Ireland, Ulster unionists and Irish nationalists. The question therefore is whether sport in Northern Ireland reflects, contributes to or indeed transcends these differences? In other words, does sport have a pronounced social role in Northern Irish society, one beyond the rhetoric of those already persuaded as to its usefulness in overcoming community division, or is it simply sport for sport's sake?

Coalter (2008) reviews the cumulative body of research which has informed both policy and practice decisions in the UK with regard to producing a tangible link between sport and its ability to deliver social as well as sporting outcomes. Coalter summarizes what he considers to be key shortcomings of these policy approaches in terms of conceptual weaknesses: How do we define 'sport' and various 'social exclusion' issues?; and methodological weaknesses. How do we 'measure' any such changes within local communities and specifically whether a particular sports intervention was responsible for any given outcome? These are valuable, if not universally welcomed, cautionary tales in the context of Northern Ireland and are equally applicable in a range of similar, divided societies. Furthermore, as Coalter recognizes, little consideration is given to those conditions thought necessary to achieve such desirable outcomes, specifically what sports processes produce which outcomes and for what types of participants under what types of circumstances? Finally, there are also limitations around current UK policy approaches in terms of the publications associated with this type of literature on social inclusion and whether the sports development programme shortcomings, the inconvenient truth to borrow a well worn phrase, are in fact hidden. Instead, the argument is advanced that the policy-makers and indeed the public at large are presented with selective success stories designed to appease funders and underpin future funding bids. In the case of Northern Ireland, it is proposed that a realist synthesis approach should be adopted, as this requires information about both successful and unsuccessful interventions that use sport for more than sport for 'sports sake'. Only then can the level of financial investment around the supposed social role of sport be more comprehensively analysed and evidence produced that points categorically to the unique outcomes that may be achieved through the deployment of sporting interventions in such divided societies.

Otherwise, there exists the benign presumption that sport can be used to help alleviate many of the social problems that exist within local communities – a metaphorical 'magic wand'. Sport can be interpreted as an instrument to reduce crime, increase employability and improve the health of the local population. Sport is also perceived to be a type of social 'glue' that will bind otherwise diverse communities together with a shared sense of belonging and pride. Coalter (2008) lists a range of academics that have identified the multitude of benefits sport supposedly possesses. These benefits range from the psychological, via the socio-psychological, to the exclusively social advantages offered by sport. The potential benefits of participation in sport are thought to include the following: improved physical fitness and health; improved mental health and psychological well-being; personality development via improved self-concept; socio-psychological benefits such as empathy, integrity, tolerance, cooperation, trustworthiness and the development of social skills; and finally, broader societal impacts, such as increased community identity, social cohesion and integration. It is thought that all of these desired outcomes can be achieved through participation in targeted sports programmes of a variety of forms (Coalter 2008).

Coalter (2008) confirms that, in the development of UK sports policy, several research reviews have been commissioned by the British government to examine the extent of the available evidence in support of the claim that sport may indeed exercise a wider social impact beyond the level of mere participation. These reviews were also tasked with identifying 'good practice' as a basis for the development of future policies designed to exact clear, measurable and ultimately positive outcomes around sport. The UK appears to have been at the forefront of undertaking such academic reviews, with Canada and Australia (Australian Sports Commission 2006) following their initial lead. The purpose of these documents was to inform a more evidence-based approach to policy-making, specifically in addressing the use of sport to ameliorate a range of social ills.

Coalter (2008) also outlines the arguments that exist in academic literature regarding the lack of understanding among practitioners – and some policy-makers – about how outcomes are achieved in real-life situations and not simply as the result of complicated theorizing on the part of bureaucrats or academics. In Weiss's vivid phrase, much (sports) policy and practice has been, and continue to be, not 'aim, steady, fire!' but 'fire, steady, aim!' (Coalter 2008, 26). Pawson (2004) also argues that definitions of what constitutes 'desired outcomes' for various policy documents in the sporting realm have been extremely vague, the use of ambiguous terminology and the deployment of erroneous phraseology around the social inclusion agenda being particularly widespread. Previously Weiss (1996) had argued persuasively that these ambiguous and indeed often overly optimistic promises are a product of the political processes that take place and of which such policy directions derive. Therefore, to maximize the possibility of achieving such socially desirable outcomes, Coalter (2008) draws the reader's attention to 'theory of change' approaches and also 'programme theory' as being worthy of increased attention. Both of these conceptual approaches present the opportunity for policy-makers to examine often overlooked questions concerning the intervention processes surrounding sport. For example, why do we assume that sport, or a particular type of sport, can have certain types of impacts on individuals and their local communities? What are the properties and processes associated with these types of programmes that lead to such supposed outcomes and viewpoints? Can we clearly identify the theory of the relationship between participation in specific sports programmes and a range of intermediate impacts which these may have (e.g. increased self-efficacy, increased physical self-worth and increased self-confidence)? How and to what extent will these intermediate changes convert into long-term changed behaviours (e.g. crime reduction, improved physical performance and reduction in or cessation of drug use within specific populations)?

There are, however, studies that have suggested that there may be downsides for individuals and communities in taking part in recreation schemes aimed at addressing broader social needs. For example, communities can become more divided in terms of their ethnic or cultural boundaries when engaging in sport (Coalter 2008). This of course is very appropriate to any discussion around sport in Northern Ireland, as highlighting differences that exist between the majority unionist population and their nationalist neighbours may serve only to exacerbate the degree of unease and malcontent existing between both. Similarly team sports, such as association football, may further aggravate an already fraught situation by creating additional, often nuanced divisions, on top of those community divisions which may already be on show.

Sport Northern Ireland

Sport Northern Ireland (Sport NI), the lead sports agency in Northern Ireland, has responded to the supposed beneficial role of sport by publishing and implementing 'Sport in our Community'. This is a strategic document linked to a broader strategic vision for sport in Northern Ireland. The latter is detailed in the Sport Matters (2009–2019) strategy document. The key aim of the latter was to promote a 'culture of lifelong enjoyment and success in sport which contributes to a peaceful, fair and prosperous society' (p. 4). Issues of social inclusion have been at the forefront of the local government agenda ever since the now deposed New Labour government established its social inclusion agenda of the late 1990s. Sport NI launched its 4-year 'Sport in Our Community' programme in April 2006 and invested almost £4 m in 34 different projects across Northern Ireland encompassing a range of diverse organizations. While the programme had three cross-cutting themes, interestingly using sport to ease community division is not explicitly outlined as one of them. Instead, as the Sport NI Community Sport Programme Impact Review (2005–2008) states, the programme aimed 'to improve the health and well-being of individuals and build community cohesion through increased participation of children, young people and adults in areas of high social need and groups traditionally marginalised in sport and physical activity' (p. 4). Following this statement, the document outlines four key areas of focus, with one being 'to develop capacity and build community participation and cohesion'. But there is no apparent indication around how such an ambiguous statement was to be delivered or indeed measured, either at the end of the funding period or periodically throughout the strategy's delivery.

Interestingly, by the time of the publication of the 2009–2010 annual report findings, mention of this 'key area' was absent from the 'Sport in Our Community' summary. Although 'Building Sport', a capital programme from Sport NI's Lottery Fund, also aimed 'to provide partnership funding for major capital projects designed to increase access to opportunities for sporting development and participation for as many people as possible' and by 'promoting equality of opportunity and good community relations', it was by no means clear how Sport NI planned to measure this most ambitious of outcomes. The investment by Sport NI's Lottery Fund programme was self-proclaimed as making a contribution to tackling social injustice and inequalities as 'the programme demonstrates the ability of sport to heal divided communities, improve health and well-being, and lift those most disadvantaged out of the poverty of aspiration.' Again any explanation of how this was to be achieved and how it might continue to make a contribution in the future was notably absent from this otherwise very desirable outcome. What evidence does Sport NI have to support this statement? Sport NI does admit in its annual review of 2010 that although online monitoring systems were in place, 'collecting and recording information across all projects is not consistent.' Although increases in participation figures within under-represented groups were detailed, these alone are not enough to ascertain whether sport can be used as a cohesive tool in Northern Irish society. The document does, however, recognize that, for the Sport Matters vision to be realized, a 'long-term cultural shift' in how people experience sport is required. However, whether this shift is expected to occur gradually over time or whether sport is regarded as a propellant to help make this cultural stride forward again remains unclear.

Midnight Soccer and Belfast Urban Sports

In the absence of any transparent, unambiguous and indeed validated outcomes around the investment in sport for community cohesion in Northern Ireland, it is left to the casual observer to ascertain whether some good is being achieved by a raft of externally funded projects across Northern Ireland. One of the country's best-known community sports development programmes, entitled Midnight Street Soccer (a late-night football league held at community sports venues in deprived urban areas), appears to be popular with potentially disenfranchised youth. This programme provides an alternative activity for young people aged 8–17 years at a time of the evening when communities are most vulnerable to anti-social and criminal behaviour. The leagues now culminate in the National Finals held in the JJB Soccer Dome in Dundalk, Republic of Ireland. The aims of Midnight Street Soccer are to promote new opportunities for participation in sport, especially among disadvantaged communities; to facilitate better understanding of diversity and difference within these communities; to improve youth provision at times when communities are vulnerable to anti-social activity; to maximize opportunities for improved social inclusion and community relations and to both develop sport in the community and the development of the community through sport. It would appear therefore that sports organizations target these types of young people who are simultaneously classified as being socially excluded, individuals most affected by the community divide in Northern Ireland and, so the logic follows, are most in need of some form of sporting intervention to address their potential exclusion from mainstream society.

As detailed in the annual review of 'Sport in Our Community', in order to develop the Midnight Street Soccer Programme, the original proponents of this scheme, the North Belfast Play Forum, were awarded an investment of £33,000 from Sport NI. Similarly the Brownlow Campus Sports Trust, based in Lurgan, County Armagh, was awarded funding of £15,000 for a part-time coordinator post alongside programme costs from the Sport NI Community Sport Programme investment award. A 12-week pilot league was staged at the Waterworks facility in Belfast and at Brownlow Campus Sports Trust on successive Saturday nights from 9.00 pm to midnight. More than 200 young people participated in a dedicated five-a-side league, which provided opportunities for young people from a range of communities to come together through sport, sometimes for the first time. Due to the success of this pilot scheme partnerships were established with other community sports development units and a second league commenced in August 2005 with a further two facilities becoming involved in the programme.

The main underlying element of this initiative was to educate young people, predominantly young males, about distancing themselves from sectarian and potentially racial behaviour within their local communities. Consequently, a community relations training programme was developed with the IFA for coaches and volunteers working on the programme. Anti-sectarian and anti-racism banners were also displayed at all participating facilities. Annually, on two separate occasions, 25 young people took part in 10 workshops and a number of football sessions as part of a 12-week training course. Workshops included self-reflection, shared interests, conflict and difference. After 10 weeks of team building and educational workshops, the young people of the Midnight Street Soccer Football Team travelled to Glasgow for a Good Relations Residential during which participants explored diverse cultures, toured Celtic Park and Ibrox stadiums and played a friendly match at the Ibrox Stadium against a Glasgow Rangers F.C. select team. Due to the perceived success of the programme, by the end of its second year, the Midnight Street Soccer initiative had become an established community sports development programme and had expanded to an additional 10 centres throughout Northern Ireland. The project was voted Northern Ireland National Lottery 'Best Sports Project' and a runner-up in the UK at the 2006 National Lottery Awards.

Following a seminar facilitated by Sport NI in February 2007, a number of Community Sport Programme projects expressed an interest in developing the concept of Midnight Street Soccer. The programme is currently running in seven venues across Belfast and a further eight facilities across Northern Ireland. Over 50 community organizations are now engaged in Midnight Street Soccer, in partnership with a range of statutory organizations, including district councils, the Youth Service, the PSNI, Probation Board for Northern Ireland and the Youth Justice Agency (YJA) targeting over 1000 young people during each league. The programme also provides employment for approximately 60 part-time football coaches. This type of coaching qualification initiative is also designed to improve the career prospects of these young people within their local communities.

> I started going to Midnight Street Soccer when I was 14. They run football training sessions and tournaments between 9 pm and midnight, when most of the problems happen. It doesn't matter if you're Catholic or Protestant – everyone just wants to play football and have fun. You might make a bad tackle, but you just say sorry and help them get up. When I play football I feel on top of the world and get a buzz about being able to socialise with different people. My mum says that the project has really helped my confidence and she's glad that it keeps me away from the drinking and drugs that some young people in my area are involved in. (Participant – Midnight Street Soccer Programme)

Another late-evening initiative which focuses on individual as opposed to team sport is taking place in Belfast and organized by Belfast Urban Sports (BUS), a charity which seeks to promote the lifestyle of urban sports as a form of positive intervention. BUS's 'Live It' initiative is based on the belief that urban sports are a powerful tool which can be used in some problematic communities to combat anti-social behaviour, sectarianism, social exclusion and obesity. One particular programme required 'Live It' to engage with high-risk and vulnerable young people in a rehabilitative role. Entitled the Priority Youth Offender Project (PYOP) this programme stemmed from the introduction of BUS's Saturday Night Skate Diversionary initiative, which involved diverting young people away from potentially troublesome situations where they were most vulnerable. The PYOP brings together staff from the YJA and the Probation Board of Northern Ireland who, in partnership, work with young offenders resident in the Greater Belfast area and whose offending behaviour has been deemed either persistent or serious. Up to six young offenders attend the T13 urban sports park for 3 h each week to perform community service duties, receive group counselling from their mentors and engage in the so-called urban sports. As a number of the BUS organizers are extreme and urban sports enthusiasts from around the world, they are able to talk with such young people, on their own level, as they too understood what it was like to be classed as an 'outsider' within society. One of the key messages they relay to the young people is that being different can be an advantage and that non-conforming is acceptable and achievable without breaking the law. Feedback from this scheme remains very positive, and BUS now engage in a continual rolling programme with the YJA and has been invited by the criminal justice agency to deliver a programme in the Woodlands Correctional Facility in Bangor. These young people are classed as some of the worst offending minors in Northern Ireland but BUS aims to develop their personal skills whilst also developing their confidence through engaging with urban sports, developing a respect for fellow participants and in turn their local communities.

> They channel their energy into sport, giving them the adrenaline rush they crave, but in a healthy way, helping themselves instead of harming others. By getting involved in something good in their community, they began to see themselves differently, capable of more than just being good at offending. As a worker I have noticed a real improvement in their self esteem and self confidence, a lot of which is down to the quality of the relationships the staff are able to build with young people ... the programme has diverted these young people away from anti-social behaviour and towards a happier and healthier future. (Ben Rayot, Youth Worker, YJA)

Due to the cross-community elements BUS promote within their programmes, successful funding from the European Commission's Peace III fund of £500 k was awarded for the Bridges Urban skate park in Belfast. Belfast City Council also invested £80 k while £50 k was received from the Landfill Tax Incentive scheme, as the new park utilizes what was previously waste ground. An urban sports development officer was also sought for the first time in Northern Ireland to deliver the key performance indicators required by the European funders and to help BUS fulfil their Urban Sports Development Plan. The naming of the skate park is supposed to represent using urban sports as a way of bridging the gaps between the two communities in Northern Ireland. Only time will tell if urban sports will have more success than comparatively well-established team sports, such as association football, in developing young people's attitudes to differences, in whatever form this may take, in Northern Ireland (Integrated Education Fund 2010).

Conclusion

This article has sought to contextualize the use of sport for the purposes of community integration in Northern Ireland. These efforts take place against a comparatively more peaceful political setting than was the case for most of that country's history. While mercifully Northern Ireland is no longer blighted by full-scale ethno-sectarian conflict, there remains some threat to an emerging peace from Irish republican splinter groups convinced that only a militant response to the British presence in Ireland will yield a sovereign and united Ireland. Thus, the path to peace has been far from straightforward for residents of Northern Ireland as the recent murder of PSNI Constable Ronan Kerr demonstrated. And yet this death gave rise to a remarkable outpouring of opposition by, among others, fellow members of the GAA. Mr Kerr's membership of the GAA allowed that organization the opportunity to reveal the full extent of its support for the new dispensation gaining traction in Northern Ireland. It also reminded erstwhile observers of the ongoing capacity of sport to make a considered difference to the lives of people living in all divided societies.

It was unfortunate therefore that the recently published CSI document, from the offices of the Northern Ireland executive, appeared to miss the point so blatantly by, among other obvious omissions, failing to properly reflect (or even acknowledge) sport's potential to contribute to a wider policy of community reconciliation. Of course, sport on occasions can achieve the exact opposite effect by exacerbating tensions and highlighting divisions. That said as the case studies contained in the latter part of this article confirm, used appropriately and judicially and supported by suitable levels of investment, sport really can contribute in a meaningful way to wider programmes of reconciliation and community cohesion. Of course, all these are not to overlook the very valid criticisms of others who suggest that the absence of a credible protocol in many cases to measure the exact outcome of sport's intervention is its fatal shortcoming. However, the motivation to address this must surely be present if one considers the apparent difference when programmes in some of the most troubled, indeed deprived, parts of Northern Ireland are profiled. Thus, it will be interesting to observe whether, in the future, such robust measures emerge and are included alongside other credible evidential forms of support in favour of these and other sporting programmes.

Notes

1. Submission to special issue of Sport in Society (Sport and Communities) Hassan, D. and Brown, S. (2014).
2. See, for example, *Daily Mail*, April 4, 2011, *Guardian*, April 6, 2011 and www.bbc.co.uk/ni (April 4–9, 2011).
3. In November 2001, the GAA repealed Rule 21 from its constitution, a ruling that up until this point had prevented members of the British security forces in Northern Ireland from joining the GAA. While the organization had received a great deal of criticism around the issue, it was able to point to a series of examples in Northern Ireland in which it appeared the police and British Army had been far from objective in its dealings with the nationalist community and the GAA in particular.
4. See, for example, http://www.tyronegaa.ie/2011/04/gaa-statement-on-ronan-kerr-murder/ (accessed April 03 2011).
5. PEACE III EU *Programme for Peace and Reconciliation, 2007–2013, Northern Ireland and the Border Region of Ireland Operational Programme*, SEUPB 2007.

References

Arthur, P. 1990. *Government & Politics of Northern Ireland*. London: Longman.
Coalter, F. 2008. "Sport-in-Development: Development for and Through Sport?" In *Sport and Social Capital*, edited by R. Hoy, and M. Nicholson, 34–46. London: Elsevier.
Community Relations Council. 2010. *Response to the Consultation on the Programme for Cohesion, Sharing and Integration Consultation*. Belfast: CRC.
Hamber, B., and G. Kelly. 2004. *A Working Definition of Reconciliation*. Occasional paper published by Democratic Dialogue Belfast: DD.
Hassan, D. 2005, February. "The GAA, Rule 21 and Police Reform in Northern Ireland." *Journal of Sport and Social Issues* 29 (1): 60–78.
Integrated Education Fund. 2010, September. *Developing the Economic Case for Shared Education*. Belfast: Oxford Economics.
Magill, C., A. Smith, and B. Hamber. 2010. *The Role of Education in Reconciliation*. Magee: University of Ulster.
McEvoy-Levy, S. 2006. *Troublemakers or Peacemakers? Youth and Post-Accord Peace Building*. New York: University of Notre Dame Press.
NI Executive. 2008. *Programme for Government 2008–2011*. Belfast: OFMDFM, http://www.northernireland.gov.uk/pfgfinal.pdf
NIMDM (Northern Ireland Multiple Deprivation Measure). 2010. Belfast: NISRA.

NIO. 1999. *A New Beginning: Policing in Northern Ireland. The Report of the Independent Commission on Policing for Northern Ireland*. Belfast: NIO.

OFMDFM. 2010, July. *Draft Programme for Cohesion, Sharing and Integration*. Belfast: OFMDFM.

Pawson, R. 2004. "Evaluating Ill-Defined Interventions with Hard-to-Follow Outcomes." A Paper presented to the ESRC seminar understanding and evaluating the impact of sport and culture on society, Leeds Met University, Jauary 17.

Shirlow, P., and B. Murtagh. 2006. *Belfast – Segregation, Violence & the City*. Dublin: Pluto.

Towards Sustainable Security: Interface Barriers & the Legacy of Segregation in Belfast. 2009. Belfast: Community Relations Council.

Weiss, M. 1996. "Sporting Participation Amongst Children." In *Worldwide Trends in Youth Sport* , edited by P. De Knop, L.-M. Engstrom, B. Skirstad, and M. Weiss, 25–39. Champaign, IL: Human Kinetics.

Women's toplessness on the Red Mile, Calgary, May–June 2004

Mary Valentich

Faculty of Social Work, University of Calgary, Calgary, Canada

During the hockey playoffs in May–June 2004, the Red Mile emerged, 14 blocks of 17th Ave. in Calgary, Alberta, Canada where fans congregated and partied. Much to the interest of media, onlookers and Internet followers, women began to lift their tops and reveal their breasts. Some proclaimed their behaviour as immoral and shameful; others perceived feminism as having failed. This article examines the experiences of six women who were interviewed in 2005 and raises questions about what they may have been expressing through their unusual behaviour and their right to do so.

In May 2004, the Calgary Flames ice hockey team made it to the NHL (National Hockey League) Stanley Cup playoffs. Cars were bedecked with red Flames flags and horns blared on evenings when there was a game. For many in this city of 933,495 Calgarians[1], game night was 'party-time'. In late afternoons, people would gather in the bars and restaurants of 17th Ave. which led to the Saddledome where the home games were played. After each game, fans, dressed in red shirts, poured into the street. The maximum estimate one night was 50,000 people, strolling up and down 14 blocks of 17th Ave., which the police had closed off to traffic. In this boisterous atmosphere, fans of all ages, including families would cavort and engage in super-friendly behaviour. Drinking occurred on the street although this is not legal in Canada. Police did intervene when drunken, disruptive behaviour presented a threat to persons and property. Later, there were rumours that sexual assaults had occurred in the back lanes. There was noise, music, crazy costumes and people generally having fun. The Red Mile had emerged and for some, the city finally had a heart – thousands of people, dressed in red, and eager for the Flames to win.

Burgener[2] asserted that:

> The essence of the Red Mile is about more than people shouting 'Go Flames Go'. It's about a gathering together of people as community. They are sharing a common experience of exuberance and solidarity and being a part of an event that in all the other ways the community supports and recognizes as emblematic of our city.

In the midst of this unusual phenomenon, women began to lift their tops and reveal their breasts. Possibly 40–50 women were involved: no one really knew. The men would start chanting one of the favourite chants – 'Take it off for Kiprusoff (the Flames' goalie)' – and some woman would lift her top. Cameras would flash. Another might dance and then lift her top. Some topless women were carried on the shoulders of their male friends. Usually the toplessness lasted only a few moments; the frenzy would heighten and then die down as people continued their strolling.

Word spread rapidly about the toplessness. Once pictures of topless women were on the Internet, Calgary received worldwide media attention. Women in Tampa, Florida where the Flames were playing against the Tampa Bay Lightning also began to lift their tops, seemingly in competition with the Calgary women for the most beauteous display. Calgary became a locale for the commercial 'Girls Gone Wild' phenomenon[3], much to the distress of some Calgarians whose letters to the editor suggested that these drunken, immoral women[4] were besmirching the city's positive reputation. Editorials were not kind to these women either, chastising them for their silly, immature and tasteless behaviour, likely fuelled by alcohol and low self-esteem[5].

The 2–1 loss by the Flames to the Tampa Bay Lightning in the seventh and final game on 7 June 2004 ended the breast-baring. With no reason for celebrating, the fans disappeared and the Red Mile disintegrated. Occasionally, over the next few years, there were reports of women lifting their tops at a few Canadian football games and in some bars. Reports surfaced from other countries, for example, Australia[6]. A Top Freedom Day of Pride event was held in Guelph, Ontario[7], but this was an organized event 'to help make it more acceptable for women to go topless in public'. Toplessness as presented on the Red Mile has thus far not been seen in Canada.

During the heyday of the Red Mile in 2004, reporters regularly turned to women's issues commentators to ask why the women were showing their breasts. Was it exhibitionism by women who had drunk a few too many? Were women simply responding to male pressure? What did the behaviour mean? Similar questions were raised by participants at the Canadian Sex Research Forum (CSRF) that met in the fall of 2004 and vigorously discussed a paper on Canadian attitudes towards female topless behaviour[8]. When I later learned that reporters had not talked to one woman who had lifted her top, I decided that a qualitative study was needed to understand the behaviour of going topless from the women's standpoint.

The purpose of this article is to report on the findings of a study conducted in 2005 when I interviewed six women who had responded to my request for women who had lifted their tops on the Red Mile. This study was designed to consider the experience of going topless from the perspectives of the women themselves. As a social worker involved in feminist organizing since the 1970s, I was distressed by the condemnation these women received from members of the public and media. Some people seemed to be very threatened by women's toplessness. What was the nature of the threat? Did the women's 'wildness' suggest that their sexuality was out-of-control? Would mayhem result? Personally receiving both criticism[9] and encouragement regarding the study itself, I became increasingly committed to presenting the perspectives of the women who came forward to be interviewed.

Research design and methodology

To understand the nature of the women's experience of going topless on 17th Ave. during the period of the Red Mile (May–June 2004), a qualitative method incorporating elements of a grounded theory approach was chosen[10]. Because there was little research on this topic, in-depth exploration was most appropriate. The study received institutional ethical approval from the University of Calgary Conjoint Faculties Research Ethics Board in January 2005.

Data were gained through semi-structured, face-to-face interviews lasting from one and a half to two hours at a time and place convenient for participants – a quiet restaurant, my university office or their home. Interviewees were asked to talk about their experience(s) in going topless on 17th Avenue after a playoff hockey game last May–June 2004, followed by appropriate prompts. Before the interview, participants signed consent forms to indicate their knowledge about the study and willingness to participate.

Within hours of posting flyers on the university campus in January 2005, a media furore erupted. Over the next six months, I gave 60 interviews to callers from Canada, United States, England and Ireland. Despite the occasional joking tone of sports reporters, the interviewers were courteous and respectful. Usually, after a local interview, a prospective interviewee would call. I also received five calls from women who had not been on the Red Mile, but who occasionally went topless and wanted to share their perceptions about behaviour known only in their private circles.

The sample included six women whose interviews occurred over a five-month period. There were two additional women with whom interviews were set up twice, but who did not show. There were several calls from women who met the criteria, but who chose not to proceed with a face-to-face interview. Despite considerable efforts to locate participants, only four fully met the criteria of actually lifting their tops on the Red Mile. I included two others who showed strong interest in the research topic and felt they could contribute to the study's purpose: a 75-year-old woman who called twice and had come close to taking her top off; and a woman in her twenties who had worn what she described as a very revealing top.

All interviews were audiotaped and transcribed, with the complete transcription provided to each woman for her review and written approval. The latter was obtained in a short follow-up interview with each woman. Subsequently, all transcribed interviews were coded in terms of the discrete items in the women's responses to the major question about the nature of her experience in going topless on the Red Mile. Twenty-five categories resulted which were ultimately grouped into seven major sets of responses. These major categories provided a framework for organizing and understanding the women's perspectives on their toplessness.

A literature search, conducted during the course of the research, primarily informed the analysis of the findings, thereby facilitating the emergence of the key theoretical ideas for understanding the behaviour of the participants with respect to their toplessness.

Literature review

Since the early 1990s, Herold and his research associates have been reporting on attitudes towards female toplessness in various contexts. Fischtein, Herold, and Desmarais[11] noted that while women in Canada have been able to go topless in public since Gwen Jacobs' precedent setting court win in Ontario in 1996[12], few Canadian women have actually engaged in this behaviour. They found that Canadians were most accepting of female topless behaviour on the beach and least accepting on the street; context was the important variable relating to attitudes towards female toplessness. In an earlier study of female topless behaviour on Australian beaches, Herold, Corbesi, and Collins[13] conducted a questionnaire survey of 116 female psychology students, about half of whom had been topless at a public beach. They found:

> Those who had ever gone topless were less likely to believe that going topless was sexual, had more permissive sexual attitudes, attended church less often, had a more favourable attitude to going topless, believed that the community approved of topless behaviour, believed that significant others were approving of topless behaviour, and had higher self-esteem and higher body image.[14]

The most commonly reported reasons for going topless in the study by Herold, Corbesi, and Collins[15] was to get an even tan (77%), enjoying the sense of freedom (53%) and naturalness of toplessness (42%), with very few (15%) saying they went because their friends went or to feel sexier (8%). Herold, Corbesi, and Collins identified Gagnon's[16] scripting theory, involving three levels of script, as a useful framework for understanding women's toplessness in public:

> ... *cultural scenarios* can be thought of as the instructional guides that exist at all levels of collective life ... The instructions for roles are embedded in narratives (the scripts for the specific role) and they provide the understandings that make role entry, performance and exit plausible ... *Interpersonal scripts* operate at the level of social interaction and the acceptance and use of such scripts are the basis for continued patterns of structured social behaviour...*Intrapsychic scripts* represent the content of mental life and are in part the resultant of the content of cultural scenarios and the demands of interaction and are in part, independent of them.[17]

The reasons for going topless as reported by Herold, Corbesi, and Collins[18] sound similar to those expressed by individuals in a major participant observation study of American attitudes towards nudity entitled *The Nude Beach*[19]. The researchers concluded that public nudity was a complex phenomenon, with American society in the 1970s quite ambivalent about sex and body freedom. While public nudity was quite threatening for some, Douglas, Rasmussen, and Flanagan[20] proposed that participants on the nude beach may have used their nudity as a kind of 'creative deviance' – a creative act that involves searching and creating new ways of doing things, for the purpose of solving some problem or making life better.

Forsyth[21] studied Mardi Gras parade strippers, women who exposed their breasts for 'throws', usually trinkets or beads. He also concluded that parade stripping may be a form of 'creative deviance,' observing that Mardi Gras day in New Orleans was a time when normally forbidden behaviours were permitted: not only did women show their breasts in the parade and on balconies, but people also walked around virtually nude and members of the gay community dressed in extreme costumes. Women indicated that they did it for the beads, because they were drunk and being encouraged, they liked to show off their breasts, for fun, the shock value and on a dare. Only one woman said that she did it for sexual reasons, that is, it made her feel young and seductive, with her breasts being her best feature.

Herold, Corbesi, and Collins[22], in their study of male Australian students' attitudes towards female toplessness, considered whether exposure of women's breasts or full nudity on public beaches was sexually provocative. They found that women did not necessarily see female toplessness as sexual, but both women and men tended to think that men would see it as sexual. Additionally, the majority of the 49 male psychology students agreed that women had the right to go topless, that it gave them a sense of personal freedom and meant greater liberation[23]. However, 61% of the men believed that topless women were more likely to arouse men and 30% felt that the topless women were more likely to be sexually assaulted.

A History of the Breast[24] provides the most comprehensive examination of changing societal perspectives on women's breasts. Through identification of the art and socio-political circumstances of various historical eras in Western history, Yalom identified the following chronological periods, beginning in prehistoric times: the Sacred Breast, the erotic, domestic, political, psychological, commercialized, liberated, medical and finally, the breast in crisis. Yalom asked: 'who owns the breast?'[25] and proposed that for most of Western history, women's breasts have been controlled by men, 'whether the control was exercised individually by husbands and lovers, or collectively by male-dominated institutions like the church, the state, and medicine'[26].

Yalom identified the late 1960s and 1970s as the period when second-wave feminists focused on the symbol of the breast, with 'bra-burning.' Women protested the over-eroticization of women in general and breasts in particular. Female breast-baring became a way of expressing defiance at the society that constrained women. Yalom stated that the 'breast emerged as a powerful marker of women's new situation'[27], one where women were making more choices about work and family. Then, women's health issues, especially breast cancer, became central in the women's liberation movement. Women portrayed their breasts in various art forms, even calendars of women who had experienced mastectomies and reconstructive surgery. Yalom believed that by the late 1990s women were taking charge of their own breasts, but still remained anxious about them and the future of the world.

Abu-Laban and McDaniel[28] summarized the various management strategies used historically 'to reshape women, in whatever image happens to be currently acceptable to those with the power to define it'[29]. These devices, often painful and harmful, ranged from restrictive bands to 'falsies,' 'padded bras,' 'push-up' padded bras and the current flocking to elective breast surgery to either augment or diminish one's breasts. That many persons are still upset about public visibility of women's breasts is evident by the frequent outbreaks of controversy regarding where women should be able to breastfeed their babies. The organization Topfree Equal Rights Association (TERA)[30] may be seen as a counter to those who wish to control how women present their breasts. Its purpose is to help 'women who encounter difficulty going without tops in public places in Canada and the USA, and informs the public on this issue'[31].

How women present any aspect of their bodies is usually a matter of considerable societal concern. In Canada and the United States, younger women in particular, have adopted styles of dress since the 1990s that have elicited negative comments. They started showing more cleavage, wearing low-cut jeans and t-shirts with 'sexy' messages. Whether this attire stemmed from influences such as the Spice Girls, the emergence of 'girl power' or whether younger women simply wished to assert their own way of dressing, their feminism and their sexuality is up for debate[32]. Recent research indicates that some younger women are not comfortable with clothing that suggests the 'whore' or 'slut' image and deride their peers for their inappropriate attire[33].

Dressing in a more provocative style has been considered as hypersexualization of women and a return to the objectification of women's bodies that feminists of the 1970s and 1980s derided. Levy's *Female Chauvinist Pigs: Women and the Rise of Raunch Culture*[34] has received much attention for proclaiming that women have lost their way with respect to ideals of feminism and their own self-worth. She detailed the myriad of ways in which women in the United States were manifesting their sexy selves. Some of the same skimpy attire, pole dancing and *Girls Gone Wild* productions are evident in Canada[35]. Levy found herself mistrusting her interviewees' remarks about such behaviour being 'empowering' and became disgusted by 'a tawdry, tarty, cartoonable version of female sexuality that has become so ubiquitous'[36]. Ross (as cited in Racco[37]) has a contrasting view:

> We're seeing a reincarnation of the vamp and the vixen, but this time it's on female terms ... This is solely about the sexual emancipation of women ... Today in this era of post-feminism, lots of women want to throw off the shackles of restraint and experience and explore sexuality in many different ways.

On the other hand, Sullivan, commented on the 'famous flashing girls on the Red Mile'[38] as follows: 'Those girls were taking off their shirts after mobs of guys yelled'. She was differentiating between 'exhilarating nude moments' and 'titillating nakedness', noting that 'there is a very significant dividing line between these forms of nudity'[39]. In her view, women showing their breasts on the Red Mile were simply acting as sex objects.

Findings

The women's responses to the central question about their going topless on the Red Mile were grouped into seven major categories that provide a framework for understanding their experiences.

Characteristics of the sample

Five of the women ranged in age from 18 years to early 30s, with the sixth woman aged 75 years. Two lived outside Calgary; two had resided near 17th Ave. for many years. Two were full-time university or post-secondary students and also working part-time; two others had taken some university or college courses at some point. While one was retired from the active work force, their current and past work included human services, retail and the health sector. None reported a current religious affiliation, although two had been raised as Catholics. One mentioned her indigenous status, but thought it had no bearing on her experience on the Red Mile.

Three were closely involved with their families, one being in business with her mother. Two had some contact with their families, one of whom was in another province. With two exceptions, the rest had generally supportive families. One felt her parents did not understand her, but she identified a couple of favourite aunts who were described as models of spunky women. Another had been estranged from her family for some time. She viewed her parents as 'original fun-loving hippies' who could not handle alcohol. After their divorce, the father had remarried, but the stepmother was generally disapproving of her stepdaughter. In the interview, the study participant suggested that the best route for understanding her and other women's toplessness was to explore the woman's relationship with her parents.

Two were living with their boyfriends; another two had serious relationships with men who did have some problem with their going topless. By the spring of 2005, these relationships had ended.

All had prior experience with going topless, with the most common while swimming or in a hot tub. One had gone topless on a beach in France. Another, over a decade ago, had supported Gwen Jacobs by going topless in the food area of a racing car rally. One participant had previously won a wet t-shirt contest as well as being chosen to be a newspaper 'Beauty'. Several went to the Red Mile with friends more than once, but went topless only once.

The Red Mile: a Calgary happening

The participants were quite uniform in their descriptions of the Red Mile, highlighting the fact that 'everyone's going to be there'. None had anticipated just how crowded it would be in the restaurants, bars and on the 14 blocks of 17th Ave. leading from the Saddledome to 14th St. Melrose Café, and other favourite spots were 'insanely packed'. The noise level was high with talk, shouting and music; people were moving slowly, occasionally stopping to chat, arms draped over each other's shoulders. Mostly they were young adults, but also family groups and older folks. The crowds were generally well-behaved, with the police watchful for any trouble. Most study participants reported that they, like others on the Red Mile, had at least one drink.

Participants reported that periodically, the men would begin to chant: 'show us your tits'. Sometimes, to the crowd's delight, a woman would show her breasts, if only for a moment. All noted the flash bulbs popping and the occurrence of a 'paparazzi moment'. Another woman would get up on her male friend's shoulders and then, lift her top. The crowd loved it: as one woman put it: 'who would diss you if you were showing your breasts?'

The study participants all knew that the media were present on the Red Mile. Daily news featured activities on the Red Mile, in particular, its breast-baring women who were becoming known as the Flames Girls. The Internet prompted worldwide attention and a Flames Girls website emerged. With the exception of the participant who wore the provocative top, the possibility of being on the Internet was not a deterrent, but rather an enticement.

While five women in the study found the crowd friendly, the one who wore the unique top noted that eventually she found the chanting tiresome, especially when she did not show her breasts and the chanting increased. The woman who lost her friend in the crowd also became irritated with the chanting. No participant reported fear, nor did they experience unwanted touching other than occasional bumping into people.

All participants thought that Calgary was experiencing an unusual moment in its history, perhaps never to be repeated. Three of them felt they were part of something larger, something beyond the everyday. One noted cynically that for the guys it was the best of all worlds – 'boobs and hockey!' Another mentioned proudly that women showing their breasts were doing something that the men could not do! (Actually some men did go topless, but with no particular crowd response.) A couple of the participants asserted that they (and other women) were the Flames Girls or the Girls of the Red Mile – a unique selection of women. The women believed that the Calgary Flames were 'on the edge' of hockey history and that they were a part of that special moment. They reported feeling positive about the team, some describing themselves as 'huge hockey fans'. They wanted to support them and felt badly when they lost. By showing their breasts and getting up on men's shoulders, they indicated that they were giving the team something special.

Before, during and after going topless

Before

All except one of the women knew about the toplessness before their going to the Red Mile: the prominent response was – 'that sounded like fun'. One told a friend that she was going to do it, as she had always wanted to do it. Another stated that she had not planned to do it, but might 'if the conditions were right on the street and the mood hits me'. Another commented: 'I'm not shy; what the heck!' One noted that she did not experience peer pressure. The older woman stopped short of toplessness when she imagined her grandchildren viewing her on television. She also regretted that her male companion could not lift her to his shoulders.

Only one woman was not in a particularly positive mood before going on the street. Her 'friends had been somewhat snotty and had booted them out of the condo and I was drinking before going out on the street'. This younger woman described not finding a bar where there was room to enter and finally buying some juice and liquor for street consumption. The one wearing her unique top did not intend to show her breasts, but had carefully planned her outfit, taking pride in creating something striking that reflected her position – 'not wanting to be eye-candy for men, but still anticipating attention'.

Even the woman who felt negative about the crowd had already lifted her top to friends in a passing car, possibly 'preparing herself' for a later performance. Another had carefully chosen a pink t-shirt for wearing after her toplessness so that people would recall her; she noted that her family had always said that she would be 'famous' and she could readily envision herself as a model or actor or someone whose picture was in the magazines.

Before lifting their tops, several participants recalled seeing some other women on the street going topless, some of whom they felt they could identify with – 'regular girls', but not with others who seemed less 'classy', even 'sleazy'. The women in this study differentiated themselves from those that 'showed too much of themselves', 'strutted around' or 'seemed out of control'.

One woman had pre-planned that she might dance on a raised platform in advance of lifting her top. The one who had previously supported Gwen Jacobs hesitated about lifting her top as she was no longer a 'young chick' but when the group rounded up a 'big cowboy' who could easily lift her to his shoulders, she decided to go ahead. She acknowledged that Canada, with its diversity, was mixed in its views about women's toplessness, but she felt it was important to take a stand on matters in which she believed.

During

Women interviewed in this study varied in their thoughts about the brief time they were topless: 'it was a big courage thing to do' to 'not a shy moment, but no big deal' to 'men have nipples, so do I!' to 'hard to do because of the unfair gender difference (in the crowd)' to 'unique way to celebrate'. One woman was slightly caught off guard when male friends lifted her and her friend's tops in unison, but decided it was a 'fun thing' of no particular consequence. The woman who was angered by the crowd when she could not find her friend echoed the 'no big deal' comment, but felt she had little power in the crowd as 'she couldn't shut them up, even by going topless'. A few of the others indicated feeling a power over the crowd of chanting men and they loved the paparazzi experience of all the flashbulbs popping. Another felt 'patriotic' and relished 'going on tv, taking a stand about being equals and being accountable for yourself'.

None described the toplessness as a sexual act, although the woman wearing the provocative top remarked on her attire as being 'for the pleasure of the men'. One felt the experience was 'exciting, a response to the hype in the street, and the fake Stanley Cup'. Because it was exciting, she let herself be carried around for a while, lifting and lowering her top occasionally. She indicated that her behaviour could be both sexual or a show of power 'depending on what she wanted to do' She appreciated that breasts were perceived in Canadian society as sexual objects, but for her it was a 'rite de passage' – taking a stand about who she was. Another noted that it was an 'expression of individuality and that's how she got gutsy about doing it'.

The women's perception of the street scene was that people were friendly, respectful and even protective. They were all aware that 'guys went insane as if they had never seen boobs'. A few mentioned that they gave no individual eye contact during the performance and they always knew that a friend was nearby if needed. The actual lifting of tops lasted only a few moments, except for the one who danced for several minutes capping her performance by showing her breasts. The toplessness was longest, but periodic for the woman on the man's shoulders.

All the women spontaneously commented that they felt good about their bodies and their breasts in particular. The one in her early thirties was slightly concerned about her weight, but thought she measured up pretty well when she saw the Florida women on the Internet. In her view, the Calgary women were somehow more 'wholesome'.

After

Immediately after showing their breasts, the women reported feeling a degree of elation. They had succeeded in either fulfilling their plans or doing a somewhat 'daredevilish' thing. Several mentioned 'breaking the rules' and feeling good about doing so. Another two women stated that 'there was really nothing negative about doing it'. One stated that she was not ashamed, another stated that she was not remorseful. One kept her pink top on to 'let people know she was the one' who had shown her breasts. A few said that their friends had surrounded them physically, in a kind of protective way, although they felt no risk. Most noted that the friends who had accompanied them had expressed positive sentiments, verbally or by gesture. The woman wearing her own unique top indicated that her male friends looked down on toplessness, questioning why a guy would encourage women to take their tops off, unless 'maybe he wasn't getting any'.

One woman reported getting an 'earful' from her boyfriend on her return to their apartment. She had not yet told him about her activities on the Red Mile, but her picture had gotten on the Internet and someone had told him.

Three women stated that they felt very positive the next week because their pictures were on the Internet: 'I got on the Red Mile; it's history and I'm part of it'. Another noted that it might be 'insignificant history' but she would be there in the picture books that kids might see when they studied the Red Mile. A third said that her Mom was 'proud of her'. One woman estimated that maybe 5% of her acquaintances were uncomfortable whereas the rest were 'ok'. Three said they might do it again, if the conditions were right and they felt like it.

One woman did hear some nasty remarks at work, but she confronted the person who had made reference to 'sluts' and felt that the matter was resolved when she challenged the individual to 'not judge a book by its cover'. The woman who had been drunk felt regretful about being a 'bad drunk', not about her toplessness. Her friends had been upset about her drinking, but she had, by the time of the interview, 'dealt with it'.

Overall, these women, nearly seven to eight months later, were not reporting negative consequences either from friends or family although some were initially surprised. Two said their families brushed off their topless behaviour as 'there she goes again'. The adult children of the 75-year-old women had commented that 'mother was always doing something!'

Self-perceptions of participants

Participants readily offered descriptors of their personal, physical and social characteristics. Their common self-perceptions included being people-oriented, outgoing, loving to interact, insightful about others and 'daredevilish', that is, willing to break the rules especially if they seemed overly constraining. They liked to express their views, could and would speak out if they thought a situation warranted it. A couple noted that they enjoyed the power over men that they had experienced on the Red Mile.

Four of the women mentioned liking to dress in their own unique style that resulted in their being known for a particular look. Two indicated feeling slightly insecure about what others thought, but also expecting a lot from themselves.

Four of them commented that they were usually surprising their families: they were the unusual ones in the family – either the black sheep or given to unexpected behaviour or likely to provoke people, keep others on edge or be 'crazier than the next'. A couple mentioned liking the attention on the Red Mile, but said that they did not see themselves as exhibitionists. A few saw themselves as risk takers, both physically and socially, and occasionally getting into 'trouble' but still liking the 'rush'.

Ideological perspectives of participants

Several of them expressed concern about women's status as equals: they supported women's rights, were angry about women being exploited or treated as sex objects, did not want to be ruled out of contention for a job because of being a woman, and believed in standing up for themselves.

Two said that they could be identified as feminists – the older woman and the one who had made her unique top. Another said she was not a *'crazy* feminist'. One did not see herself as a feminist although she expressed some of the above beliefs. The supporter of Gwen Jacobs called herself a liberal. They all presented themselves as women who were determined to live their lives as they saw fit, despite occasional opposition that some had experienced from family members, female friends or boyfriends. Several espoused a 'live and let live' tolerance.

None felt ashamed of their breasts or what they had done. 'I'm young and what the heck! This is my life' summed up one participant's position. Another stated: 'I'm going to have fun with my life and not let my boyfriend dictate my public life'. Two others expressed similar convictions about 'being out there and taking off my shirt' as one of those things where 'one person can make a difference'.

Discussion of findings

Given the small number of interviewees, the findings pertain only to the study participants. Nonetheless, ideas and questions about women's experience of toplessness may emerge for further consideration.

A major concept that pertains to understanding the toplessness of the interviewees involved the *context* of the Red Mile. Had it not been perceived as a very special happening in the city, where people were interacting in a friendly, party manner, these women would likely not have gone topless. In this *context*, they felt safe and generally, supported by others. Within this *context*, the study participants, with one exception, presented their act of toplessness as an act of *celebration*, featuring one or more of the following components: *having fun; making an offering/showing support or breaking the rules*. In other words, the concept of *celebration* could be manifest, according to the participants, through varying ways, but all were indicative of rejoicing in the achievement of the Flames.

In contrast to the idea of *celebration*, for one participant, going topless may be understood as an act of *defiance*, characterized by the feature of *expressing anger*. While she also experienced the Red Mile as a special event in Calgary's history, she expressed some distress about the crowd when she could not locate her friend and she became annoyed with the chanting. She recognized her anger in lifting her top, in a sense, to deal with the crowd.

The interviewees' responses regarding their toplessness on the Red Mile also suggested links between the act of lifting their tops and how the women saw themselves or who they believed they were in the process of becoming. Thus, their toplessness, in their views, pertained to their *identity*, with one or more of the following aspects involved: *being a celebrity such as an actor or model; being a part of history; being a Flames Girl; making a political statement* and *seeking a remedy*. Such facets of *identity* were known by some participants at the time of their going topless on the Red Mile; others surfaced later, when the women reflected on their act of toplessness.

None of the interviewees fit the prevailing stereotype of the thoughtless, drunken woman responding primarily to the pressure of the crowd, ready to subject herself to the demands of the men, without consideration of her own sense of self. Even the woman who acknowledged her excessive drinking at the time viewed her behaviour in lifting her top as somehow related to unresolved issues in her relationship with her parents.

All the women in this study saw themselves as having a *choice* about how they presented themselves on the Red Mile and all supported a woman's *right to choose*. The study participants believed themselves to be conscious agents and valued their capacity to make choices about how to present themselves. However, they all recognized that men would likely see toplessness as sexual, although some also believed they controlled the extent to which they wished to present their behaviour as sexualized. Further, most of the interviewees could appreciate that their behaviour might be viewed by others as an objectification of their bodies in response to male demands.

In this regard, Levy's perspective[40] on the development of a raunch culture, especially among younger women, may be relevant: are women simply falling back into traditional gender role behaviours that involve sexual objectification of women's bodies? The commercialization of women showing their breasts is quite evident in the *Girls Gone Wild* videos, some of which focused on women on the Red Mile.

Yalom's[41] question comes to mind: who owns the breast? The women in the study did not see themselves as simply succumbing to the crowd's pressure. Possibly they were more typical of women in Yalom's era of the 'liberated breast'. They were, in a sense, acting in spirit with the women of both second- and third-wave feminism in asserting the right of women to present their bodies as they saw fit. A journalist, Blatchford[42] captured the relative ease that the participants experienced in going topless on the Red Mile as well as the variability in purpose:

> There is hardly a woman of my acquaintance who has not flashed her bra, or more. I have witnessed it done in bars, cars, parties, restaurants and certain offices. It may express any number of things. It may be about showing off a new or particularly nice bra. It may be about flirting; it may be a gesture of contempt, born in a sort of, look-what-you can't have spirit.[43]

Vogels[44] offers a moderate sex-related perspective on young women and their current, somewhat flamboyant, sexual expression. She wonders if young women are leading a new sexual revolution or are they just trying to have fun[45]. She sees younger women as less guilty about sexual expression, more liberal about premarital sex, and currently more accepting of sexual behaviour such as oral sex.

The findings in this study, although limited by sample size, may lead to the question of whether women's 'wildness' as expressed by showing their breasts on the Red Mile is indicative of some dissatisfaction that women have with the constraints still in place with respect to women's sexuality. Breast cancer survivors through their topless portraits have proclaimed their dissatisfaction with being relegated to asexuality. However, men of any age in North America have no qualms about taking their shirts off in numerous contexts. Women may well be saying[46]: what is wrong with our bodies that we must stay covered up? Does the 'covering up' and remaining mysterious, forbidden, available only under pre-determined conditions, foster the sexual objectification of women?

Finally, at the cultural level, the Red Mile was an unusual, thus far never repeated phenomenon in Calgary. Reports in the media regularly confirmed the fact that Calgary had never experienced such an outpouring of emotion and a show of loyalty to the Calgary Flames. Fortney[47] summed up the scene and its significance as follows:

> While Calgarians have always been known for getting behind our teams, this was over the top (even for us): in addition to screaming our lungs out for a crew that made us believe hard work and heart could trump big-market money, we showed our colours every way we could. The city became a sea of red... Was it a metaphor for the oil boom, the prosperity spilling into Canada's most vibrant city? Or was it just a manifestation of our basic nature: we are a young, enthusiastic city fuelled by joie de vivre, this time lit with a flaming C.[48]

It has been a long time since the Calgary Olympics in 1988 when the city had also come to life, but this was different. For the women in this study, the Red Mile was a once in a lifetime experience and it was, in that context, that they dared to engage in their unusual behaviour.

Conclusion

The study findings, albeit based on the responses of only six women, have shown that every behaviour should be evaluated within its context. Generalization of findings to seemingly similar behaviours is risky, given that the behaviour may have different meanings to the participants. Nonetheless, women's breasts and where they can be visible in today's world remains a contentious issue, one where public judgments easily assign women to the 'slut' category characterized by reliance on her sexual attributes to achieve her goals. Were some women on the Red Mile daring society to let women make their own decisions about their bodies? Not men, the medical profession, media or academic experts on women's issues. It behoves researchers and social workers whose clientele are largely women, to listen and discern their messages, without moralizing. The journey for women to own their breasts and make their decisions about them is ongoing.

Notes

1. 2009 Civic Census Summary, Historical Population Summary, http://www.calgary.ca/DocGallery/Bu/cityclerks/city.pdf (accessed February 24, 2011).
2. P. Burgener, 'Red Mile Opportunity for the Community', *Calgary Herald*, May 4, 2006, B4.
3. L. Dohy, 'Red Mile Showcases for 50,000 Smiles', *Calgary Herald*, June 4, 2004, A2.
4. R. Stapher, letter to the editor, 'Just Acting Like Boobs', *Calgary Herald*, December 31, 2005, A25.
5. 'No mystery on Red Mile', *Calgary Herald*, January 21, 2005, A18.
6. 'Mob Demands Women Flash at "Family Event"', *Calgary Herald*, January 8, 2008, A9.
7. '200 Women to Doff Shirts in Guelph', *The Globe and Mail*, August 28, 2010, A5.
8. Fischtein, Herold, and Desmarais, 'Canadian Sex Research Forum'.
9. 'No mystery on Red Mile', *Calgary Herald*, January 21, 2005, A18.
10. K. Charmaz, 'Grounded Theory: Objectivist and Constructivist Methods'.
11. Fischtein, Herold, and Desmarais, 'Canadian Sex Research Forum'.
12. D. DeCloet, *Another Blessing from Ontario, Alberta Report*, 24, No. 28, June 23, 1997, 38.
13. Herold, Corbesi and Collins, 'Psychosocial Aspects of Female'.
14. Ibid., 133.
15. Ibid., 133–142.

16. Gagnon, 'The Explicit and Implicit'.
17. Ibid., 9, 10.
18. Herold, Corbesi, and Collins, 'Psychosocial Aspects of Female'.
19. Douglas, Rasmussen, and Flanagan, *The Nude Beach*.
20. Ibid.,239.
21. Forsyth, 'Parade Strippers'.
22. Herold, Corbesi and Collins, 'Attitudes Toward Female Topless'.
23. Ibid., 179.
24. Yalom, *A History of the Breast*.
25. Ibid., 3.
26. Ibid., 241.
27. Ibid., 248.
28. Abu-Laban and McDaniel, 'Beauty, Status, and Aging'.
29. Ibid., 118.
30. Topfree Equal Rights Association (TERA), http://www.tera.ca (accessed January 24, 2005), 1–34.
31. Ibid., 1.
32. Munford, 'Wake up and Smell the Lipgloss'.
33. S. Proudfoot, 'Teenage Girls Walk Tightrope over Clothing', *Calgary Herald*, April 17, 2009, A15.
34. Levy, *Female Chauvinist Pigs*.
35. J. Timson, 'Girls Gone Raunch', *Macleans*, September 26, 2005, 38–42.
36. Ibid.
37. M. Racco, 'Good Girls Do', *The Globe and Mail*, April 8, 2006, L2.
38. K.H. Gray, 'I Am so Naked', *Swerve*, February 4, 2005, 13.
39. Ibid.
40. Levy, *Female Chauvinist Pigs*.
41. Yalom, *A History of the Breast*.
42. C. Blatchford 'Flashing's Busting Out All Over', *Globe and Mail*, December 18, 2004, A. 23. [AQ 2005/2004]
43. Ibid.
44. J. Vogels, 'Campus Gone Wild', *Destinations*, August/September, 2006, 301–41.
45. Ibid., 301.
46. '200 Women to Doff Shirts in Guelph', *The Globe and Mail*, August 28, 2010, A5.
47. V. Fortney, 'Painting the Town Red', *Swerve*, December 24, 2004, 6–7.
48. Ibid., 6.

References

Abu-Laban, S.M., and S.A. McDaniel. 'Beauty, Status, and Aging'. In *Feminist Issues: Race, Class and Sexuality*, edited by N. Mandell, 108–33. Toronto: Prentice-Hall, 2001.
Charmaz, K. 'Grounded Theory: Objectivist and Constructivist Methods'. In *Handbook of Qualitative Research*, edited by N.K. Denzin and Y.S. Lincoln, 509–35. Thousand Oaks, CA: Sage.
Douglas, J.D., P.K. Rasmussen, and C.A. Flanagan. *The Nude Beach*. Beverly Hills, CA: Sage, 1977.
Fischtein, D., E. Herold, and S. Desmarais. 'Canadian Sex Research Forum: Conference Abstracts'. 2004 Fredericton, New Brunswick, 8–10 October.
Forsyth, C.J. 'Parade Strippers: A Note on Being Naked in Public'. *Deviant Behavior: An Interdisciplinary Journal* 13 (1992): 391–403.
Gagnon, J.H. 'The Explicit and Implicit Use of the Scripting Perspective in Sex Research'. *Annual Review of Sex Research* 1 (1990): 1–43.
Herold, E., B. Corbesi, and J. Collins. 'Psychosocial Aspects of Female Topless Behavior on Australian Beaches'. *The Journal of Sex Research* 31 (1994): 133–42.
Herold, E., Corbesi, B., and J. Collins. 'Attitudes Toward Female Topless Beach Behavior: A Study of Male Australian University Students'. *Canadian Journal of Human Sexuality* 4 (1995): 4177–82.
Levy, A. *Female Chauvinist Pigs*. New York: Free Press, 2005.

Munford, R. ''Wake Up and Smell the Lipgloss': Gender, Generation and the (A) Politics of Girl Power'. *Third Wave Feminism*, edited by Stacy Gillis, Gillian Howe and Rebecca Munford, 142–53. New York: Palgrave MacMillan, 2004.

2009 Civic Census Summary. 'Historical Population Summary'. http://www.calgary.ca/DocGallery/Bu/cityclerks/city.pdf (accessed February 24, 2011).

Topfree Equal Rights Association (TERA). 2005 http://www.tera.ca (accessed January 24, 2005), 1–34.

Yalom, M. *A History of the Breast*. New York: Ballantine Books, 1997.

Volunteer roles, involvement and commitment in voluntary sport organizations: evidence of core and peripheral volunteers

Caroline Ringuet-Riot, Graham Cuskelly, Chris Auld and Dwight H. Zakus

Department of Tourism, Hotel and Sport Management, Griffith Business School, Griffith University, Nathan, QLD, Australia

The nature and scope of volunteer involvement in sport is well established; however, research indicates that involvement in community sport volunteering is under threat (Cuskelly, G., 2005. 'Volunteer Participation Trends in Australian Sport.' In *Volunteers in Sports Clubs*, edited by G. Nichols and M. Collins. Eastbourne: Leisure Studies Association; Cuskelly, G., T. Taylor, R. Hoye, and S. Darcy, 2005. *Volunteers in Community Rugby*. Sydney: ARU). Trends indicate that volunteer hours per individual are decreasing and this can have significant implications for the successful operation of voluntary sport organizations (VSOs) and the subsequent benefits for participants and the communities in which they operate. This paper extends knowledge of the nature of volunteer engagement in sport by exploring the categorization of sport volunteers as 'core' or 'peripheral' based on self-reported levels of involvement and commitment within VSOs. Using a survey of 243 sport volunteers across three sports, we identified significant differences between core and peripheral volunteers based on their levels of involvement and commitment in their self-identified primary sport organization roles. Implications of these findings for volunteer recruitment and retention and for the provision of sport participation opportunities in the community are addressed.

Introduction

The basic premise of this paper is the central and important role of sport volunteers. Without volunteers, no sport or sport system is possible. Volunteers are the heart of the wide base of developmental sport and a key factor underpinning the viability of sport events, whether weekly or major competitions. To further understand, develop and advance the sport system, the contribution of volunteers must be nurtured and supported. This paper seeks to extend knowledge of the nature of volunteer engagement in sport and suggests initiatives to enhance the sport volunteer experience.

Understanding the voluntary sport sector and volunteer participation is critically important for the long-term sustainability of most sport delivery systems (Stewart et al. 2004). Stewart et al.'s (2004) typology of sport practice suggests that volunteering is a central factor in the operation of all aspects of the national sport systems of westernized democracies and thus provides a key element for all four segments of sport practice: recreational, spontaneous, exercise and high-performance sport. The significance of the volunteer contribution is further emphasized through the policy focus and degree of policy attention on sport and its potential role in delivering a wide range of social goals. Recent reviews of both sport and health policies in Australia (e.g. Australian Sports Commission 2008a, 2008b, 2009), and amongst most Western nations, highlight the importance and contribution of the voluntary sport sector, thereby providing a focus on the sector as a means to increase participation in sport and physical activity for preventative physical and mental health, amongst a broader set of goals.

Voluntary sport organizations (VSOs) are the community entities that are generally considered to comprise the base of sport delivery systems. To analyze volunteers in this study, VSOs were operationally defined as:

> nonprofit organizations formally constituted to provide members with opportunities to participate in organized sport and physical activities within particular team or individual sports. VSOs are separate from the state, independently governed and operated by volunteer management committees or boards, and do not return profits to their members. (Cuskelly, Hoye, and Auld 2006, 17)

In other words, they are non-profit, voluntarily managed and governed, and member-driven organizations. These organizations are populated with human resources who provide their time and labour for the delivery of sport, most often for no remuneration.

Further, in this research, sport volunteers were classified as those persons in 'roles undertaken to support, arrange and/or run organized sport and physical activity' (Australian Bureau of Statistics 2002, 39). The number of these persons, as recent evidence suggests, is not only decreasing but volunteers also exhibit less willingness to engage in certain aspects of volunteering (Engelberg, Skinner, and Zakus 2010). Added to this is evidence that those currently volunteering are contributing less time (as measured by hours per week) to their volunteer activity (Cuskelly et al. 2005). Evidence derived from a recent sport industry-wide consultation in the Australian state of New South Wales (NSW) (NSW Department of Sport and Recreation 2007) and other research (Cuskelly 2005) indicated that volunteer involvement in community sport is decreasing. This is problematic as lower levels of volunteer engagement may constrain the capacity of the voluntary sport sector to sustain national sport delivery systems, deliver more opportunities for participation in organized sport and achieve other social and health goals.

Two groupings of sport volunteers are typically evident: those who hold managing, governing or administrative roles and those who participate in operational roles such as coaches, team managers and event organizers. Both sets of roles are integral to the operation of sport clubs and events. Pearce (1993) first coined the term 'core' volunteer to describe the involvement and commitment levels of volunteers in non-profit organizations. Cuskelly, Hoye, and Auld (2006) applied this conceptualization to sport volunteers and contended that core volunteers usually hold a formal office, often as a board or committee member, are seen as the leaders and typically commit to higher levels of involvement and commitment. A reduction in 'core' volunteer (e.g. committee members and administrators) numbers, as noted above, will have significant implications for the effective and efficient functioning of VSOs. Furthermore, a review of organized sport and physical activity involvement between 1996 and 2007 in NSW revealed a general decline in the number of committee members/administrators involved in local community sport clubs, although the numbers of those in predominantly operational roles, such as scorers/ timekeepers and medical support volunteers, remained relatively stable or had increased (Australian Bureau of Statistics 2004).

This latter group, in contrast, is described as peripheral volunteers. These volunteers tend to commit less time and can be classified as steady or occasional contributors whose involvement and commitment levels are lower than those of core volunteers (Pearce 1993). However, no previous research has examined the differences between core and peripheral volunteers in sport and how such roles are conceptualized and defined by volunteers.

The key purpose of this paper was to determine how and to what extent sport volunteers identify and categorize themselves as either core or peripheral volunteers, even where they hold multiple roles, a common occurrence in VSOs. Categorization was based on self-reported levels of involvement and commitment to roles within a VSO. To realize the purpose of the study, three research questions were addressed:

1. To what extent are volunteers involved in a primary and/or secondary VSO volunteer role?
2. To what extent do involvement and commitment levels in primary roles determine differences between core and peripheral volunteers?
3. Are there differences in the demographic and behavioural characteristics of core and peripheral volunteers?

Literature review

The size and importance of the volunteer sector in sport

Volunteers are integral and essential to society and are an especially valuable resource in the sports sector (Rochester 2006; Sports and Recreation New Zealand 2006). 'Voluntary contribution to sport is of such a scale that when quantified it outstrips all other voluntary activity and dwarfs the amount of paid employment in sport' (Sport England 2003, 2). Volunteerism has reached an extent whereby sport has become dependent on it (Australian Bureau of Statistics 2006; Sport England 2003). Rochester (2006, 2) noted that 'the great expectations of politicians and policy makers and the rising aspirations of the many organizations which promote volunteering and involve volunteers in their work has been accompanied by a growing research interest.' A number of studies from various countries illustrate the significant contributions volunteers make to the community sport and recreation sector (Australian Bureau of Statistics 2006; Rochester 2006; Sport England 2003; Sports and Recreation New Zealand 2008). While a comparison of these studies poses questions relating to definitional and methodological differences, their overall findings reinforce the scale and importance of voluntary involvement and commitment on a national and international scale.

Findings from a series of Citizenship Surveys in England between 2001 and 2006 suggested that 76% of those questioned had taken part in some kind of volunteering activity, with 50% of those questioned having been involved in volunteering at least once a month (Rochester 2006). In 2003, England recorded 5,821,400 sport volunteers, a number that represented nearly 15% of the adult population. These volunteers were noted as contributing over 1.2 billion hours each year to sport, or the equivalent of 720,000 full-time paid workers (Sport England 2003).

In New Zealand, in 2007, over 829,735 members of the population volunteered for a sport or recreation activity, equating to a participation level of 25.3% of the total population. The most popular roles were that of parent helpers and coaches (Sports and Recreation New Zealand 2008). Of those people who volunteered in the sport and recreation sector, 79% volunteered for a sports club, 36% volunteered for a sports team and 13% volunteered for a recreational organization.

A number of other international jurisdictions also exhibited high levels of sport volunteering. For instance, Boraas-White's (2006) research on volunteer activity in the USA revealed that in 2004–2005, 3 out of 10 people participated in some form of volunteering activity, and almost 10% of those volunteers coached, refereed or supervised sports teams. Similarly, in Canada in 2005, 7% of Canadians were involved in amateur coaching. However, the number of adult Canadians who volunteered as referees, officials or umpires decreased by 15% to 800,000 in 2005 after peaking at 937,000 in 1998.

Furthermore, over two million Canadians volunteered their time as administrators or helpers in amateur sports in 2005 (Ifedi 2005).

In Australia, the substantial contribution of volunteers is well documented, and the statistics on volunteering demonstrate its importance to governments and national economies (Zakus 2009). Data indicate that 11% of the adult population aged 18 years and over were involved as volunteers in sport and recreation organizations in 2006. This figure equated to over 1.7 million Australians, with many volunteers involved in more than one role for a sport and recreation organization (Australian Bureau of Statistics 2006). Zakus (2009, 231–232) noted that:

> Volunteers contributed approximately 187 million hours/year in 2006 in one or more sport or recreation organizations. At the current national minimum wage of AUD 14.31, this equates to over AUD 2,676 million. And 84% or 1.4 million did not receive any form of pay or only limited reimbursement for volunteer-related expenses.

Role, performance and role theory

Volunteers participate in a diverse range of formally and informally designated roles and positions including coach, manager, committee member or administrator, referee or umpire, scorer, timekeeper or as a medical support person. Furthermore, many volunteers often have more than one role with data revealing that while about 60% take on one volunteer role, a further 25% are active in two volunteer roles, almost 10% in three and around 5% take responsibility for four or more volunteer positions (Australian Bureau of Statistics 2007). The commitment volunteers make in terms of their time is also substantial. Australian Bureau of Statistics data reveal that 48% of those with a non-playing involvement contribute three hours or less per week, 42% contribute between three and nine hours and a further 7% spend between 10 and 19 hours per week (Australian Bureau of Statistics 2007, 19).

Some studies suggest that particular roles in an organization are more critical to organizational performance than others (Delery and Shaw 2001; Emery and Trist 1969). For instance, Humphrey, Morgeson, and Mannor (2009) suggest that the career experience and job-related skill of strategic core role holders are more strongly related to performance than the experience and job-related skill of non-core role holders. Furthermore, Humphrey, Morgeson, and Mannor (2009) suggest that one or more roles are often more tightly linked to the overall performance of the organization than are other roles. Drawing evidence from team design literatures and the work of Humphrey, Morgeson, and Mannor (2009), it can be concluded that core volunteers are more critical for the successful operation of VSOs than peripheral volunteers because they encounter more of the problems that need to be overcome in the organization, have a greater exposure to the tasks that the organization performs and are more central to the workflow of the organization. This has significant implications for VSOs facing a trend towards declining numbers of core volunteers. Role theory was utilized to understand why individuals choose to take on (and remain in) roles that are either more central or peripheral to an organization.

Role theory can be considered from two main perspectives. The first approach suggests that roles are situated within social systems and become institutionalized clusters of normative rights and obligations (Linton 1936). This structural account of roles describes most of everyday activity to be the acting out of socially defined categories (e.g. manager, teacher and coach). These categories carry associated rights and duties that are created by socially based expectations.

The second perspective is a social-psychological approach to 'role' based on the traditions of symbolic interactionism (Stryker and Statham 1985). This approach focuses on the active processes involved in making, taking and playing at roles, and examines the interactions in which people come to play their roles rather than describing the place of these roles in the social structure. Here, emphasis is on the ways in which people come to take the role of the other, construct their own roles, anticipate the response of others to their roles and finally play at their particular roles. Sometimes people may embrace their parts fully and play out the details of their role in cherished detail. Therefore, some roles are more intimately linked with a person's sense of identity than others.

Over time, the roles that individuals play can become part of their personal identity, how they see themselves and how others see them. Through socialization individuals become social identities with recognizable roles to play. Social interactions and settings have a tendency to positively reinforce a person's role, subsequently heightening his/her role identity and sense of attachment to the role. For example, becoming a socially competent person, someone who fits in, feels at ease with others and relates to others in socially acceptable ways, is a complex task. When this is realized, a greater sense of attachment to the 'role' may evolve.

When roles become intimately linked with a sense of identity, individuals may become more involved and committed to their role. For instance, Laverie and McDonald (2007, 285) suggested that 'dedicated volunteers strongly identify with the organization to which they donate their time and energy.' Although role identity may strengthen a person's commitment and involvement to a role, it may also stem from the social interactions that arise from involvement in and commitment to a role in the first place. Organizational involvement literature can be used to predict volunteer role choice in an organization and the degree of commitment to an organization.

Volunteer involvement and commitment

Based on the constructs of behaviour, activity or attitude, the relationship between involvement and commitment has been well explored by social scientists and theorists since the late 1950s and the early 1960s (Becker 1960; Etzioni 1961; Kanter 1968; Kelman 1958). Etzioni (1961, 1975) conceptualized the term 'involvement' that can be applied to understanding volunteer involvement in VSOs. The macro-organizational theory of involvement proposed by Etzioni also offers a useful way to conceptualize individual's commitment to and behaviour in organizations. Generally, organizational involvement is described as the willingness of a person to engage in activities that are consistent with and to support the organization's objectives (Gould 1979). Drawing on Etzioni's 1961 work, Etzioni and Lehman (1980) proposed three specific types of involvement: moral (strong and positive commitment), alienative (strong and negative commitment) and calculative (weak commitment).

Moral involvement is an acceptance of and identification with organization goals (Etzioni 1961, 1975). An individual's sense of identification with an organization may influence the extent to which that person becomes involved in the organization and his/her intention to remain involved (Penley and Gould 1988). Gould (1979) argued that moral involvement may be most closely related to the concepts of organizational commitment that involves the internalization of organizational roles and values. Similarly, Mowday, Porter, and Steers (1982, 27) suggested that organizational commitment 'is the relative strength of an individual's identification with and involvement in a particular organization'. From a volunteer perspective, Laverie and McDonald (2007, 285) concluded that 'a volunteer's identity supports volunteer behavior to the point of dedication.'

Like moral involvement, alienative involvement reflects an affective attachment to the organization, the difference being that alienative involvement exists on the basis of

(1) a lack of control over the internal organizational environment and (2) the perceived absence of alternatives for organizational commitment. This form of involvement is a negative organizational attachment and is associated with situations in which limited intrinsic rewards may be obtained from one's work (Aiken and Hage 1966). The lack of control implicit in alienation becomes a perceived inability to change or control the organization that can influence decisions to forfeit (or reduce) organizational involvement. Therefore, those involved in more strategic than operational roles in an organization may have a stronger sense of ability to change or control the organization that, in turn, may influence their involvement in and commitment to the organization. Furthermore, Blauner (1964) linked alienation with conditions of meaninglessness, powerlessness, self-estrangement and social isolation. On the basis of motivations for volunteer participation, these conditions could significantly alter a volunteer's decision to begin or continue involvement. For example, Phillips, Little, and Goodine (2002) identified that meaningful volunteer experiences were an important factor in volunteer retention, and Davies (1998) argued that a number of 'generic' motives influence volunteer involvement including social contact, having a sense of accomplishment, self-expression and personal enrichment.

Etzioni and Lehman's (1980) third type of involvement, calculative involvement, describes an individual's involvement in an organization based on the individual receiving inducements to match contributions. This form of organizational attachment is based on an exchange process and is conceptually rooted in March and Simon's (1958) exchange theory. The 'exchange process' can be responsible for behavioural intentions and ultimately behavior, which is closely associated with retention of organizational membership (Penley and Gould 1988). This may explain an individual's intensity of involvement to their role. An individual may devote greater energies and commitment to the organization if inducements for role participation increase. From a sport volunteer perspective, these inducements may include personal and social rewards such as gaining work experience, tapping into community networks, and recognition rewards and incentives. In the field of volunteer motivation, Knoke and Prensky (1984) described this as a utilitarian (or material) incentive aligned with self-interest and the personal benefits gained from volunteering. Other forms of motivation (affective and normative) and their association with involvement and commitment are described in the following paragraphs.

The organizational involvement literature can be used to predict role choice and continued participation (retention) in an organization. It is also instrumental for understanding the degree of commitment to an organization (Etzioni 1961; Gould 1979). Organizational commitment can be described as a behaviour, or affective response to the organization, that depends on what the organization means personally to the individual and the individual's perceptions of the values and ideology that may be actualized through participation in the organization. Kelman (1958) proposed that commitment results from one of three processes: compliance (in order to gain reward or avoid punishment), identification (to develop or maintain a satisfying relationship) and internalization (because there is congruence between the individual's value system and the induced behaviour). Other theorists (e.g. Penley and Gould 1988) used Etzioni's three dimensions of involvement to explain organizational attachment as a form of affective commitment (based on moral and alienative involvement) or instrumental commitment (based on calculative involvement).

On the one hand, organizational commitment is conceptualized as a form of affective attachment to an organization, characterized by Buchanan (1974) as a sense of identification, involvement and loyalty to an organization or to a role within an organization. Because of this affective form of organizational attachment, a person may remain highly committed to an organization even when inducements diminish. In sport volunteering, affective commitment may stem from an affective incentive (such as the social benefits associated with interpersonal relationships, group identification and group status) that serves to motivate many sport volunteers and influence involvement and retention (Knoke and Prensky 1984). Affective incentives are different from normative incentives that align with altruism as a motive for volunteering.

On the other hand, instrumental sources of commitment refer to a bond that develops between the organization and an individual as a result of the exchange process – when an individual exchanges his or her contributions for the inducements provided by the organization. Penley and Gould (1988, 44) described that the extent of the instrumental commitment depends on the 'intensity of the bond, and the intensity of the bond depends on the degree to which an employee's intentions to behave are consistent with the organization's behavioral demands'. Meyer and Allen (1997) further advanced the conceptualization of organizational commitment by proposing a three-component model including affective commitment, continuance commitment and normative commitment. From their perspective, affective commitment refers to how individuals want to become committed to an organization because of the strength of identification with and involvement in the organization. Continuance commitment develops from a lack of alternatives or the potential loss of positive benefits if one was to leave an organization. Finally, normative commitment is based on socialization, organizational investment and the strength of reciprocity norm.

Overall, the various components of commitment relate to different reasons for becoming committed to an organization. Catano, Pond, and Kelloway (2001, 256) acknowledged the 'many factors which can influence whether individuals join a voluntary organization, or once they have joined, actively assume leadership roles and participate fully in the life of the organization'. These factors can determine the difference between volunteer involvement and volunteer commitment. Clearly, there is conceptual alignment between the volunteer motivations or incentives described earlier (affective, utilitarian and normative) and the three-component model of organizational commitment (affective, continuance and normative, respectively), which may explain why some volunteers decide to stay with a VSO while others leave. For example, Cuskelly, Hoye, and Auld (2006, 91) argued that 'volunteers motivated by utilitarian incentives are likely to develop a stronger sense of continuance commitment than volunteers motivated by normative or affective incentives'.

Another important theoretical model of volunteers is that of Robert Stebbins, in particular, the concept of 'serious leisure' (Stebbins 1992, 1996, 1997). Stebbins (2001, 3) indicated that:

> serious leisure is the systematic pursuit of an amateur, hobbyist, or volunteer activity that participants find so substantial and interesting that, in the typical case, they launch themselves on a career centred on acquiring and expressing its special skills, knowledge, and experience.

Such volunteer work demands sustained, positive commitment that leads to 'career volunteering'. In the sample and the cases studied here, a clear demarcation was evident in the career of serious leisurists and those not on boards (cf. Engelberg, Skinner, and Zakus, 2010).

The interactions between involvement, commitment and motivation are complex. Balduck, Van Rossem, and Buelens (2009) suggested that volunteers having a strong commitment to an organization displayed an increase in their active involvement (e.g. donating hours, attending meetings, serving on committees and/or making financial contributions to the organization). Therefore, the concept of organizational commitment helps explain the involvement in (level of involvement and duration of involvement) and attachment to social organizations and the development of organizational commitment.

In summary, volunteer involvement and commitment can be described on the basis of individual behaviours and attitudes to volunteering, and are mutually dependent concepts that act to reinforce one another through processes of satisfaction and retention. However, the application of involvement and commitment concepts to core and peripheral volunteer roles in VSOs has not been previously explored. This study progresses knowledge in this area by identifying the nature and extent of core and peripheral volunteer involvement and commitment to VSOs.

Within VSOs, the commitment of core volunteers and the extent to which they are satisfied with volunteer experiences is particularly important for organizational effectiveness and stability. Cuskelly, Hoye, and Auld (2006, 90) suggested that 'organizational commitment provides a basis for understanding the linkages that develop between volunteers and VSOs and it is both a factor in the retention of volunteers and, to some extent, their performance.' However, it should be noted that while a high level of commitment can result in more loyalty, increased teamwork, reduced turnover and absence, along with a greater sense of self-worth, dignity, psychological involvement and feeling of being integral to the organization, there is no clear link to performance (Arnold, Robertson, and Cooper 1991; Bishop, Scott, and Burroughs 1997).

The present study uses self-reported levels of involvement and commitment within VSOs as a basis for categorizing sport volunteers as 'core' or 'peripheral'. This research contributes to the relatively unexplored area of core and peripheral volunteer roles in social organizations, first, by identifying the extent to which volunteers are involved in a primary and/or secondary VSO volunteer role; second, by examining the extent to which involvement and commitment levels in primary roles determine differences between core and peripheral volunteers; and, third, by examining the extent to which there are differences in the demographic and behavioural characteristics of core and peripheral volunteers. Further understanding the nature of volunteer involvement and commitment, the reasons that volunteers choose to take on certain roles and why they behave as they do within VSO settings can be better enunciated.

Methods

To address the three research questions, a sample of volunteers drawn from three state sporting organizations, from metropolitan and regional NSW, was surveyed. All research was conducted in accordance with human research ethics approval through Griffith University, Queensland, Australia. The following sections describe the sampling of participants, development of the survey instrument, and the collection procedures and analysis techniques employed.

Participants

The sampling frame comprised volunteers from local community sport clubs involving three sports. The sport organizations were selected in consultation with the NSW Department of Sport and Recreation and represented a broadly representative cross section of male- and female-dominated sports, inner and outer metropolitan centres and regional areas, summer and winter sports, team and individual sports, and large and small sports (determined by the total number of participants).

The sample was drawn from volunteer members of VSOs formally affiliated with each of the three selected sports who agreed to an invitation from their respective state sport organization (SSO) to participate in the study. A final sample of 243 volunteers was derived from a total of 632 possible volunteers initially invited to participate (see 'Procedures' section) realizing a final response rate of 38%. The study participants were predominantly from the Sydney (capital city) metropolitan area (58%), with smaller proportions from other metropolitan centres (15%), and rural areas (26%).

The average age of respondents was 43.2 years (SD=9.0), 58% of respondents were male and 81.5% of respondents described themselves as employed outside the home. Of those employed, 30% were managers or administrators, 24% were professionals or para-professionals and 16% were clerical, service or sales workers. This sample was very representative of the national population in terms of sport volunteers. For instance, Australian statistics on sport volunteers indicate that 61% of sport volunteers are male, compared with 58% in this study (Australian Bureau of Statistics 2009).

Survey instrument

A self-administered survey instrument was designed and developed for the purpose of this study to collect data regarding self-reported volunteer involvement, commitment and roles, and selected demographic characteristics. Commitment and involvement were of primary interest and were operationalized using seven statements developed from the literature and in consultation with representatives of the three SSOs involved in the study. The seven survey items developed aimed to capture the perceived levels of volunteer involvement and commitment to their VSO, to their role within it, and their perceived level of participation in planning, decision-making and service delivery. Organizational commitment and involvement scales such as the organizational commitment questionnaire (Mowday, Steers, and Porter 1979; Porter et al. 1974) and the three-component instrument developed by Meyer and Allen (1997) were considered inappropriate for measuring these constructs with volunteers as they were quite complex, solely developed for work organizations and included a large number of items.

To deal with these difficulties, Engelberg (2008) developed and tested a questionnaire constructed specifically for the sport volunteer sector. Three types of commitment and three targets of that commitment were tested. Engelberg's initial study and the adaptation of the questionnaires for further use in her dissertation revealed good reliabilities (Cronbach's α of 91 for the total scale and of 82, 89 and 76 for the three subscales) and intercorrelations between the scales and background variables of the volunteers. This provides support for the scale implemented in this study.

Volunteer involvement and commitment were measured using a four-point unidirectional Likert-type scale that ranges from 'low' to 'very high'. The internal consistency of the involvement and commitment scale was high with a Cronbach's α coefficient ($\alpha=0.92$) for the seven items used in the scale.

Other survey items gathered demographic data (e.g. age, sex, employment and education), volunteers' perceived primary and secondary roles within their VSO, and the number of years and average hours per week they contributed to these roles. The survey instrument was piloted amongst nine experts in the field, including the project managers, researchers and sport representatives (e.g. Chief Executive Officers, Coaching and Development Officers, VSO Presidents and Secretaries), to identify possible problems of ambiguity with instrument wording and to assess survey completion time.

Procedures

Representatives of the three identified SSOs recruited volunteers to participate in the study. Each SSO contacted volunteers listed on their respective organizational and member databases via email to explain the purpose and procedures of the study to seek their participation. Of the 632 SSO contacts, the sample of 243 (38%) consented to receive the survey, while only 13 declined to participate.

The sample that consented to have their email addresses provided to the research team and participate in the study were emailed an invitation to complete an online survey. An incentive and follow-up strategies recommended by Dillman (2000) were used to enhance the response rate. Participants had four weeks to complete the survey. The first follow-up email was sent to participants ten days after the initial distribution. The final follow-up email was sent to participants one week before the survey closed.

Data analysis

Data were translated from the online survey database to an SPSS data file and analyzed using SPSS descriptives, crosstabs (χ^2), t-test and cluster analysis. Because the primary purpose of the study was to examine differences between core and peripheral volunteers, hierarchical cluster analysis using Ward's method was applied to the involvement and commitment scale item data. The purpose of the cluster analysis was to identify relatively homogeneous and exclusive groups of volunteers based on their self-reported levels of involvement and commitment. The cluster analysis was used to statistically maximize group differences between mean involvement and commitment scores for core and peripheral volunteers. Ward's method of hierarchical agglomerative clustering using standardized Z-scores and squared Euclidian distances was applied to identify group differences. This method was selected to minimize within-cluster differences and to avoid problems with 'chaining' of observations found in the single linkage method (Hair et al. 1998). As Ward's method is sensitive to outliers, Z-scores for the volunteer motivation index dimensions were checked for outlying cases (more than 3 SDs from the mean) prior to cluster analysis. A drawback of cluster analysis is the lack of a standard or objective procedure to determine the final number of clusters to be formed. Hair et al. (1998, 503) argued that large increases in the agglomeration coefficient 'have been shown to be a fairly accurate algorithm'.

Results

Primary and secondary volunteer roles

The first research question sought to identify the extent to which volunteers were involved in a primary and/or secondary role in a VSO. The primary and secondary volunteer roles reported by the survey respondents are summarized in Table 1. A majority of the survey respondents (85%) reported that they were involved in their VSO both in primary and secondary volunteer roles. Of the 16 roles listed in the survey, the most frequently reported roles overall were secretary (40.8%), trainer/instructor/teacher/coach (36%) and president or chair (30.4%).

When the total responses were broken down into either primary or secondary roles, it was quite evident that president or chair and secretary were more likely to be reported as the primary volunteer role (26% and 34% of respondents, respectively) than were more operational roles such as trainer/instructor/teacher/coach. These latter role types were categorized by a larger proportion of respondents as their secondary (22.7%) rather than as

Table 1. Primary and secondary VSO volunteer roles.

	Primary volunteer role (%)	Secondary volunteer role (%)	Total (%)
President or chair	26.1	4.3	30.4
Secretary	34.0	6.8	40.8
Treasurer	2.5	1.0	3.5
Registrar	3.7	1.4	5.1
Volunteer coordinator	0.8	3.9	4.7
Competition/event coordinator	2.1	4.3	6.4
Ground coordinator/marshal	–	1.9	1.9
Team manager	5.8	9.2	15.0
Trainer/instructor/teacher/coach	13.3	22.7	36.0
Official/referee/umpire	3.7	12.6	16.3
Timekeeper/scorer	2.9	7.2	10.1
Medical support person	1.2	3.4	4.6
Marketing/PR/news/fund raiser	1.7	6.3	8.0
Canteen and bar	–	2.9	2.9
General help	1.7	8.7	10.4
Other	0.4	3.4	3.8
Total	100.0	100.0	200.0
Number of cases	241	207	

their primary role (13.3%). Similarly, roles such as official/referee/umpire (total 16.3%) and team manager (total 15%) were amongst the more frequently listed roles but were most likely to be perceived as secondary (13% and 9%, respectively) by respondents.

The respondents were also asked to identify the nature and degree of their involvement in their primary and secondary volunteer roles in the club. Providing further support to the notion of distinct primary and secondary roles, volunteers contributed significantly more *hours* per week and more *years* in their primary roles, compared with their secondary roles [χ^2 (df 6) = 33.9, $p < 0.001$]. Volunteers were more likely to report contributing more than five hours per week (52%) to their primary roles compared with their secondary roles in which only 20% of volunteers contributed more than five hours per week. Significant associations were also evident between the *years* volunteers had been involved in their primary and secondary roles [χ^2 (df 9) = 123.0, $p < 0.001$], although the patterns were different in terms of hours contributed per week. Volunteers who had spent more years in their primary role were also more likely to have spent more years in their secondary role (tables not shown).

Cluster analysis

The second research question focused on whether volunteer self-reported involvement and commitment levels in their primary roles would further differentiate between core and peripheral volunteers. The mean scores for the variables used to categorize the survey respondents as either core or peripheral volunteers are displayed in Table 2. Scores on each item ranged from 1 'low' to 4 'very high'. In comparison with peripheral volunteers, core volunteers were more highly involved and committed and made greater contributions to planning, decision-making and 'hands-on' work within their clubs in their primary volunteer role. Not surprisingly, given that the function of cluster analysis is to statistically maximize group differences, there were significant differences between the core and peripheral volunteer groups (Wilks' λ (7,231) = 80.25, $p < 0.001$). Significant differences

Table 2. Mean scores (and standard deviation) for core and peripheral volunteer categories on variables used in cluster analysis (Ward's method).

Level	Core volunteers	Peripheral volunteers	Univariate F (1,237)
Involvement in primary volunteer role	3.79 (0.44)	2.86 (0.41)	144.9*
Involvement in club	3.82 (0.41)	2.73 (0.74)	209.8*
Commitment to primary volunteer role	3.76 (0.44)	3.04 (0.70)	95.9*
Commitment to club	3.80 (0.42)	2.91 (0.73)	142.7*
Contribution to decision-making in the club	3.79 (0.41)	2.31 (0.77)	373.7*
Contribution to planning in the club	3.77 (0.44)	2.22 (0.79)	368.6*
Practical (hands-on) work done in the club	3.89 (0.32)	2.81 (0.82)	201.2*
Total	100%	100%	
Number of cases	141	98	

Note: *$p < 0.001$

between core and peripheral volunteers were also identified for each of the seven variables used in the cluster analysis procedure (see Table 2).

The third research question sought to identify whether differences in demographic and behavioural characteristics of core and peripheral volunteers would support the differentiation of roles. Differences between core and peripheral volunteers were examined by testing for between-group differences based on demographics, primary role, and hours and years of participation. There were no significant differences between core and peripheral volunteers based on their gender, age, current employment status or highest level of educational attainment.

Before testing for significant differences between core and peripheral volunteers in terms of their primary volunteer role, those roles with a frequency of less than 10 cases were recorded as 'other'. There were significant differences [χ^2 (df 4)$=$31.3, $p < 0.01$] between core and peripheral volunteers in what they self-reported as their primary role (see Table 3). Core volunteers were more likely to report VSO board positions such as president or chair (35.3%) or secretary (38.3%) than to report operational positions such as team manager (2.8%) or trainer/instructor/teacher/coach (6.4%).

In contrast, peripheral volunteers reported their primary role predominantly as an operational one, such as team manager (10.2%), trainer/instructor/teacher/coach (22.4%) or other (25.5%). In summary, core volunteers were more likely (74%) to identify a leadership or policy role (president, chair or secretary) than were peripheral volunteers who more likely identified (58.1%) holding an operational or helping roles in their VSO including team manager, trainer/instructor/teacher/coach or other (see Table 3).

Table 3. Differences between core and peripheral volunteers by primary volunteer role.

	Core (%)	Peripheral (%)
President or chair	35.3	13.3
Secretary	38.3	26.8
Team manager	2.8	10.2
Trainer/instructor/teacher/coach	6.4	22.4
Other	17.0	25.5
Total	100.0	100.0
Number of cases	141	98

Note: χ^2 (df 4)$=$31.3, $p < 0.01$

Table 4.   Hours per week in primary volunteer role by core and peripheral volunteer category.

Hours per week	Core (%)	Peripheral (%)
Up to 5	31.9	71.4
6 to 10	34.8	20.4
More than 10	33.3	8.2
Total	100	100
Number of cases	141	98

Note: χ^2 (df 2) = 38.8, $p < 0.001$

Hours per week

The self-reported hours per week that volunteers contributed to both their primary and secondary roles are summarized in Tables 4 and 5. In the primary role, there were significant differences [χ^2 (df 2) = 38.8, $p < 0.001$] in the hours contributed per week between core and peripheral volunteers. Amongst the core volunteers, there was a relatively even distribution of hours contributed (31.9–34.8%). In contrast, peripheral volunteers were much more likely to contribute up to five hours per week (71.4%) than they were to contribute more than 10 hours per week (8.2%) (see Table 4). Similarly, there were significant differences in the hours per week contributed by core and peripheral volunteers [χ^2 (df 2) = 19.9, $p < 0.001$]. Core volunteers were five times more likely than peripheral volunteers to contribute more than five hours per week (30.3% vs. 6.0%) to their secondary role whereas peripheral volunteers were twice as likely to contribute less than one hour per week (10.7%) than were core volunteers (4.1%) (see Table 5). Overall, it appears that core volunteers contribute significantly more hours per week than peripheral volunteers to both their primary and secondary volunteer roles.

Years involved

Data for years of involvement in primary and secondary roles were also tested for differences between core and peripheral volunteers (tables not shown). There were no significant differences between core and peripheral volunteers in the years they had been involved in either their primary or secondary roles. Similarly, there were no significant differences between core and peripheral volunteers in terms of the years they had been a member of their VSO or the years they had been involved in their sport. These findings may indicate similar patterns of retention between core and peripheral volunteers. However, the majority of volunteers (more than 60%) reported involvement of five years or less in both primary and secondary roles. From another perspective, almost two thirds of

Table 5.   Hours per week in secondary volunteer role by core and peripheral volunteer category.

Hours per week	Core (%)	Peripheral (%)
Up to 5	4.1	10.7
6 to 10	65.6	83.3
More than 10	30.3	6.0
Total	100	100
Number of cases	122	84

Note: χ^2 (df 2) = 19.9, $p < 0.001$

VSO volunteers continue in their primary or secondary roles for five or less years irrespective of being categorized as a core or peripheral volunteer.

In summary, a majority of survey respondents (85%) were involved in their VSO both in a primary and a secondary volunteer role. Board roles (president, chair and secretary) were more likely to be reported as the primary volunteer role rather than operational type roles (e.g. trainer, teacher and coach). However, operational roles were reported by a larger proportion of respondents as their secondary rather than their primary role. Overall, volunteers contributed significantly more hours per week to their primary role than to their secondary role.

Findings also indicate that volunteer involvement and commitment levels in primary roles can be used to classify volunteers as core or peripheral volunteers. Significant differences between core and peripheral volunteers were identified for level of involvement and level of commitment in primary volunteer role and club, contributions to decision-making and planning in the club, and practical work done in the club. Core volunteers were significantly more involved and committed to their primary roles than were peripheral volunteers. They also made greater contributions to planning, decision-making and hands-on work within their clubs in their primary role. As such, core volunteers were more likely to be involved in a leadership or policy role (e.g. board positions) than an operational position, whereas peripheral volunteers were more likely to hold operational roles.

Finally, no significant differences were found between core and peripheral volunteers based on demographic characteristics including gender, age, current employment status or highest level of educational attainment. However, significant differences were found between core and peripheral volunteers in terms of behavioural characteristics such as hours contributed to volunteering. The following section will address the practical and theoretical significance of these findings for volunteer involvement in non-profit sport.

Discussion

The overall objective of this study was to examine the perceptions of sport volunteers in relation to the nature and extent to which they categorized themselves as either core or peripheral volunteers. While all roles filled by volunteers are integrally important, there are differences in involvement, commitment and output in each of the above types. Three research questions were addressed and the findings relevant to each of these will be discussed in turn.

Involvement in primary and secondary VSO volunteer roles

The data clearly revealed that many volunteers are involved in multiple roles in VSOs. However, respondents were able to clearly distinguish between what constituted their primary and secondary roles. Importantly, in terms of distinguishing between core and peripheral volunteers, respondents tended to identify roles such as president or chair and secretary as their primary role rather than more operational-level activities such as trainer/instructor or coach. Furthermore, congruent with the self-reported categorizations outlined above, volunteers also indicated that more hours per week were contributed to those roles perceived as primary in nature compared with those categorized as secondary.

Commitment levels and core and peripheral volunteers

The cluster analysis revealed that core volunteers tended to be more highly involved and committed to both the more specific elements of volunteering (i.e. with their sport club) and the broader and typically longer term elements of their generic overall volunteer experience than were peripheral volunteers. This behaviour was manifested across different levels of volunteering in VSOs including not only management and governance roles in areas such as organizational planning and decision-making, but also operational-level work. However, as indicated above, core volunteers were more likely to identify the management and governance activities as their primary function.

Demographic and behavioural differences between core and peripheral volunteers

The analysis indicated that there were no significant differences in key demographic characteristics between core and peripheral volunteers. Importantly, the results suggested that there were no significant differences between the two groups in terms of the years they had been involved in either their primary or secondary roles, with the majority of volunteers reporting involvement of five years or less in both primary and secondary roles. This is a key finding as it suggests that core volunteering is not 'evolutionary' in nature and/or necessarily a natural consequence of longer periods of engagement with the organization or socialization. Furthermore, this finding implies that some individuals may come to the initial volunteer experience more disposed and/or willing to commit. For example, the social-psychological approach to understanding roles suggests that some roles are more strongly associated with a person's sense of identity than others. In addition, the core or peripheral volunteer behaviour may be a function of any previous volunteer experience and this issue also warrants further investigation.

As may be expected, given the higher level of engagement expected of leadership roles in management and governance, core volunteers contributed more hours per week than peripheral volunteers to their primary roles. Engelberg (2008) noted that 'committee members were significantly more committed to their role than volunteers in other roles' (p. 114), which also emanated from a similar behaviour of a larger time commitment. However, core volunteers also contributed more hours per week to their secondary roles underlining the overall greater level of organizational engagement and commitment exhibited by core volunteers. The results confirm Pearce's (1993) finding that core volunteers contribute significantly more hours per week than peripheral volunteers in both primary and secondary roles.

The key issue for VSOs is how to better engage their volunteers such that more peripheral volunteers are converted into core volunteers. VSOs rely on relatively high levels of volunteer involvement and are likely to be affected by the trends towards declining volunteer numbers. Furthermore, with lesser hours and fewer years of experience, the knowledge and 'informational disadvantage which may affect their understanding of procedures, organizational issues and priorities' (Engelberg, Skinner, and Zakus 2010) will likewise affect the efficiency and effectiveness of voluntary management. Therefore, given the trend towards volunteers contributing fewer hours, a lower conversion rate of core to peripheral volunteering not only has implications for VSOs in terms of capacity derived from hours of volunteer work but also the quality of VSO services as peripheral volunteers are likely to have only a superficial understanding of VSO operations due to less exposure to organizational issues, tasks and workflow.

This may also have liability implications. The literature supports the notion that certain organizational roles are more critical to organizational performance than others (Delery and Shaw 2001; Emery and Trist 1969; Humphrey, Morgeson, and Mannor 2009). Humphrey, Morgeson, and Mannor (2009) suggested that core volunteers are more critical for the successful operation of VSOs than peripheral volunteers, because they encounter more of the problems that need to be overcome in the organization, have a greater exposure to the tasks that the organization is performing and are more central to the workflow of the organization. Furthermore, the results suggest that given that most respondents first identified a core function as their primary role and yet also identified secondary peripheral roles that more is being done by fewer volunteers thus placing more stress on these valuable people. Other research (e.g. Taylor et al. 2006) has suggested that workload issues (largely under the control of VSOs) play a significant role in the decision of volunteers to leave but such concerns may also be relevant in the peripheral to core conversion process. This issue also needs more research, that is, not just focusing research on the decision to leave or stay but the decision to maintain involvement at the peripheral level rather than 'stepping up' to a core level of commitment.

But questions remain as to what extent conversion from peripheral to core volunteering behaviour is a function of interactions between the volunteer and the organization, the personal attributes/dispositions (including previous volunteer experiences) of the volunteers or a combination of both.

Conclusion

This research contributes to a better understanding of the differences between core and peripheral sport volunteers and how these differences emerge through role differentiation. Knowing whether there are sufficient differences between core and peripheral volunteer involvement in, and commitment to, VSOs can assist the development of recruitment strategies and volunteer management methods designed to better target each type of volunteer. Furthermore, a better understanding of the roles fulfilled by core and peripheral volunteers and the nature of their involvement and commitment is essential to protect and develop the role of this vital group of people who form the foundation of a cohesive network enabling sports clubs to deliver services to its members, sustain the sport system and consequentially build social capital.

References

Aiken, M., and J. Hage. 1966. "Organizational Alienation: A Comparative Analysis." *American Sociological Review* 31: 497–507.

Arnold, J., I. T. Robertson, and C. Cooper. 1991. *Work Psychology: Understanding Human Behavior in the Workplace.* London: Pitman.

Australian Bureau of Statistics. 2002. *Involvement in Organised Sport and Physical Activity.* Cat. No. 6285.0. Canberra: Commonwealth of Australia.

Australian Bureau of Statistics. 2004. *Involvement in Organised Sport and Physical Activity 2004 Survey.* Cat. No. 6285.0. Canberra: Commonwealth of Australia.

Australian Bureau of Statistics. 2006. *Voluntary Work Australia.* Cat. No. 4441.0. Canberra: Commonwealth of Australia.

Australian Bureau of Statistics. 2007. *Involvement in Organised Sport and Physical Activity.* Cat. No. 6285.0. Canberra: Commonwealth of Australia.

Australian Bureau of Statistics. 2009. *Sport and Recreation: A Statistical Overview.* Cat. No. 4156.0. Canberra: Commonwealth of Australia.

Australian Sports Commission. 2009. "Addendum to the Submission of the Australian Sports Commission to the Commonwealth Government's Independent Review of Sport in Australia." Accessed February 16, 2009. http://www.ausport.gov.au/__data/assets/pdf_file/0008/269459/Addendum_to_the_ASC_Submission_to_Sport_Panel.pdf

Australian Sports Commission. 2008a. "Australian Sport: Emerging Challenges, New Directions." Accessed September 8, 2008. http://www.health.gov.au/internet/main/publishing.nsf/Content/4BEFA13FF8128886CA2574410012101A/$File/australian-sport.pdf

Australian Sports Commission. 2008b. "Submission to the Commonwealth Government's Independent Review of Sport in Australia." Accessed November 15, 2008. http://www.ausport.gov.au/__data/assets/pdf_file/0018/246411/Submission_-_Independent_Review_Final_20_Oct_1.pdf

Balduck, A., A. Van Rossem, and M. Buelens. 2009. "Identifying Competencies of Volunteer Board Members of Community Sports Clubs." *Nonprofit and Voluntary Sector Quarterly* 39 (2): 213–235.

Becker, H. S. 1960. "Notes on the Concept of Commitment." *American Sociological Review* 66: 32–42.

Bishop, J., K. Scott, and S. Burroughs. 1997. "Support, Commitment, and Employee Outcomes in a Team Environment." *Journal of Management* 26 (6): 1113–1132.

Blauner, R. 1964. *Alienation and Freedom*. Chicago: Univeristy of Chicago Press.

Boraas-White, S. 2006. "Volunteering in the United States 2005." Accessed January 12, 2010. http://www.bls.gov/opub/mlr/2006/02/ressum.pdf

Buchanan, B. 1974. "Building Organizational Commitment: The Socialization of Managers in Work Organizations." *Administrative Science Quarterly* 19 (4): 533–546.

Catano, M., E. Pond, and K. Kelloway. 2001. "Exploring Commitment and Leadership in Volunteer Organizations." *Leadership and Organization Development Journal* 22 (6): 256–263.

Cuskelly, G. 2005. "Volunteer Participation Trends in Australian Sport." In *Volunteers in Sports Clubs*, edited by G. Nichols and M. Collins. Eastbourne: Leisure Studies Association.

Cuskelly, G., R. Hoye, and C. Auld. 2006. *Working with Volunteers in Sport: Theory and Practice*. London: Routledge.

Cuskelly, G., T. Taylor, R. Hoye, and S. Darcy. 2005. *Volunteers in Community Rugby*. Sydney: ARU.

Davies, J. 1998. "The Value of Volunteers." *Australian Parks and Recreation* 34 (1): 33–35.

Delery, J. E., and J. D. Shaw. 2001. "The Strategic Management of People in Work Organizations: Review, Synthesis, and Extension." In *Research in Personnel and Human Resource Management*, edited by G. R. Ferris, Vol. 20, 165–197. New York: Elsevier.

Dillman, D. A. 2000. *Mail and Internet Surveys: The Tailored Design Method*. New York: Wiley.

Emery, F. E., and E. L. Trist. 1969. "Socio-Technical Systems." In *Systems Thinking*, edited by F. E. Emery, 281–296. London: Penguin Books.

Engelberg, E. 2008. "The Commitment of Volunteers in Junior Sport Organizations: A Mixed Methods Study." Unpublished doctoral dissertation, Griffith University.

Engelberg, E., J. Skinner, and D. H. Zakus. 2010. "Exploring the Relationship Between Commitment, Experience, and Self-Assessed Performance in Youth Sport Organizations." *Sport Management Review* 14 (12): 117–125. DOI: 10.1016/j.smr.2010.05.003

Etzioni, A. 1961. *A Comparative Analysis of Complex Organizations*. New York: Free Press.

Etzioni, A. 1975. *A Comparative Analysis of Complex Organizations*. Revised and enlarged edition. New York: Free Press.

Etzioni, A., and E. W. Lehman. 1980. *A Sociological Reader on Complex Organizations*. 3rd ed. New York: Holt, Rinehart and Winston.

Gould, S. 1979. "An Equity-Exchange Model of Organizational Involvement." *The Academy of Management Review* 4 (1): 53–62.

Hair, J. F., Jr, R. E. Anderson, R. L. Tatham, and W. C. Black. 1998. *Multivariate Data Analysis*. 5th ed. Englewood Cliffs, NJ: Prentice-Hall.

Humphrey, S., F. Morgeson, and M. Mannor. 2009. "Developing a Theory of the Strategic Core of Teams: A Role Composition Model of Team Performance." *Journal of Applied Psychology* 94 (1): 48–61.

Ifedi, F. 2005. "Sports Participation in Canada 2005: Research Paper for Culture, Tourism and the Centre for Education Statistics." Accessed January 12, 2010. http://www.statcan.gc.ca/pub/81-595-m/81-595-m2008060-eng.pdf

Kanter, R. M. 1968. "Commitment and Social Organization: A Study of Commitment Mechanisms in Utopian Communities." *American Sociological Review* 33: 499–517.

Kelman, H. C. 1958. "Compliance, Identification, and Internalization: Three Processes of Attitude Change." *Journal of Conflict Resolution* 2 (1): 51–60.

Knoke, D., and D. Prensky. 1984. "What Relevance do Organizational Theories have for Voluntary Associations?" *Social Science Quarterly* 65 (1): 3–20.

Laverie, D., and R. McDonald. 2007. "Volunteer Dedication: Understanding the Role of Identity Importance on Participation Frequency." *Journal of Macromarketing* 27 (3): 274–288.

Linton, R. 1936. *The Study of Man*. New York: Appleton-Century.

March, J. G., and H. A. Simon. 1958. *Organizations*. New York: Wiley.

Meyer, J. P., and N. J. Allen. 1997. *Commitment in the Workplace: Theory, Research, and Application*. Newbury Park, CA: Sage.

Mowday, R. T., L. W. Porter, and R. M. Steers. 1982. *Employee-Organization Linkages: The Psychology of Commitment, Absenteeism, and Turnover*. New York: Academic Press.

Mowday, R. T., R. M. Steers, and L. M. Porter. 1979. "The Measurement of Organizational Commitment." *Journal of Vocational Behavior* 14 (2): 224–247.

NSW Department of Sport and Recreation. 2007. *Industry Strategic Directions, a Five Year Plan: Key Issues Discussion Paper. 'People and Volunteers' Priority Area; Cited in Volunteers in Sport Research Brief June 2007*. Sydney Olympic Park, NSW: NSW Department of Sport and Recreation.

Pearce, J. 1993. *Volunteers: The Organizational Behavior of Unpaid Workers*. London: Routledge.

Penley, L. E., and S. Gould. 1988. "Etzioni's Model of Organizational Involvement: A Perspective for Understanding Commitment to Organizations." *Journal of Organizational Behavior* 9 (1): 43–59.

Phillips, S., B. Little, and L. Goodine. 2002. *Recruiting, Retaining, and Rewarding Volunteers: What Volunteers Have to Say*. Toronto, ON: Canadian Centre for Philanthropy.

Porter, L. W., R. M. Steers, R. T. Mowday, and P. V. Boulian. 1974. "Organizatinal Commitment, Job Satisfaction, and Turnover Among Psychiatric Technicians." *Journal of Applied Psychology* 59: 603–609.

Rochester, C. 2006. *Making Sense of Volunteering: A Literature Review*. London: Volunteering England.

Sport England. 2003. *Sports Volunteering in England in 2002: A Summary Report*. London: Sports England.

Sports and Recreation New Zealand. 2006. *Finding and Keeping Volunteers: What the Research Tells Us*. Wellington: Sports and Recreation New Zealand.

Sports and Recreation New Zealand. 2008. *Volunteers the Heart of Sport: The Experiences and Motivations of Sports Volunteers*. Wellington: Sports and Recreation New Zealand.

Stebbins, R. 1992. *Amateurs, Professionals and Serious Leisure*. Montreal: McGill-Queens University Press.

Stebbins, R. 1996. "Volunteering: A Serious Leisure Pursuit." *Nonprofit and Voluntary Sector Quarterly* 25: 211–224.

Stebbins, R. A. 1997. "Casual Leisure: A Conceptual Statement." *Leisure Studies* 16: 17–25.

Stebbins, R. A. 2001. *New Directions in the Theory and Research of Serious Leisure: Mellen Studies in Sociology*. Vol. 28. Lewiston, NY: Edwin Mellen.

Stewart, B., M. Nicholson, A. Smith, and H. Westerbeek. 2004. *Australian Sport: Better by Design? The Evolution of Australian Sport Policy*. London: Routledge.

Stryker, S., and A. Statham. 1985. "Symbolic Interaction and Role Theory." In *Handbook of Social Psychology*, edited by G. Lindzey and E. Aronson, 3rd ed., Vol. 1, 311–378. New York: Random House.

Taylor, T., S. Darcy, R. Hoye, and G. Cuskelly. 2006. "Using Psychological Contract Theory to Explore Issues in Effective Volunteer Management." *European Sport Management Quarterly* 6 (2): 123–147.

Zakus, D. H. 2009. "Sustainability of Community Sport Organizations." In *Social Responsibility and Sustainability in Sports*, edited by P. Rodriguez, S. Kesenne and H. Dietl, 229–256. Oviedo, Spain: Ediciones de la Universidad de Oviedo.

Epilogue: the not-so-hidden complexity of the sport-community connection

During the first-class meeting of an Introductory Sociology course, I was teaching at George Mason University in Virginia, a student asked me to sum up the findings of the discipline in one sentence. I considered equivocating on the matter and trying to explain the complexity of the field and all of its constituent parts, but instead I opted to try and provide a relevant answer. Ultimately, I decided on the following two-word answer: 'It depends.' When the student asked me what depended, I replied that, actually, my answer was 'It depends.' I believe that – from an empirical standpoint – is the essence of sociology, and perhaps all of the social sciences. Anyone who has tried to derive universal laws of human behaviour should sympathize. Outcomes, whether they be sporting outcomes, policy outcomes or life outcomes, simply depend. This answer, while wholly unsatisfactory, does much to untangle the complicated nature of the community-sport question. The study of sport and communities has produced (predictably) decidedly mixed results. Indeed, why would we as sport scholars expect anything different? Within the field of sport and community studies, we detect two distinct issues: 'sport' and 'community'. Within sport sociology, scholars have studied various forms of engagement with sport: participation as a player, spectatorship, fandom, volunteerism or policy. It stands to reason that different forms of engagement with sport as an institution would yield empirically distinct results and, thus, should almost certainly be theorized separately. Should we believe that a volunteer in a youth sport league and a season-ticket holder at the Emirates in North London would have similar experiences *vis-à-vis* community? Even if their outcomes may be similar, it would be foolish to assume that the outcomes came about through identical pathways. Yet I believe that, when not in direct proximity, they could both reasonably be explored in terms of community creation. Yes, part of the problem is how scholars think of community (see below), but the exceedingly diverse experiences contained within the larger rubric of 'sport' is also implicated here. To that extent, it seems quixotic to interrogate – within the few pages we are allotted here – *any* connection between sport and community – let alone *the* connection between the two. Future volumes in this area must come to grips with and begin to break down these different experiences. It seems appropriate in this sense that a comprehensive theory of sport and community – nay, sport and *anything* – be built from the ground up. Having said that, it is important not to lose the forest for the trees. Specialization produces depth, but not breadth. The challenge of the social sciences is to try and embrace both; it does, after all, inhere in the longstanding micro–macro tension that exists particularly in sociology.

As David Hassan very astutely noted in the Prologue to this volume, the concept of community is, as it has been for over half a century, problematic. By 1955, Hillery had noted nearly 100 distinct definitions of community in the sociological literature.[1] This, of course, predated the innovations to the concept of community that would later emerge from the work of eminent scholars such as Sarason,[2] Webber[3] and Wellman,[4] among others. Now it is perhaps not the time to delve into the merits of these various and occasionally competing forms of community, but only to point out that, rather than building towards any sense of scholarly consensus about the nature of community, we instead seem to be following the well-worn path of entropy. Fortunately, within this volume, we are generally confronted with the place-bound nature of community. Without exception, the articles contained within conceive of the community (mostly implicitly) as some arrangement of relationships *within a geographically defined place*. Pre-emptively, I would like to concede the point to critics who would (and should) find fault with this collection on the basis that it makes this assumption of community. I am not entirely sure whether it does this or whether instead this is just the state of social research into sport at this moment in time. In either event, a volume embracing the connection between sport and some form of 'community liberated' would be a revelation in this field.

However, perhaps the more trenchant remark within his opening comments referred to the *desirability* of community through sport (or through any social institution), and whether or not this is a noble pursuit or outcome of the sporting experience. I see two particularly relevant strands of this question that we as sports scholars should address: community as exclusionary and insular, and community as constraint on individual freedom. I shall give each idea a brief treatment in the following.

While colloquially, many tend to think of community as a 'warm and fuzzy' place where all are known and all are accepted, scholars have written on the mechanisms by which communities are defined, namely, through boundaries. Communities are often identified less on what they are and more on what they are *not*. Gerald Suttles wrote perhaps the definitive statement on the exclusionary element of communities through his notion of the defended neighbourhood.[5] Anthony Cohen has also written extensively on how the definition of community comes from the boundary, because here the distinctions between 'us' and 'them' are more pronounced and easy to spot.[6] Sport, through institutionalized practices such as competition and, especially in organized team sports, different uniforms, highlights boundary construction and maintenance starkly, and also emphasizes the exclusionary practices inherent in the modern sporting experience. Of course, this element can be overcome, but sport scholars should be cautious in believing that something inherent in the nature of sport brings people together, as it also contains elements that keep them apart *by design*.

Despite the tendency of classical social theorists to bemoan the loss of community due to the social and economic forces that drove the founding of sociology as an academic discipline (namely, urbanization and the Industrial Revolution), one element that these researchers tended to agree on was that this move, be it from Mechanical to Organic Solidarity (Durkheim)[7] or from *gemeinschaft* to *gesellschaft* (Tönnies),[8] was accompanied by an increase in individual freedom. The city, it was noted, offered anonymity that small communities, rural areas and clan groupings simply lacked.[9] Later on, social capital theorists, as a branch of intellectual offspring of classical community theorists, noted much the same thing.[10] Strong ties, the kind which facilitate Putnam's 'bonding' social capital,[11] also create obligations, which naturally act as a constraint on individual freedom. Portes and Landolt specifically noted emerging trends of individuals altering their allegiances and core elements of their identities (such as their religious preference) in the face of mounting group pressures entailed in such bonding social capital relationships. Weak ties, the kind favoured by scholars such as Granovetter,[12] while less onerous in terms of group pressure, still are built upon shared norms, particularly that of reciprocity. The general reluctance of both community and social capital theorists to adequately deal with the downside of social interaction and dense networks characterized by strong, affective ties, represents both a distressing hole in the general theory and an immense opportunity for further impactful research.

All of the above are neither to denigrate the work contained within nor to undermine its importance, but instead to point out the difficulty in assessing with any sense of comprehensiveness 'community' as a monolithic framework that has some discrete intersection with 'sport', also as a monolithic entity. Just within the parameters I have delineated above, one can think of sport in terms of (a) participation, (b) spectatorship, (c) fandom[13] or (d) volunteering. Doubtless, one could also divine others with little effort. Thinking of community, the major distinction seems to be between that of place-bound community versus 'community unbound', though even that is a simplistic distinction. A simple exercise in permutations gives us no fewer than eight different combinations of research areas addressing some aspect of 'sport' with some other aspect of 'community', Obviously, then, one single volume cannot any longer even pretend to cover these institutions adequately. The questions remains then: what have we contributed within this volume?

I believe first and foremost that sports scholars can put to bed the question of whether or not sport can be used to build networks or community. In large part, we have. However, because it does not always do this – in fact, it can and does serve the opposite purposes – we have moved to an era defined less by 'What' questions, and more by 'When,' 'Why' or 'How' questions, as well as their negative counterparts. This is an advance, to be sure. In my own piece, I argued that sport was likely to build relationships where it provided opportunities for people to meet, a focus for their interactions and a cooperative environment (drawing heavily from Mario Small's work in daycare centres in New York City). Theoretically, then, activities providing these elements – whether they be sport related or not – could also be used to build similar networks, which is the crux of Matthew Nicholson's informative piece. Sport is not a unique institution, he argues. I would agree, adding that activities providing for opportunity, focus and cooperation in similar respects would offer similar returns. It may be natural for sport sociologists, particularly in the USA (where sport sociology is still somewhat marginalized) to want to assign a unique place for sport as practice to build networks and community sentiment. In the light of the work presented here, however, it seems prudent to abandon that notion. This may be a source, then, of disagreement among sport scholars regarding the ability (or inability) of sport to build networks and community. Mary Valentich's work offers another related perspective. The sociability provided by a highly focused (but ultimately imagined) communal interactions and environment allows her to provide strong evidence that, even in the imagined community, opportunity, focus and cooperation provide a powerful impetus for the expression of what otherwise might be thought of as intimate behaviours. When grappling with questions of sport and community (particularly those studying fans and spectators), scholars will always have to wrestle with the question of actual versus imagined community (or even communitas).[14]

Another embodiment of such disagreement comes in the preceding articles dealing with specific interventions at the local community level, either by municipalities or by organizations embedded in local communities. These studies represent one of the two primary empirical cores of the volume. As the authors show, we see in specific interventions the embodiment of the contradictions present in sport and community as a research body up to this point. The prevailing question that comes out of these works is instructive: for whom? This question has been asked repeatedly by scholars, but work presented here suggests that it is still a relevant and trenchant question. Where sport has been used for community creation, it has been successful only selectively and in ways that replicate power differentials found throughout the larger society, namely race and gender. Cleland, Roult, and Hassan and Telford's pieces all reiterate the point that intervention is a necessary but not sufficient condition for the *equitable* creation of community in local areas. As they stand, such interventions are extremely prone to benefitting the already privileged in an area. However, Hassan and Telford show that careful design and implementation with a specific eye towards equitable distribution of benefits can produce desirable results across social differences.

A comprehensive theory of successful interventions across classical divisions – race, class and gender – has yet to be written.

Last, but by no means least, contradictions emerge when addressing sport as a volunteer activity (rather than as a participatory or legislative one). This comes about when we examine the differences between classes of volunteers, as Ronguet et al. do. Engelberg, Skinner and Zakus show the next logical progression in such an analysis: different types of volunteers view themselves as distinct from others, and this becomes the basis for mutual animosity. Add to this mix the differing motivations for volunteering in the first place, and the seemingly stratified moral weight and legitimacy given to such reasons, and the two pieces establish that volunteering and involvement in itself is no guarantee that participants will find greater satisfaction, friendships and communal sentiment through such activities. In a separate section of my own research (the project that spawned my contribution to this volume), I also witnessed firsthand the destructive elements of heavy involvement in sport governance.

The contributions to this volume, if they are to be considered successful, need to stimulate additional research and theorization. They need to inspire questions. I believe that they have done this. Sports scholar need first to find sport's rightful place in a panoply of activities which enhance – through design or through by-product – networks and feelings of community. It might be prudent first, however, to explicitly separate various aspects for both sport and community into overlapping but not identical spheres. Doubtless, much can be gleaned from the application of conclusions from one sphere to another, but these need to be theorized and examined separately before they can be brought back together in a more comprehensive theory. If sport sociology as a discipline has been guilty of anything, it is the crime of breadth over depth. Perhaps, it is my inductive training talking, but I believe that better theorization of these issues will come from the ground up. The contributions of this volume are a step in the right direction. There is still much work to be done and, despite how much ink has been spilled over the sport–community connection, it is still a very fruitful area of exploration, and future scholars have a lot to unpack, and they also have a great deal to contribute.

Notes

1. Hillery, 'Definitions of Community'.
2. Sarason, *Psychological Sense of Community*.
3. Webber, 'Order in Diversity'.
4. Wellman, 'The Community Question'.
5. Suttles, *The Social Construction of Communities*.
6. Cohen, *The Symbolic Construction of Community*.
7. Durkheim, *The Division of Labor in Society*.
8. Tonnies, *Community and Society*.
9. Simmel, 'The Metropolis and Mental Life'.
10. See, for example, Portes and Landolt, 'Social Capital'.
11. Putnam, *Bowling Alone*.
12. Granovetter, 'The Strength of Weak Ties'.
13. For the distinction between fandom and spectatorship, see Wann et al., *Sport Fans*.
14. Ingham and McDonand, 'Sport and Community/Communitas'.

References

Cohen, Anthony P. *The Symbolic Construction of Community*. London: Tavistock, 1985.
Durkheim, Emile. *The Division of Labor in Society (with an Introduction by Lewis Coser)*. Translated by W.D. Halls. New York: Free Press, 1997 [1933].

Granovetter, Mark S. 'The Strength of Weak Ties'. *American Journal of Sociology* 78 (1973): 1360–80.

Hillery, George A. 'Definitions of Community: Areas of Agreement'. *Rural Sociology* 20 (1955): 111–23.

Ingham, Alan G., and Mary G. McDonald. 'Sport and Community/Communitas'. In *Sporting Dystopias: The Making and Meaning of Urban Sport Cultures*, ed. R.C. Wilcox, 17–33. Albany: State University of New York Press, 2003.

Portes, Alejandro, and Patricia Landolt. 'Social Capital: Promises and Pitfalls of Its Role in Development'. *Journal of Latin American Studies* 32 (2000): 529–47.

Putnam, Robert D. *Bowling Alone: The Collapse and Revival of American Community*. New York: Simon and Schuster, 2000.

Sarason, Seymour B. *The Psychological Sense of Community: Prospects for a Community Psychology*. San Francisco, CA: Jossey-Bass, 1974.

Simmel, Georg. 'The Metropolis and Mental Life'. In *The Sociology of Georg Simmel*, ed. H.K. Wolff, 409–24. New York: Free Press, 1964 [1902].

Suttles, Gerald. *The Social Construction of Communities*. Chicago, IL: University of Chicago Press, 1972.

Tönnies, Ferdinand. *Community and Society (Gemeinschaft und Gesellschaft)*. Translated by C.P. Loomis. Mineola, NY: Dover Publications, 1957 [1887].

Wann, Daniel, Merrill J. Melnick, Gordon W. Russell, and Dale G. Pease. *Sport Fans: The Psychology and Social Impact of Spectators*. New York: Routledge, 2001.

Webber, Melvin M. 'Order in Diversity: Community without Propinquity'. In *Cities and Space: The Future Use of Urban Land*, ed. L. Wingo, 23–54. Baltimore, MD: Johns Hopkins Press, 1963.

Wellman, Barry. 'The Community Question: The Intimate Networks of East Yorkers'. *American Journal of Sociology* 84 (1979): 1201–31.

Sean F. Brown*

*Northeastern University,
Department of Sociology and Anthropology*

*Current affiliation: University of Chicago, Department of Sociology.

Index